Kant

AND CURRENT PHILOSOPHICAL ISSUES

Kant

& CURRENT PHILOSOPHICAL

ISSUES: *Some Modern Developments*

of His Theory of Knowledge

By BELLA K. MILMED

NEW YORK UNIVERSITY PRESS · 1961

ACKNOWLEDGMENTS

QUOTED MATERIAL is used with permission as follows:

From *Immanuel Kant's Critique of Pure Reason,* translated by Norman Kemp Smith, 1953. Reprinted by permission of the publishers, Macmillan and Co., Ltd., London, and St. Martin's Press, Inc., New York.

From Immanuel Kant: *Prolegomena to Any Future Metaphysics,* translated by Lewis W. Beck, New York, 1951. Reprinted by permission of the publishers, The Liberal Arts Press, Inc.

From C. I. Lewis: *An Analysis of Knowledge and Valuation,* 1946. Reprinted by permission of the publishers, The Open Court Publishing Company, La Salle, Illinois.

From Clarence Irving Lewis: *Mind and the World Order,* 1956. Reprinted by permission of Dover Publications, Inc., New York 14, New York ($1.95).

From C. I. Lewis: *A Survey of Symbolic Logic,* 1918. Reprinted by permission of the publishers, University of California Press, Berkeley.

From Hans Reichenbach: *Elements of Symbolic Logic,* 1947. Reprinted by permission of the publishers, The Macmillan Company, New York.

From Hans Reichenbach: *Experience and Prediction,* 1938. Reprinted by permission of the publishers, University of Chicago Press, Chicago.

From Hans Reichenbach, *The Rise of Scientific Philosophy,* 1951. Reprinted by permission of the publishers, University of California Press, Berkeley.

From Albert Einstein, *Ideas and Opinions,* New York, Crown Publishers, Inc., 1954. Reprinted by permission of the Estate of Albert Einstein.

PREFACE

THE "CURRENT PHILOSOPHICAL ISSUES" with which the present discussion deals are two: how and why is abstract logic applicable to concrete experience? and what do we mean by existence independent of knowledge, in a world of sense perceptions and conceptual constructions? These problems are analyzed in terms of their Kantian origins and solutions, and then in terms of the adaptation and expansion of these solutions by C. I. Lewis and Hans Reichenbach to meet current conceptual needs.

The discussion is intended as selective and not exhaustive, its subject matter being chosen solely for its bearing on the problems at issue. It is intended, further, as explicative and not historical. The proposed interpretation of Kant is advanced not as an exposition of his sole or even "real" intent, but as a translation of his concepts into modern ones—as an interpretation which may, consistently with his premises, make him intelligible and helpful today; and the later writers are discussed, not to trace Kant's direct influence but to illustrate his current significance. It is hoped that in this way Kant and his successors may render each other more thoroughly understandable, with a resulting clarification of problems that are crucial for philosophy at the present time.

Whatever the degree to which these intentions may have been fulfilled, the project could not have been carried out at all without the encouragement and advice of Professor Sidney Hook at every stage from preliminaries to publication, over a period of time whose length might well have caused him to despair of the attempt. And it is no mere formality if I also thank my husband, without whose co-operation in many concrete ways the project would never have been possible, without whose active prodding it would not yet have been actual, and without whose cordial approval it would not now be so gratifying in spite of its flaws.

B. K. M.

CONTENTS

Kant Today: *A Preliminary View*

THE PHILOSOPHY of Kant is not very fashionable today. Tradition-
ally labeled as "rationalist" and "idealist," it may easily be regarded as outmoded and irrelevant at a time when philosophers of almost all schools, however conflicting, unite in using these epithets as
terms of abuse. Even the rationalists of today tend to use "idealist" as
a term of abuse. Yet, oddly enough, once our attention is turned in the
requisite direction, it is not at all difficult to see that this virtual expul-
sion of rationalism and idealism from the philosophical field finds its
major theoretical validation in premises established by Kant himself.
Indeed, it is the establishment of these premises that constitutes the
almost incalculable contribution of Kant to philosophy since his time.
Surely it is apparent at the outset that such a situation, if it indeed
obtains, is not one to ignore. Let us see, then, first of all, just what
the situation is.

The existence of the empirical, naturalistic approach as a peren-
nial one in philosophy, as well as the close correlation between its
ascendancy and that of natural science, may be regarded as obvious.
There have always been impressive grounds and powerful motives,
and at times a concentration of cultural factors as well, behind the
view that the world as experienced (and as further known by means
of a science based on experience) is in some important sense primary
and in some important sense exhaustive. Currently, however, the
strength of such a view is founded upon theoretical grounds much
more precise and conclusive than the mere prevalence of a naturalistic or scientific temper. Indeed, it is questionable whether there is
any such prevalence today. The solid theoretical foundation of all
philosophical naturalism at the present time is provided by one of

the few definite and almost universally accepted advances that philosophy has ever made, the recognition of the abstract, nonexistential character of logic. The rationalist notion, of long standing and vast influence, that logic and mathematics, by virtue of their certainty and universality, have priority as means of insight into the nature of things is thereby deprived of its foundation; and with it that major branch of idealism which, equating the mental with the rational, regards the mental element in the world as primary on rationalistic grounds.

In this sense, there can be little doubt as to the validity of Reichenbach's analysis of "the rise of scientific philosophy" as a progressive "disintegration of the synthetic a priori." [1] The discovery of non-Euclidean geometries, of the relativity of space and time, and of the element of indeterminacy in subatomic phenomena are analyzed by Reichenbach as successive demonstrations that principles once regarded as logically necessary laws of the physical world (i.e., as synthetic a priori) are either not logically necessary or not about the physical world (i.e., not a priori or not synthetic). Finally, Reichenbach concludes, Russell's "reduction of mathematics to logic" completes the "disintegration of the synthetic a priori" by showing that mathematical necessity, like logical necessity, "is of an analytic nature." For logic is "necessary" because it is "empty; that is, it does not express properties of physical objects," but merely "connects sentences in such a way that the resulting combination is true independently of the truth of the individual sentences." [2] This view, avowedly derived from Wittgenstein's analysis of logic as "the domain of tautological formulas" and Carnap's analysis of logic as "the syntax of language," Reichenbach identifies as the "formalistic interpretation" of logic, in contrast with the "aprioristic interpretation" which he attributes to Kant, the view that "logic is a science with its own authority, . . . founded in the a priori nature of reason . . ." [3]

All of this may seem to be quite commonplace and hardly in need of repetition, although its importance can hardly be overestimated. Yet, when the contrast with Kant is introduced into the picture, we may suddenly remember that it is precisely the distinction between the analytic and the synthetic, the formal and the existential, that provides the logical starting point of Kant's entire philosophy. Moreover, while the distinction itself does not by any means originate with Kant, there does originate with him an understanding of its implications for the nature of logical and empirical knowledge and their interrelation.

Kant's definition of analytic and synthetic statements is relatively simple.

In all judgments in which the relation of a subject to the predicate is thought . . . Either the predicate B belongs to the subject A, as something which is (covertly) contained in this concept A; or B lies outside the concept A, although it does indeed stand in connection with it. In the one case I entitle the judgment analytic, in the other synthetic.[4]

Naturally, this definition is expressed in terms of the subject-predicate logic of Kant's day; Reichenbach speaks rather of "transformation of one proposition into another without any addition to its intension."[5] But surely the significant sense in which these two formulations are equivalent is obvious. For we are not here concerned with the question of where we get the "concepts"; indeed, Kant himself states that "In whatever manner the understanding may have arrived at a concept," the distinction between analytic and synthetic treatment of it will still hold.[6] Nor are we here concerned with the still more complicated question of where we get the rules of logic by which equivalences between concepts or propositions are determined. The significant distinction for present purposes is that which holds between analytic statements as "merely *explicative,* adding nothing to the content of knowledge," and synthetic statements as *"expansive,* increasing the given knowledge";[7] and this distinction has assuredly not been obliterated by new developments in logic.

(Such attacks on the analytic-synthetic distinction as that of Morton G. White, based on the view that the distinction depends on the concept of synonymy, which is not precise in natural languages,[8] serve merely to indicate that, in terms of the kind of logical and linguistic analysis currently used, a formulation like Reichenbach's is more suitable than one like Kant's. The distinction is the same, however, in both formulations.)

More interesting than the distinction itself, which Kant shares with Leibniz and Hume before him, is his keen recognition of its significance. For Kant is perfectly clear, first of all, as to the fact that "general logic," by which he means what we ordinarily call "formal logic," is the "part of logic, which may . . . be entitled *analytic.*"[9] "If we reflect in a merely logical fashion, we are only comparing our concepts with each other . . . ," [10] i.e., not dealing with facts at all. General logic is, secondly, purely formal, setting forth the "formal conditions of agreement with the understanding"; thus, being applicable to all knowledge whatsoever, it "teaches us nothing whatsoever regarding the content of knowledge" and therefore cannot serve as "an instrument . . . to extend and enlarge our knowledge." [11] It cannot even provide "general instructions how we are to subsume" empirical objects under its own rules; i.e., Kant distinguishes formal from applied logic, recognizing that a series of formal rules for the application of rules, *ad infinitum*, would never enable us to infer a single specific fact.[12]

A third point recognized by Kant in connection with the analytic-synthetic distinction is most significant of all. It is not Wittgenstein nor Russell, but Kant himself, who first makes the explicit declaration that "all existential propositions are synthetic," on the ground that " *'Being'* is obviously not a real predicate . . ." [13] If it were, he argues, we could not have a concept of any existing object, because the concept would have to lack a predicate possessed by the object.[14] It is on this basis that Kant establishes his famous disproof of the ontological argument for the existence of God; but the point is made for *all* assertions of existence. "In the *mere concept* of a thing no mark of its existence is to be found." [15] But the "mere concept" is the subject matter of logic, as already noted. It is clear, therefore, that "no one can venture with the help of logic alone to judge regarding objects, or to make any assertion. We must first, independently of logic, obtain reliable information . . ." [16] The source of such information is, of course, experience; "the perception which supplies the content to the concept is the sole mark of actuality." [17] And "Judgments of experience, as such, are one and all synthetic. For it would be absurd to found an analytic judgment on experience," since no experience is required for its validation.[18]

It must be recognized at the outset, then, whatever the complicating role of the "synthetic a priori," that a clear distinction is set up between the analytic, the formal, the purely conceptual, on one hand, and the synthetic, the existential, the empirical, on the other; and further, that Kant draws the explicit conclusion that no existential assertion can be derived from or validated by logic alone. If we are inclined to ask, under these circumstances, "How are a priori synthetic judgments possible?" this is no more than Kant himself asks, making of this question, indeed, the central "problem of pure reason." [19] If we are further inclined to reply that, *on the basis of Kant's own premises*, such judgments are obviously *not* possible, it is at least worth while to find out what a philosopher so well aware of these premises could have meant by "a priori synthetic judgments"; and in what sense he regarded them as possible; and also whether his solution can contribute anything at all toward solution of the philosophical dilemmas (for certainly there are crucial ones) that acceptance of these same premises has created today. It will be worth while to investigate how Kant could say explicitly that "All knowledge of things merely from pure understanding or pure reason is nothing but sheer illusion," [20] and also, on the very next page, that his theory is "designed for the purpose of comprehending the possibility of our *a priori* knowledge of objects of experience . . ." [21]

A major step toward at least a reawakening of interest in Kant —and also, I think, toward an understanding of Kant in twentieth century terms—is taken when we note as the salient feature of his approach to this question not his belief in the existence and validity of synthetic a priori propositions but rather his recognition of the difficulties involved in that belief. Kant is fully aware that the possibility both of analytic a priori propositions and of synthetic a posteriori ones is easily understandable, while in the case of synthetic a priori propositions "the possibility must be sought or investigated . . ." [22]

A second very great contribution of Kant to subsequent philosophy is the recognition of a conceptual element in experience, and therefore in all knowledge; and along with this, as a most important corollary, the recognition of a deductive element in all science. This represents not a weakening but rather a strengthening of the analytic-synthetic distinction, a reconstruction of knowledge in terms of it, a transfer of the rational factor (which turns out to be in some sense indispensable after all) from the ontological to the epistemological field. Just because logic is analytic and nonexistential, and just because, conversely, existence and immediate passive awareness of it are extralogical, (or, in Kantian language, just because "Thoughts without content are empty," while "intuitions without concepts are blind,") [23] both elements must be present together in experience, i.e., in the world as we are conscious of it, if our experience is to be at all comprehensible or coherent. The wider the gap between logic and existence, the more urgently we are compelled to find within "experience" an element of logic as well as of existence, if experience is to be dealt with at all in conceptual terms.

The irrational, existential factor alone, the sense "impressions" which are merely given and the faint "images" or reproductions of them which for Hume constituted the sum total of our knowledge, could not, as Hume himself found, be put together in any manner that would approximate even our everyday experience of things, much less science. For Kant, however, "experience is itself a species of knowledge which involves understanding"; [24] and a consciousness of distinguishable *objects*, as contrasted with an undifferentiated awareness of "a rhapsody of perceptions that would not fit into any context," [25] is equated with experience in this sense. For experience of determinate, identifiable objects and events, it is not enough to see colors and shapes and to hear sounds, or even to remember them besides; we must also *understand* these by interpreting them in terms of physical objects in a physical world. For Kant, therefore, the distinctive mental function is not reproduction, although this, too, plays its part, but "understanding," in a quite literal sense. It is astonishing how far the ccomprehension of Kant is facilitated, if we think of "understanding" not as merely the technical name of a so-called "faculty" but as an ordinary word, meaning just about what it always means. Our "understanding" is the means by which we "can . . . *understand* anything in the manifold of intuition." [26] We understand something if we have a concept available to apply to it, a place for it in our conceptual scheme of things; and if we have not, we try to make such a place for it, or *explain* it. Indeed, if we cannot do this, we cannot even apply words to it, for language is itself a conceptual scheme.

As Kant puts it,

Objects are *given* to us by means of sensibility, and it alone yields us *intuitions;* they are *thought* through the understanding, and from the understanding arise *concepts*. But all thought must . . . relate ultimately to . . . sensibility, because in no other way can an object be given to us.[27]

When we provide *reasons* for events, we provide premises from which they are deducible. Thus explanation is conceptual, deductive, and hence analytic. What there *is* to explain, on the other hand, can be learned only by sense perception, without which, indeed, there would be nothing to understand. Where the two coincide, where the sequence of perceptions turns out actually to illustrate (or "conform to") a conceptual structure, we have neither abstract logical analysis alone nor blank awareness alone, but knowledge in the full sense.

But how is this conformity possible? Sense data merely occur; they are as they are; they are not deducible from anything, nor can anything be deduced from them. They must, therefore, be organized into the kind of structure in which logical relations are possible; it is "the activity of our understanding" that must "work up the raw material of the sensible impressions into that knowledge of objects which is entitled experience." [28] It would not be possible to form concepts which merely *describe* the data; for each perception in turn, being unique, would require a new *ad hoc* concept, which would of course serve no purpose, if indeed it could be called a concept at all. As Kant puts it, if our "*concepts . . .* conform to the object," we are incapable of "determining something in regard to" objects "prior to their being given." [29] Nor is the conceptual structure *inferred* from the data; Kant habitually speaks of the activity of the understanding as "spontaneous" and is well aware that we can construct systems of "empty" concepts if we so desire. However, we also can and do build up *a conceptual structure into which the data can be incorporated*; and when appropriate perceptions do in fact occur, the concepts are no longer empty but rather combine with these perceptions to constitute knowledge, or experience, in the full sense. "What experience gives is the instance which stands under the rule." [30] It is in this manner "that the objects, or what is the same thing, that the *experience* in which alone, as given objects, they can be known, conform to the concepts."

That this conformity, as so interpreted, seems to be analytic need not be too disconcerting; Kant himself says as much when he points out that "we can know *a priori* of things only what we ourselves put into them." [31] The question of an analytic element involved here and of the extent and importance of its role, and the related question as to just what there is in this situation that Kant nevertheless finds it necessary to interpret as synthetic a priori, will require extended investigation later on; indeed, we have here the crucial point in the interpretation of Kant. At the moment, however, the important point is simply the fact that a conceptual element, an organizing and explanatory factor contributed by the human mind, is shown to be involved in any coherent experience, particularly in the kind that distinguishes physical objects.

Terminology aside, it is difficult to think of a philosopher at the present time who does not accept this view in some form and to some extent. Most obviously, one of the fundamental principles of pragmatism in all its forms is the doctrine of the active role of the knower in creating the object of knowledge. Taking Dewey as our example of this view, we find the repeated denial "that the object of knowledge is already there in full-fledged being and that we just run across it . . ." Of course, such a denial as it stands is quite ambiguous; and Dewey, it is true, often seems to mean that we know an object only to the extent that we physically produce or at least change it, or even that the physical change itself constitutes knowledge. An example of this is his assertion that the discovery of America was not knowledge until it changed the map.[32] He may even seem to indicate that there *is* no object—indeed, that there is nothing at all—unless we literally produce it; it is difficult to find any other meaning in his habitual denial of knowledge of "antecedent facts." Nevertheless, many passages make clear that this is not what Dewey means; at least, not always.

He does *not* mean, he says, that there is no "bare occurrence" except as a result of our operations, but rather that certain events will be *observable* if certain operations are performed; and the operations include "reasoning" and "observation" as well as overt physical experiment.[33] In fact, we experiment in order to apply hypotheses to events, and in this way to supply reasons for them, order them in a coherent system, understand them. A physical object is such an ordering hypothesis applied to actual and potential events; if we did not include the potential, or predictable, events, the actual ones could not be systematized nor the hypothesis verified. And if we did not so systematize experiential events, Dewey points out (in full accord with Kant), "Objects observed and dealt with would be a shifting panorama of sudden disconnected appearances and disappearances." [34]

It is the hypothetical, conceptual element in the physical object, then, that distinguishes it from a string of "bare occurrences," although the hypothesis must be applicable to the bare occurrences. Similarly, the changes brought about by knowledge may be conceptual; indeed, the changes that really count in epistemological terms, those that determine that something *is* an object of knowledge, *must* be conceptual. When Dewey declares that immediate qualities, which are "had" rather than "known," become incorporated in knowledge only when they are "tremendously modified," the required modification is merely that the qualities be "linked together by 'physical objects'—that is, by means of the mathematical-mechanical objects of physics" in an "ordered series." [35]

Dewey's definition of the object as "a set of qualities treated as *potentialities* for specified existential consequences," [36] then, need not require that the qualities be so "treated" in a physical sense or that the consequences actually occur; it is sufficient if the qualities are so treated conceptually, just because the "existential consequences" are *"potentialities"* by definition. The physical object is, as Kant would say, "possible experience."

In the positivist view, rigidly "empiricist" as it may be in the eyes of its exponents, the conceptual element in all knowledge of the physical world is still clearer, because less obscured by that close entanglement with the operational element that in pragmatism is often inextricable to the point of confusion. A good example, among the many available, is Margenau's analysis of physical objects as logical "systems," so constructed that the "object" functions in a "substantival role as a carrier of observable properties." In this view even the properties (e.g., "the property, blue" assigned to objects, as distinguished from "sensed blue") are themselves constructs.[37] It is interesting that this conception is accepted by Einstein. For him a physical object is "a free creation of the human (or animal) mind," which we "correlate" to "repeatedly occurring complexes of sense impressions . . ." The concept of an object provides a "mental connection" between sense impressions, enabling us to "orient ourselves in the labyrinth" of such impressions. Einstein, moreover, unlike professional positivist philosophers, openly declares his derivation from Kant of the view that the "postulation of a real external world" *means* that our sensory experience "can be put in order" by concepts.[38]

Turning from analyses of our everyday knowledge of objects to analyses of scientific knowledge, we find a general recognition of the latter as an application of the same conceptual process on a higher level, or rather a series of higher levels.[39] This is almost inevitable as soon as knowledge of objects is regarded as a kind of concept formation for dealing with given data. Again, therefore, the starting point is Kant, whose discussion shuttles back and forth rather indiscriminately between the application of "laws" to "nature" and the application of "concepts" to "objects." [40] Both in Kant and in the more recent writers, recognition of the conceptual element in experience is allied to recognition of the deductive element in science.

Since "modern science," automatically identified as "empirical science," is often said to have rendered Kant and all his works obsolete, it may be worth while to read his famous introductory statement of the scientific method (there labeled by him, as is too rarely noted, "the experimental method") [41] side by side with parallel statements by the recognized chief protagonist of "experimental method," Dewey himself. The results are extremely interesting.

KANT:	DEWEY:
The epoch-making discovery of Galileo and other early experimenters was the discovery that reason has insight only into that which it produces after a plan of its own, and . . .	. . . laws . . . are means of *prediction* only as far as they operate as means of *production* of a given situation . . .
must itself show the way with principles of judgment based upon fixed laws, constraining nature to give answer to questions of reason's own determining.	. . . laws . . . are instrumentalities in determining, through operations they prescribe and direct, the ordered sequences into which gross qualitative events are resolved.[42]
Accidental observations, made in obedience to no previously thought-out plan, can never be made to yield a necessary law . . . Reason, holding in one hand its principles, according to which alone concordant appearances can be admitted as equivalent to laws, and in the other hand the experiment which it has devised in conformity with these principles, must approach nature in order to be taught by it.	[Unless we] *prepare* existential material so that it has convincing evidential weight with respect to an inferred generalization . . . no number of cases, no matter how extensive, will ground an inference, or occasion anything other than a more or less happy guess.[43]

Kant adds, moreover, the warning that "reason must seek in nature, not fictitiously ascribe to it, whatever as not being knowable through reason's own resources has to be learnt, if learnt at all, only from nature"; [44] and we have already seen that we cannot, in his view, learn the *existence* of anything whatsoever "through reason's own resources."

Without minimizing the difference between Kant's reference to "fixed laws" and Dewey's reference to "operations" in the second pair of parallel items above, it is obvious that the similarity of pattern far outweighs any differences of emphasis or language. It is our own concepts, our own methods of understanding, both writers assert, that determine, not what shall or shall not happen in the world at large (although Dewey's manner of statement is the more misleading on this score), but how we are to *understand* what happens, how we are to organize it conceptually so as to *make* it understandable. It is not the recurrence of sequences of events, however frequent, but the deducibility of such recurrence from a general law that gives us genuine scientific knowledge; and the law is not found as a direct result of any experiment but must be formulated in advance, so that the experiment may be arranged as an application and test of it. It should be added, too, that although Dewey introduces his *Logic* as an attempt to identify logic with experimental inquiry, he finds it necessary, in the course of his analysis, to provide for a special stage of inquiry, called "reasoning," which performs the deductive function of deriving from laws or hypotheses their testable consequences [45] and which has all the characteristics of what is commonly called "logic."

Turning now to analyses of science by the current positivist writers, we find nothing very different—except, perhaps, for further differences in language and emphasis. The method of "the more advanced branches of empirical science" is described by Hempel, for instance, as a "hypothetico-deductive-observational procedure," in which, "Guided by his knowledge of observational data, the scientist has to invent a set of . . . theoretical constructs" and use them in hypotheses to "establish explanatory and predictive connections between the data of direct observation." [46] Feigl, too, points out that the "more general assumptions (laws, hypotheses, theoretical postulates)" are used as a "*set of premises*," and facts are derived from them as conclusions of deductive inferences; so that the element of necessity in scientific laws is a logical one, the necessity of "the *implication* underlying the inference from assumptions to conclusions." [47] This interpretation of the role of "necessity" will help us to understand Kant, who comes far closer to it than his terminology would lead us to expect. We have here the admission into empirical science of a very extensive and essential a priori element, with which the element of necessity is identified; and while this element is further identified as strictly analytic, its *relevance* to the synthetic, existential, empirical aspects of science is clearly maintained.

Here again we have the agreement of Einstein. No concept, he says, is derived from experience, either by abstraction [48] or by deductive [49] or inductive inference.[50] Empirical data "suggest" a concept or theory, but they are not its *premises;* [51] it is rather the *deducible conclusions* of a theory that make the contact with empirical data. The theory itself is a "free invention," so constructed as to provide a logical scheme into which empirical data will fit.[52] Empirical data provide the content or subject matter of knowledge, and therefore must provide the confirmation without which a conceptual structure is "empty" [53] (i.e., inapplicable, a theory about nothing). But it is the function of logical reasoning to explain and order this subject matter; [54] and each set of concepts in turn acts as data for a conceptual system of the next level, "a system retaining the primary concepts and relations of the 'first layer' as logically derived concepts and relations." [55]

It is noteworthy that the conceptual element in science is here accepted not only as extremely far-reaching (as a premise for deductive inference on a large scale), but also as *independent* of the empirical element in origin and structure, though not in validity as an account of the existing world. Since the purpose of science is achievement of such validity, we construct the theory that the known empirical facts "suggest," hoping to find many empirical facts that conform to it. This agrees perfectly with Kant's dictum that "though all our knowledge begins with experience, it does not follow that it all arises out of experience." [56] Or, in the very similar words of Reichenbach, the protagonist of "scientific philosophy" in opposition to the alleged "rationalism" of Kant, "Observational data are the starting-point of scientific method; but they do not exhaust it." [57]

Clearly, this interpretation is a far cry from the view of science put forward by Francis Bacon [58] and perpetuated into the twentieth century by Karl Pearson, for whom science is a "classification of facts and the formation of absolute judgments upon the basis of this classification," [59] while facts are sense impressions, "immediate" or "stored." [60] As Reichenbach himself notes, "Einstein's empiricism is not the one of Bacon and Mill," which limited science to "simple inductive generalizations." It is rather an "empiricism of mathematical construction, which . . . connects observational data by deductive operations and enables us to predict new observational data." [61]

This, of course, is standard positivist doctrine. Indeed, paradoxical as it may at first seem, it may well be argued that the major contribution of the logical positivists, however radically empiricist their intentions and criteria, is the restoration of abstract, deductive logic to a fundamental role in the interpretation both of science and of knowledge generally. In this respect, at least, we can already see that they are genuine successors of Kant. Nor should this aspect be underestimated in Dewey, whose operational interpretation of logic turns out, as we have seen, to be just as much a logical interpretation of scientific operations.

Kant's present influence, then, acknowledged or unacknowledged, shows itself in two main ideas virtually ubiquitous in current philosophy: *1*] the view that logic and deductive reasoning in general are analytic and can yield no existential knowledge, while all existence propositions are synthetic, and *2*] the view that all knowledge, both in "common sense" experience of objects and in science, contains an abstract, conceptual element constructed by the mental activity of the knower and amenable to deductive manipulation. We have seen that no exception need be made (that the first of these two main ideas, indeed, acquires a special polemical significance) for those aggressively naturalistic writers to whom the name of Kant epitomizes the rejected "rationalism" and "idealism."

Surely this anomalous situation can only lead to confusion. We shall have occasion, in the course of discussion, to observe a few of the many instances in which philosophers apply Kant's ideas implicitly while condemning him explicitly, or even take pains to point out that any resemblance is purely coincidental. Obviously, we ought to understand this situation more fully. Is Kant an idealist and rationalist, or not? Recognition of the analytic character of logic and the synthetic character of all existence propositions is ordinarily regarded as the very antithesis of rationalism; while recognition of a conceptual element in all knowledge, although expressible in idealistic terms, makes Kant no more an "idealist" than the pragmatists and positivists of our own day. But how, then, has the usual classification of Kant arisen?

As a step toward clarification, let us note first the elements of empiricism to be found in Kant, not to exaggerate them but to start with full awareness of an aspect of his doctrine often overlooked. First, there is Kant's explicit insistence that "In the order of time . . . we have no knowledge antecedent to experience." [62] Even as to the source of the categories, those concepts upon which Kant bases the a priori element in knowledge, he declares that "We can . . . seek to discover in experience, if not the principle of their possibility, at least the occasioning causes of their production." That is, although "they cannot, indeed, be derived from experience, since in that case they would not be knowledge *a priori*," our concepts "could never arise even in thought" if they were empirically "without data." [63] We may readily compare Einstein's view that the concepts of science are suggested by experience though not derived from experience.

More important than this genetic priority of experience is its priority in terms of that structural analysis of knowledge which is, after all, Kant's primary concern. Once we do have concepts at our disposal, all knowledge must still take as its point of departure some empirical subject matter to which the concepts are to be applied. Any other use of concepts is not knowledge at all, if by knowledge we mean existential cognition and not mere abstract construction. "If we do not start from experience, or do not proceed in accordance with laws of the empirical connection of appearances, our guessing or enquiring into the existence of anything will only be an idle pretence." [64] Surely this is the basic principle of empiricism.

Further, in line with this principle, Kant shows a clear recognition that neither the rules of logic nor abstract reasonings based on them can yield truth; that they are only "the negative touchstone of truth." [65] No self-contradictory statement can be true; but no "objective reality" can be "proved by the fact that reason requires it." [66] Indeed, "only in experience is there truth." [67] For Kant thinks of "truth" in terms of its traditional Aristotelian definition as "agreement of knowledge with its object"; [68] and the only "object" that we know is the object of experience. That is why Kant rejects any inference, by means of reason alone, which is inherently incapable of em pirical application. "Reason . . . never teaches us anything more than objects of possible experience, and even of these nothing more than can be learned in experience." [69]

Occasionally Kant goes still further, indicating that a concept without empirical applicability lacks not only truth but meaning. "We demand in every concept . . . the possibility of giving it an object to which it may be applied. In the absence of such object, it has no meaning . . ." [70] Kant even demands, at one point, an *actually experienced* object, if not for all concepts, "at least for the elements of which they are composed," if they are to have "meaning." [71] Although it would be a distortion of Kant's intention to interpret any of this too narrowly or rigidly, we can hardly fail to recognize at least a strong ingredient of something approaching a verifiability theory of meaning, a theory ordinarily associated with full-fledged empiricism.

It would be strange, then, if similar elements of empiricism were to be absent from Kant's treatment of science. Whatever we may find to be his precise meaning when he speaks of the "pure science of nature" (where "pure" is interchangeable, according to his usage, with deductive, or a priori), he does *not* mean a science which can "altogether refuse and dispense with the testimony of experience"; for no "science of nature," he recognizes, can "rival mathematics" in this respect. The "transcendental deduction" required to *account for* the a priori element in science is not required to *validate* it; for validation in regard to science "rests . . . upon experience and its thorough confirmation." [72] If this remark appears incompatible with Kant's "pure science" as ordinarily interpreted, it is at least there to be taken into account. It is true enough, of course, that Kant requires the application of concepts or laws to "possible experience" more often than to actual experience, i.e., verifiability more often than verification; but any doubts which this raises as to the extent of Kant's empirical aspect may serve to remind us of something often forgotten in more modern contexts—that the verifiability theory of meaning is not automatically synonymous with one-hundred-per-cent empiricism, since verifiability is not itself verifiable.

We have not yet exhausted, however, the empirical aspect of Kant. We must note, further, his view of the nature of scientific explanations. "A *transcendental hypothesis*, in which a mere idea of reason is used in explanation of natural existences, would really be no explanation . . ." [73] says Kant. We cannot merely invent an arbitrary hypothesis, even though it could logically serve as a ground for the facts to be explained. The only explanations admissible to science are those which can be "grounded upon that which . . . can belong to experience, and be brought into connection with our actual perceptions and empirical laws." [74] In other words, the facts to be explained must not merely be deducible from the hypothesis; they must also be related by it to other empirical facts (i.e., there must be additional empirical justification beyond the facts to be explained), and the hypothesis must tie in with other empirically established laws. It is on this basis that explanation of empirical phenomena by the concept of the soul as a simple substance, by the "cosmological Ideas" about the universe as a whole, and by the "will of a Supreme Being" is rejected as no explanation at all. [75] Moreover, ad hoc (or "auxiliary") hypotheses to explain particular cases are ruled out as firmly as empirically irrelevant hypotheses; if they are needed, the entire explanation becomes suspect as fiction. [76]

All of this is good empiricist doctrine in regard to admissible hypotheses. It is true that Kant's statements of the requirements tend to emphasize previous rather than subsequent empirical justifications, and that some empiricists would regard only the latter as constituting "confirmation" in the strict sense. Kant's statements, however, seem to evince lack of interest in temporal distinctions of this kind rather than outright rejection of the need for confirmation; and he appears to come reasonably close to Reichenbach's criterion according to which a science "will always remain empiricist as long as it leaves the ultimate criterion of truth to sense perception." [77]

Needless to say, the empirical features of Kant's doctrine singled out here—the origin of all knowledge in experience, the recognition of experience as sole criterion of truth and even of meaning, the requirement of empirical confirmation even for "pure natural science," the limitation of scientific explanation to empirically relevant hypotheses—are not the most fundamental or pervasive features of that doctrine. Kant does not emphasize or dwell upon them particularly; nor do they represent a major aspect of his influence upon later philosophers, who derive these ideas from quite other sources. Nevertheless, they are definitely there. When we note them in conjunction with the analytic-synthetic distinction and its interpretation, ideas which *are* fundamental, pervasive, and influential in a sense in which these other empirical features are not, we are prepared to understand that Kant need not always be classified as a rationalist. Weldon, for instance, does not so regard him; rather, he asserts that Kant's

. . . achievement was to expose once and for all the pretensions of "ontology" and "rational" science and to set philosophy on the right road . . . by . . . making a steady . . . attempt to elucidate the implications of contemporary scientific methods and doctrines . . .[78]

Nevertheless, the rationalist classification is the usual one, and we shall have to find out why.

One very simple but powerful reason is historical—the fact that Kant's immediate followers, and their followers in turn, developed his ideas in an idealistic direction; indeed, if we include Hegel and his disciples among them, they constituted the idealistic philosophy of the post-Kantian period. This development, it is well known, depended upon the elimination from the Kantian structure of the doctrine of the "thing in itself"; and controversy as to whether this change is extremely fundamental, hardly worth mentioning, or virtually conceded by Kant himself has been a welter of conflicting opinions ever since. Heinrich Cassirer remarks, in commenting on Kant's section on "Phenomena and Noumena," that those who themselves reject the thing in itself believe that Kant here at last rejects it also, while those who accept it interpret the section as making no essential modification; and that Kant's final view is therefore not definitely determinable.[79] Even a decision on this matter, however, would not give us the whole story; for some interpreters (including Cassirer) who do accept the importance of the thing in itself tend to attribute to this very doctrine a thoroughly idealistic character.

Kant, then, is blamed both for the presence of the thing in itself in his scheme and for its absence; and he is interpreted as an "idealist" on both counts. I believe that the first count involves a misinterpretation of the thing in itself, while the second count involves an underestimation of its importance. This is a matter to which we must return. It may seem, at first glance, that there is little relation here to the question of Kant's alleged rationalism; that clarification as to the thing in itself would determine only whether he should be regarded as an idealist in the Berkeleyan sense, i.e., whether he believes that the mental element as identified with *consciousness* is primary and ubiquitous in the universe. Yet there is also a relation to the question of idealism in the Platonic sense, in which the mental element as identified with *rational structure* is primary and ubiquitous in the universe. For we have already seen that Kant regards the mental element, taken in both senses, as ubiquitous in *experience;* but this may be quite another matter *if* a nonexperiental existent, such as the thing in itself, is admitted. It is clear, in any event, that exponents of idealism (in both senses) and of rationalism have claimed derivation from Kant; with how much justification, remains to be seen.

Of course Kant could not be so widely identified as a rationalist without some foundation in his own writings; and indeed there is such a foundation. Superficial, perhaps, but by no means uninfluential in this respect, are the personal mannerisms found throughout, mannerisms which do not in themselves make any particular philosophical views attributable to him but which may well have been enhanced by the rationalist climate in which he worked. Kant undoubtedly writes with an air of the utmost self-confidence and psychological certainty, although even in this respect the extent of his published revisions and various autobiographical references in his letters present quite another picture.[80] So do his posthumously published private notes,

. . . in which, with frequent failure and at best with only comparative success, constantly restating and modifying, with words and sentences crossed out, and with notes added on the margins, . . . he endeavoured to arrive at a satisfactory formulation of certain new positions to which he was tentatively feeling his way.[81]

However this may be, we may be sure that no philosopher today would "venture to assert that there is not a single metaphysical problem which has not been solved, or for the solution of which the key at least has not been supplied," [82] in his own treatise, or, for that matter, in any other; yet such a statement, as well as such claims for the absolute certainty of his conclusions as Kant occasionally puts forward,[83] can hardly be explained in terms of rationalist assumptions alone. The assumption of immunity to errors of commission and omission is not rationalism but simple egotism.

In addition to the matter of temperament, there is the matter of verbal usage. This, too, must be regarded as adding to the rationalistic impression produced and as encouraged by the rationalistic climate of Kant's time, but as fundamentally irrelevant. When Kant assumes that "metaphysics" (or any other knowledge, for that matter) must be certain and a priori in order to be regarded as a "science," [84] no particular light is thrown on anything except his use of the term "science"—a use, moreover, which is not consistently maintained, since he also observes that "In natural science . . . there is endless conjecture, and certainty is not to be counted upon," because here we deal with "objects which are given to us independently of our concepts." [85] Much more important than the application of the term "science" is this recognition that in dealing with the existent we cannot obtain certainty. Nevertheless, there are complications here, as we shall find when we turn, as we must now do, to the rationalistic elements in Kant's thought itself.

In some sense which it will be worth while to determine with care, Kant lays great stress on his belief that certainty *is* possible; also, that universality, completeness, and knowledge independent of all experience are possible. "As to *certainty*," he says, "I have prescribed to myself the maxim, that in this kind of investigation it is in no wise permissible to hold *opinions*"; nor is any "hypothesis" to be admitted to his argument.[86] Kant habitually speaks of knowledge short of certainty in this same derogatory tone, perpetuating the Platonic distinction between knowledge and opinion. He finds it "absurd . . . in metaphysics, a philosophy from pure reason, to think of grounding our judgments upon probability and conjecture . . . Conjectures . . . can be suffered in an empirical science of nature only . . ." [87]

Yet, before jumping to conclusions, we should note the reason given for the rejection of less than certain knowledge and for the belief that certainty is obtainable. In the first case, Kant explains that "Any knowledge that professes to hold *a priori* lays claim to be regarded as absolutely necessary"; and in the second, since we are speaking of "a philosophy from pure reason," the same explanation holds. In other words, the absolutely certain is equated with the a priori and with the necessary. This is correct from any point of view, including the currently prevalent one which equates all three with the analytic; and Kant, in further equating this kind of knowledge with knowledge derived from "pure reason," often comes very close to exhibiting it as analytic. We have already noted his view that conceptual knowledge is "empty" unless sense experience provides a "content" for it. We should further note that in the "unique" field of pure reason, "the object is not to be met with outside the concept . . . Our sole question is as to what lies in the idea . . ." [88] If Kant means, then, that some knowledge is certain because it is a priori (i.e., nonempirical and therefore nonexistential), because it is necessary (i.e., independent of empirical facts), and because it is analytic (i.e., deals only with "what lies in the idea"), there can thus far be no objection to his view.

The same considerations apply when Kant insists that "we shall understand by *a priori* knowledge, not knowledge independent of this or that experience, but knowledge absolutely independent of all experience," [89] and when he makes various claims as to universality and even as to completeness (if the latter can be interpreted in terms of the completeness of a logical system). All such claims cannot be summarily dismissed as "rationalism" until we decide exactly *what* knowledge Kant has in mind as certain, a priori, necessary, or complete; and this question is not easy to decide. It is true that Kant regards some of this knowledge as somehow "synthetic"; but, in attempting to explain what he means by this, we can only confuse matters if we fail to note how much of this knowledge is clearly or obscurely analytic and how important is the role of such analytic, deductive apparatus in empiricist interpretations today.

There are, however, certain features of Kant's views which may definitely be regarded as rationalistic in character. There can be no doubt that Kant believed in the availability of a unique system of knowledge into which everything in experience must fit. There is for him one and only one correct system of logic which establishes the conceptual structure, a system fully set forth by Aristotle.[90] We have a "completely coherent experience," [91] always organizable in terms of that conceptual structure with nothing left over. And there is one completely coherent system of physical laws, to be discovered and expressed by one completely coherent system of physical science. "That all events in the sensible world stand in thorough-going connection in accordance with unchangeable laws of nature is an established principle . . . and allows of no exception." [92] The "objectively valid" is equated with that which is "valid universally for all time." [93] In such a world and such a science, neither probability nor alternatives appear to have any place. Kant often mentions, of course, that there are "empirical rules" in science, but he does not seem to regard them as very interesting or fundamental. Obviously, it is precisely the all-inclusive, totally coherent structure of science that Kant regards as the supreme example of "a priori synthetic judgments"; so that once more we come to this concept as the crucial one.

Its thorough interpretation, particularly in the light of Kant's own clear-cut distinction between the analytic and the synthetic, is the chief requirement, then, for the understanding of Kant, especially now that this very distinction has taken on a greatly augmented importance.

I think it will be possible to make sense of such an interpretation. It will be found that the genuine rationalistic assumptions involved, the assumption as to a rigid and complete system of nature and the correlative assumption as to a rigid and complete system of mind, are drawn not from Kant's own philosophical premises but from the logic, the mathematics, and the physics of his time, which he naturally accepted; that, apart from the assumptions so derived, the a priori elements in Kant's scheme are the analytic elements; and that Kant meant by "synthetic a priori" nothing other than *applied logic,* which presents essentially the same problem today as it presented to Kant. If logic is analytic and nonexistential, and the data of experience are entirely extralogical, how do the two elements come together? How is it possible to systematize our sense perceptions in terms of those abstractions, "physical objects," or, more generally, to reason deductively about the existent world? If we balk today at Kant's term "pure natural science," we speak of "mathematical physics" without a qualm; but surely nothing is changed by this substitution.

Clarification along these lines, moreover, may make it evident that Kant's own philosophical premises—as distinct from the logic, mathematics, and science to which he applied them—are even more readily applicable to the logic, mathematics, and science of the twentieth century; that, indeed, philosophers of our own time have made this application, not always with due recognition of the Kantian origin of their premises; that they have sometimes done so, moreover, in such a way as to contribute highly valuable expansions and adaptations of the Kantian scheme. In particular, we must consider the contribution of C. I. Lewis, who has so revised the Kantian approach as to introduce the required loosening of the mental and conceptual structure; and the contribution of Hans Reichenbach, who has extended to the field of probability logic and its application the same approach that Kant brought to the field of deductive logic and its application, and thus has introduced the required loosening of the structure of nature and of science.

The purpose of a detailed consideration of the "synthetic a priori," then, is not merely to find out whether Kant should properly be called a rationalist. It is rather to find out, in so doing, what contribution Kant can still make to the solution of the problem which he himself introduced and which is even more acute in philosophy today—the problem of bridging the gap between the analytic and the synthetic, between logic and existence, to such an extent that the application of logic to the empirical world is possible. Similarly, a detailed consideration of the doctrine of the thing in itself will also be required, not merely to decide whether Kant should properly be called an idealist, but rather to understand Kant's proposed solution of the second pressing problem which his own contributions to current philosophy have created—the problem of locating independent, existential reality in a world of conceptualized experience. If the world of physical objects, as objects of knowledge, is in some sense created by our knowledge of it; if it is in some sense an abstraction, a conceptual construct, with no existential content apart from the occurrence of the sense data which it organizes; what *is* there independently of our sensations and our constructions alike? If it is not apparent, at first glance, that this question presents a problem for Kant's successors as it did for him, if they are not themselves conscious of any difficulties in this connection, we shall see that they do nevertheless run into such a problem—and into considerable confusion because of their reluctance to recognize it. And I think we shall find that here, too, Kant can make sense; that the thing in itself is neither an irrelevancy best overlooked nor a constituent of a mental world separate and different from the physical, but rather the thing of *our* world, the experienced world, as it exists independently of being experienced.

If these conclusions should be established, the Kantian view will turn out to be neither rationalism nor idealism in any sense in which such views are decisively repudiated by naturalist philosophers today. We shall then be in a position to understand what Kant's fundamental scheme, divested of the scientific and mathematical assumptions of his time and expanded by genuine successors who adapt it to the science and mathematics accepted today, may still have to offer toward the working out of crucial philosophical issues.

2

The Synthetic A Priori

THE TYPES of synthetic a priori knowledge that Kant regards as possible, and whose possibility he therefore finds it necessary to explain, are listed in the *Prolegomena* as "pure mathematics," "pure natural science," "metaphysics in general," and "metaphysics as a science." [1] Other forms of knowledge regarded as a priori by Kant are formal ("general") logic, which is definitely not synthetic, and ethics, which, although he slips into calling it a "pure rational science," [2] is fundamentally not considered knowledge at all, since it is assigned to "practical" rather than "theoretical reason." The *Prolegomena* list, therefore, may furnish an adequate preliminary clue as to what the knowledge is that Kant identifies as synthetic a priori.

In regard to "metaphysics in general" and "metaphysics as a science," we must understand that for Kant metaphysics, as most writers (though not he himself) use the term, is *not* possible. A dominant theme of the entire *Dialectic* is the demonstration that there is no ultimate or uniquely fundamental knowledge, ontological in content, about the universe as a whole; that we know nothing about existence except in terms of experience. The "metaphysics" which Kant regards as possible, together with the "transcendental philosophy" which "necessarily precedes it" [3] and which Kant also includes among "pure rational sciences," constitute what we should be more likely to call "epistemology"; they take the form of an analysis of concepts and mental procedures inherent in human knowledge, on the levels which he assigns to "reason" and "understanding" respectively. Metaphysics in this sense may be regarded as a priori, and is so regarded by Kant, in its role as an *analysis* of the a priori; i.e., there is an element in knowledge whose grounds are a priori, and its epistemological analysis and justification are therefore also a priori. If we are to find out what Kant means by synthetic a priori knowledge, then, we must turn to the role of such knowledge in mathematics and science.

In regard to "pure" mathematics, surely there need be no problem for us as to its nonempirical (a priori) character. It is rather the alleged synthetic character of such knowledge that we may question. It is important to realize, however, that for Kant the situation is different; for him the synthetic character of mathematics is a virtually indubitable assumption, and with this its a priori character must be reconciled. Prior to the discovery of non-Euclidean geometries, there was no reason, after all, not to regard the one known geometry as "necessary," and therefore also as necessarily descriptive of space; and it indeed appeared to be so in the Newtonian physics of Kant's day. Thoroughly relevant here is the useful warning of Weldon:

It is not always remembered that since Kant was thinking and writing in 1781 and not in 1940, the . . . views of Descartes, Leibniz, and Newton, not those of Einstein, Heisenberg, and Schrödinger, provided his problems.[4]

Indeed, Einstein himself recognized Kant's "erroneous opinion" of mathematics as "difficult to avoid in his time," pointing out that, when allowances are made on this score, his fundamental doctrine of the indispensability of *"concepts and 'categories' "* for our thinking is genuinely sound.[5]

Weldon's point is equally well taken in regard to Kant's view of science, where the difficulty is reversed. We are well aware today of the empirical and therefore synthetic element in physics, and correspondingly distrustful of the view that there can be a "pure natural science" independent of all experience. Here too, however, we find Kant, naturally enough, accepting other assumptions than ours. He takes science as he finds it, as anyone except the few real innovators in the field of science itself must do. Whenever he formulates the "a priori principles" of nature in specific scientific terms, they are standard "universal laws" of Newtonian physics—the conservation of matter, the equality of action and reaction, the law of inverse squares.[6] Expressed in somewhat more general and also more metaphysical terms, but still part of standard intellectual equipment in Kant's day, are the traditional principles concerning "nature" for which Leibniz was then the current authority [7]—that "nothing happens through blind chance," that "no necessity in nature is blind, but always a conditioned and therefore intelligible necessity," that there can be no "leap in the series of . . . alterations" and no "gaps or cleft between two appearances" (i.e., no "vacuum").[8] Obviously, none of this is original with Kant.

All such laws are habitually described by Kant as "necessary," "universal," and "a priori." The laws of Newtonian physics indeed purported to be "valid universally for all time"; [9] and Kant, accepting this claim at its face value, reasons very plausibly that these laws must therefore be a priori and thus necessary independently of any experience, because otherwise they would have to admit of the possibility of some exception which experience might present. On the other hand, he also recognizes that, since science claims to tell us something about the actual empirical world, its statements must be existential and therefore synthetic. Kant believes, therefore, that in "unanimously recognized" laws of science "there is actually given certain pure a priori synthetical cognitions. . . . We . . . need not ask *whether* it be possible, for it is actual, but *how* it is possible . . ." [10]

Both the alleged synthetic character of mathematics and the alleged absolute universality of physics, then, are initial intellectual equipment with which Kant operates. They are perplexing features assumed to exist in knowledge, and he sets out to explain them as best he can. The surprising feature of Kant's work is not his acceptance of the body of knowledge regarded as established in his time, but rather his ability to penetrate, by means of it and through it, to something far more fundamental and permanent. His philosophy is a clear confrontation and attempted solution of the broader and more enduring problem underlying those presented by the now obsolescent physical and mathematical notions of his time. The supposed question as to how deductive, conceptual, a priori mathematics can at the same time be "synthetic," i.e., existentially informative; the supposed question, conversely, as to how physical laws formulating the structure of the empirical world can at the same time be absolutely valid, universally and necessarily; indeed, the need to regard these supposed situations as problematic at all; all of this is seen by Kant as part of one fundamental problem. It is the problem of explaining how *any* conceptual structure and any logical reasoning in terms of such a structure can help us to know anything about empirical events; or, conversely, how the empirical data presented by our senses can possibly make sense to us in conceptual terms; the problem, in short, of *the applicability of logic to experience and the experienced world.* "The question . . . arises, how it can be conceivable that nature should have to proceed in accordance with categories which yet are not derived from it," or, in other words, "why everything that can be presented to our senses must be subject to laws which have their origin *a priori* in the understanding alone." [11] This is the question to which Kant reduces his initial one, "How are *a priori* synthetic judgments possible?" [12] and which the entire *Critique of Pure Reason* is designed to answer.

This dilemma, moreover, in the form in which we have now seen it appear in Kant's own words, arises even if we assume that mathematics is not synthetic, that physics is not a priori, and that a mistaken view of the status of logic is involved when Kant states the question in the form, "how *subjective conditions of thought* can have *objective validity* . . ." [13] Kant's views on the status of logic in relation to mind will require discussion later. The present dilemma, however, arises directly from the two major elements in Kant's doctrine which, as we have seen, are widely accepted today—the distinction between analytic and synthetic judgments and the recognition of a conceptual element in all knowledge. First of all, a conceptual system can be developed analytically, according to rules of logic, without any guarantee that the system will be applicable to anything empirical. As Kant puts it, "An analytic proposition . . . is concerned only with what is already thought in the concept . . . it is indifferent as to the object to which the concept may apply." [14] Indeed, "if no intuition could be given corresponding to the concept . . . there would be nothing, and could be nothing, to which my thought could be applied." [15] Why, then, should the actual empirical world behave according to any rules of logic at all? How can we be assured that our empirical perceptions ("intuitions") will correspond to our concepts?

Secondly, what can we mean by an "intuition . . . corresponding to the concept"? Kant recognizes the conceptual element in our knowledge as independent of, and different in kind from, the sensory element. He sees that our abstract concepts, especially those by which we order and explain our experience, are not directly descriptive (or "representative") of the sense data which constitute the existential element in that experience. "How, then, is the *subsumption* of intuitions under pure concepts, the *application* of a category to appearances, possible?" [16]

Seeing clearly that analysis of concepts can never lead to recognition of the existence of anything or (consequently) to the incorporation of any existent in the logical structure, and seeing also that the Aristotelian method of "subsumption" of the more particular under the more general can never lead from events to the laws of physics or even from particular sense data to physical objects, Kant recognizes that neither formal logic alone nor empirical observation alone can solve his problem. He therefore sets out to develop a theory of *applied logic,* a theory general enough to apply logic to *all* experience but as firmly anchored to experience on one hand as to logic on the other. This is what he calls "transcendental logic."

That by "transcendental logic" Kant means a general theory of applied logic is readily apparent from his own explanations of the terms involved. He is quite clear in his assertion that "*transcendental logic* . . . concerns itself with the laws of understanding and of reason solely in so far as they relate *a priori* to objects." [17] Or again, "Understanding and judgment find . . . in transcendental logic their canon of objectively valid and correct employment" (with "objectively" meaning, as it usually does for Kant, in relation to genuine physical objects). For "formal logic abstracts from all content of knowledge . . . and deals solely with the form of thought in general . . ." while "transcendental logic" has "a certain determinate content" (although that content is "limited to . . . those modes of knowledge which are pure and *a priori* . . .").[18] Moreover, although Kant uses the term "applied logic" for something which he explicitly distinguishes from transcendental logic, it is quite obvious that he does not mean by it what we should normally mean by it today, the analysis of logical reasoning about empirical subject matter. "What I call applied logic," he says,

(contrary to the usual meaning of this title, according to which it should contain certain exercises for which pure logic gives the rules) is a representation of the understanding . . . under the accidental subjective conditions which may hinder or help its application . . .

such as "attention, . . . doubt, hesitation, and conviction, etc." [19] Thus Kant reserves the term "applied logic," in his own usage, for certain aspects of psychology, while he interprets the term as used by others in an extremely narrow manner, confining its scope to "certain exercises." His distinction between "transcendental" and "applied" logic, therefore, does not involve "applied logic" as the term is commonly used today.

The problem, then, that "transcendental logic" or "transcendental philosophy" is designed to solve, the problem (more specifically) that the notion of the synthetic a priori is designed to solve, is the question of how the a priori can be *applied to* the synthetic—how concepts can be applied to objects—how logic can be applied to experience. This is true in Kant's treatment of mathematics, in connection with which he states,

When in *a priori* judgment we seek to go out beyond the given concept, we come in the *a priori* intuitions upon that which cannot be discovered in the concept but which is certainly found *a priori* in the intuition corresponding to the concept, and can be connected with it synthetically.[20]

In other words, a statement becomes synthetic (i.e., goes "out beyond the given concept") only when it is "connected with" (i.e., *applied to*) "intuition"; and the application to "intuition," Kant goes on to explain, is an application to "objects of the senses." Kant recognizes this fact in spite of his assumption that even the most abtract formulations of mathematics must be synthetic, an assumption which leads him to complicate matters by introducing the notion of "a priori intuition" as an intermediary.

As for the categories, where the complicating assumptions involved in Kant's view of mathematical concepts are absent, their role as means of applying logical concepts to sensory material is even clearer. For here, as Kant points out, no "a priori intuition" is required, but only "an application to some intuition by which an object of them is given us." [21] It is the applicability of the categories that constitutes their role in knowledge; in themselves they "do not afford us any knowledge of things; they do so only through their possible application to *empirical intuition*." [22] It is the element of applicability, moreover, that constitutes the "synthetic" element; for Kant is quite definite as to the fact that without it "the concepts would be void of all content, and therefore mere logical forms" [23] (i.e., definitive, not synthetic);

they are "merely functions of the understanding for concepts; and represent no object. This [objective] meaning they acquire from sensibility . . ." [24]

Indeed, Kant's starting point for the derivation of his categorial structure is a "table" classifying all the types of "judgment" recognized by the logic of his time. The "table of categories" is this same system of classification as applied to the same logical types of judgment *about empirical data*. I.e., "the *categories* are just these functions of judgment, in so far as they are employed in determination of the manifold of a given intuition." [25] Through each of them "the intuition of an object is regarded as determined in respect of one of the logical functions of judgment." [26] For instance, a "universal" judgment about empirical data is a statement asserting some sort of "unity" in these data; a "hypothetical" judgment about empirical data is a statement asserting a "relation" of "causality and dependence" between two sets of data; and similarly with the others. The categories are derived from logic, but they refer to experience; they are logical concepts so interpreted as to be capable of application to sense perceptions, if appropriate ones occur.

Whether there will actually be any such sense perceptions, the categories cannot tell us; for they cannot inform us of the existence of anything at all. As Kant says, "the categories are not in themselves knowledge, but are merely *forms of thought* for the making of knowledge from given intuitions"; [27] they "cannot yield any determining synthetic proposition" (i.e., "determining" that something exists), "but only a principle of the synthesis of possible empirical intuitions" [28] (i.e., a *definition*, or criterion, for selecting sensory data and organizing them into a system). And since the structure which the categories interpret in terms of empirical application is the structure of logic itself, it is quite clear that in the "transcendental philosophy" which studies the categorial system, "Our sole question is as to what lies in the idea . . ." [29] In other words, the conceptual framework of knowledge is analytic.

Analysis of this structure can, however, give us general knowledge about the nature of experience, *because this structure defines experience*. Kant does not apply the term "experience" to mere uninterpreted sense data, but only to the kind of cognitive awareness of a physical world in which our daily life is carried on and in which, as he continually points out, the application of systematic concepts plays a fundamental role. Thus all of his statements distinguishing between the "raw material of the sensible impressions" and "that knowledge of objects which is entitled experience" [30] may properly be regarded as definitions of experience. The categorial structure is knowledge about experience, because any subject matter that does not conform to it is (by definition) not experience.

The criteria which define experience also define the objects of experience (i.e., physical objects). The categories are "concepts of an object in general," [31] concepts which set up a general criterion of an object. They are "modes of thinking an object for possible intuitions, and of giving it meaning . . . in conformity with some function of the understanding, that is, of *defining it*." [32] An objective, physical house, for instance, is distinguished from our successive subjective perceptions of it by the fact that "it stands under a rule" which defines it, i.e., "which distinguishes it from every other apprehension . . ." [33] In other words, when we speak of a physical object, we mean not only various sense perceptions, but also a conceptual construction which can function as a "rule" for relating the sense perceptions, actual and possible; and the nature of the relationships which can be established by rule is stipulated by the categories.

It is this interpretation that enables us to include in the physical object more than the sum total of our actual perceptions of it; and indeed, to include in the physical world more than the sum total of actually perceived objects. For "the knowledge of things as *actual* does not, indeed, demand immediate *perception* . . . of the object whose existence is to be known," but merely "the connection of the object with some actual perception" under the categories. From a categorial principle and an actual perception (both, we may note, are indispensable), we may *infer the possibility* of other perceptions; and in this way we have a concept of a physical object. The "existence" of a thing means that it may "be so given us that the perception of it can, if need be, precede the concept"; i.e., the actual existence of an object is equated with the possible experience of it, in terms of real physical (not abstract logical) possibility.[34] That is why "nature," as Kant uses the term, can be identified with the totality both of actual physical objects and of possible experience.

Experience, then, is the kind of conscious process in which the categories are applied to sense perceptions; and physical objects, the objects of experience, consist of sense perceptions plus the conceptual structures into which they are organized when the categories are applied to them. It is the coincidence of sense data and categorial constructs that defines objectivity and constitutes the objective world; for these two elements of our knowledge "can supply objectively valid judgments of things only in *conjunction* with each other." [35] Thus we can assert a priori that the system of categories will be applicable to *any particular* experience only because they are applicable to *all possible* experience; and we can assert that they are applicable to all possible experience only because they are part of our definition of experience. It is not logically possible to call anything "experience" to which the categories do not apply; and therefore it is not possible for anything properly identifiable as "experience" to occur without their applicability. We must note, however, and keep in mind for future reference, that on this basis it is quite possible for *something* to occur that cannot properly be called "experience" in this sense.

Thus the "principles of pure understanding," all of which are statements that the individual categories, taken in turn, are applicable to all experience, turn out to be analytic in spite of their empirical reference. Although stated as generalizations about experience, they are actually definitions of experience, derived not from sense perception but from the logical system which we wish to apply to sense perception in order to understand it. According to Kant himself, "The table of categories is quite naturally our guide in the construction of the table of principles. For the latter are simply rules for the objective employment of the former." [36] It is not logically necessary that any particular experience should occur, or indeed, that anything at all should exist; and therefore, whenever we make use of these rules in the organization of actual empirical occurrences (i.e., whenever they are not "empty"), they acquire synthetic meaning; we may then interpret them as statements about all *existing* experience. Their justification, however, is analytic; and the actual occurrence of the opportunity to use them is not known a priori, and is never regarded by Kant as being known in such a manner. It may be inferred, but empirical premises are always required; i.e.,

the existence of any object of the senses cannot be known completely *a priori*, but only comparatively *a priori*, relatively to some other previously given existence . . . from connection with that which is perceived, in accordance with universal laws of experience.[37]

It is only within experience, only by inference from one occurrence to another when both fall within the definition of experience and when the rules for universal application of the categories are therefore operative, that we can reason about an occurrence of which we have no actual perception.

The "principles," then, together constitute a definition of experience, and the justification of their application to "all experience" is analytic; it is their actual application, the recognition of appropriate material for their application, that is synthetic; and it is the applicability of the a priori to the synthetic that Kant calls "synthetic a priori."

It may be worth while to single out, as examples of this interpretation, those categorial principles that usually are singled out for discussion (probably because of their significant roles both in common sense knowledge and in science), the principles of substance and causality. The principle of substance is presented by Kant in at least three forms, of which the most enlightening is the statement "that in all appearances there is something permanent." This statement is called "synthetic a priori" by Kant, in contrast with "the proposition that substance is permanent," which he regards as "tautological." [38] We may note, however, that "appearances," as distinguished from mere "representations," are sense perceptions "viewed . . . in so far as they stand for an object"; [39] and an object, as we have seen, is by definition subject to the categories. In the long run, then, the principle is circular and analytic after all.

This circularity, however, does not render the principle unimportant, as the entire analysis of substance is a very far-reaching elucidation of what is involved in knowledge. Most prominently, it elucidates the kind of knowledge that organizes the world of our everyday experience as a world of things, enduring and changing in time. For Kant shows, in discussing the concept of substance, that this concept is required for such coherent experience; that we make implicit use of it whenever we interpret the occurrence of a variety of sense data not as a "bare succession" in which "existence is always vanishing and recommencing," but as the occurrence of changes in *things* (i.e., as a succession in which "the permanent is the object itself, that is, substance as phenomenon").[40] We cannot conceive change without conceiving permanence, and we cannot conceive identifiable things or events without conceiving both change and permanence. If we could not conceive things in this way, however, our experience would be very different from the experience that we actually have, so different that we are amply justified in regarding any such occurrences as no experience at all, by definition. We should indeed be living in a different world; and it would be a world to which no rational inference would be relevant.

This concept of substance, then, is not at all the traditional pre-Kantian concept of a fundamental existent. The existential material is provided solely by sense perception; and substance is a conceptual structure for organizing this material into logical form, with no "objective reality" unless there is such material for it to organize (i.e., unless we "have an intuition").[41] Interestingly enough, Kant's analysis not only does not contradict but rather anticipates Russell's criticism of the concept of substance and attribute as a hypostasis of the subject-predicate relation fundamental to Aristotelian logic.[42] According to Kant's doctrine, this is precisely what the concept of substance is intended to be. The logical "form of judgment" from which it is derived is that of the "categorical judgment," which asserts the relation "of the predicate to the subject"; [43] and substance is "something which can exist only as subject and not as mere predicate." [44] But Kant points out, further, that this hypostasis is required for our experience to be what it is; that a physical object *is* this same hypostasis, with actual existence only to the extent that actual sense perceptions fill the role of predicates. And although subject-predicate logic is no longer the only logic, as it was for Kant and all his contemporaries, it is certainly still the logic of our conceptual dealings with our sense perceptions in terms of the physical objects of everyday experience.

The status which Kant accords to the concept of causality is similar; and to understand this, it is not necessary to disentangle in detail his involved and often questionable argument for the causal principle. The important point seems to be that the distinction between a permanent object and a series of transitory occurrences, since our sensory awareness of both consists of a string of successive sensations, is a conceptual distinction; and that this conceptual distinction is dependent on the application of "rules" explaining *why* one sensation follows another in the sequence in which it actually does follow. In the mere sequence of sensations,

nothing is distinguished from anything else. But immediately I perceive or assume that in this succession there is a relation to the preceding state, from which the representation follows in conformity with a rule, I represent something as an event, as something that happens; that is to say, I apprehend an object . . .[45]

In other words, it is the conceptual relation of causality between successive sensations that gives them their place in the objective physical world; indeed, it is this relation, this place in the physical framework, that constitutes their objectivity as events.

Does this mean that the objectivity of an event is so constituted *by definition?* Logically and in terms of Kant's general theoretical structure, it does; but as to the question whether it means this to Kant, one can only conclude that he himself is not quite sure. It is noteworthy that, in the very passage just quoted, he is undecided as to whether we "perceive or assume" the causal relation. At one point he states specifically that the proposition, "Everything which happens has its cause," cannot be analytic, because "the concept of a 'cause' lies entirely outside the other concept, and signifies something different from 'that which happens' . . ."[46] At another point, however, he says that he has "derived the principle that everything which happens has a cause, from the condition under which alone a concept of happening in general is objectively possible."[47] It would be quite in order, one might suppose, to reconcile these two statements on the grounds that the first refers to everything which merely "happens," including purely subjective happenings, while the second refers to that which happens "objectively"; it is from the latter concept, then, that causality, as a criterion of objectivity, is analytically derivable. Such a distinction may indeed be in the back of Kant's mind. Unfortunately, however, we have just seen him speak of the cognition of "an event, as something that happens," as *equivalent* to the apprehension of "an object," and as *distinguished* from the mere succession of sensations.

There is, of course, an obvious reason for Kant's indecision in this matter. It lies in the fundamental role, in the science of his time, of the assumption that there are specific physical laws inherent in the nature of things, whose applicability to everything, past, present, and future, can be known with certainty; in other words, that the physical universe could not possibly be other than it is. To justify such an assumption, Kant would have to attribute to causality an absolute existential status which he cannot consistently maintain for it. It is both precarious and presumptuous to assume that any writer, especially one as profoundly convinced as Kant of the importance of his own words, means one part of what he says and not another. Yet it is at least evident that the analytic interpretation of causality (as a relation which *defines* an objective event) is one that Kant has in mind, whether or not he also has others in mind; that this interpretation is most coherent with his premises; and that it represents his most original thinking in contrast with the assumptions which he takes over from the intellectual background of his time.

It is on this basis, indeed, that Kant attempts in the *Prolegomena* to clarify his stand, perhaps to reconcile a possible inconsistency of which he himself has become aware. "It is all the same," he says explicitly,

> whether I say: "A judgment of perception can never rank as experience without the law that, whenever an event is observed, it is always referred to some antecedent, which it follows according to a universal rule," or: "Everything of which experience teaches that it happens must have a cause."

And surprisingly, in view of his frequent use of the second of these formulations, he adds, here,

> It is, however, more suitable to choose the first formula. For we can *a priori* and prior to all given objects have a knowledge of those conditions on which alone experience of them is possible, but never of the laws to which things may in themselves be subject . . .[48]

Causality, in other words, is not something that exists independently of human consciousness; it is part of the experienced world because it is part of the means by which we experience that world, a means which includes conceptual as well as sensory equipment. An event is not somehow tied ontologically to an antecedent cause, but "referred to some antecedent" in being known as an event; and the fact of being so "referred" is a definitive criterion determining that it may "rank as experience."

If this analysis is correct, however, we cannot know that a similar cause, occurring at some other time, will be followed by a similar effect. The relation between cause and effect may indeed be "necessary" in terms of the "rule" which we apply to the particular case; but how do we know that our rule will apply to any other case? Kant definitely recognizes that, in terms of sense perceptions actually given, the anticipated effect may fail to follow. This eventuality, however, merely means that the *same* rule cannot be applied, not that *no* rule is applicable; and if indeed no physical rule is applicable, the sensory material is excluded from the physical world, *by definition*. In Kant's own words,

. . . were I to posit the antecedent and the event were not to follow necessarily thereupon, I should have to regard the succession as a merely subjective play of my fancy; and if I still represented it to myself as something objective, I should have to call it a mere dream. Thus . . . the relation of cause to effect—is the condition of the objective validity of our empirical judgments, . . . the condition of experience.[49]

It is by construction of causal systems that we separate our sensations into a physical world, a dream world, and a "play of . . . fancy," and probably other parallel classifications as well. In deciding to which of these any particular sense perception must be assigned, however, we must consider the strictly *empirical* facts as to what sense perceptions precede and follow it, and see where the actual sequence will fit into the rules; so that in this sense *the application is synthetic,* although the justification is analytic. This is true not only of causality but of all the categorial principles.

This conclusion, however, leaves a very fundamental and far-reaching question unanswered. How do we know that our definition is applicable at all, rather than empty—that there is any experience whatsoever, in the sense in which the application of the categories defines experience? How do we know that any of our sense perceptions will be capable of such organization as to meet our definition, or, conversely, that our method of understanding will enable us to understand the existing world? It may well appear that we reach here the crucial point of the whole discussion; for if we are concerned, as Kant undoubtedly is, with explaining the applicability of logic, an explanation in analytic terms is, in a sense, no explanation at all. Kant may have shown that logic, through the categories, is applicable to "experience," if experience is defined as that to which logic is thus applicable; but what does this prove? We still need the supplementary assertion that *there is experience* in terms of such a definition. Thus Reichenbach is almost right in his assertion that "The postulate that experience in the frame of the a-priori principles must always be possible is the unwarranted assumption of Kant's system . . ."[50]

It would be more accurate, however, to assert that the postulate that there *is* (not that there must always be) such experience is the fundamental *synthetic premise* of Kant's system; and in this form the assumption is hardly "unwarranted," since it would be difficult to deny that we do have such experience as a matter of empirical fact. Kant himself is well aware both that this premise is needed for the applicability, or "synthetic" feature, of his a priori system, and that *it is not itself true a priori*. His "principles," he says, as instances of "synthetic judgment," cannot be established

directly from concepts alone, but always only indirectly through relation of these concepts to something altogether contingent, namely, *possible experience*. When such experience (that is, something as object of possible experiences) is presupposed, these principles are indeed apodeictically certain; but in themselves, directly, they can never be known a priori.[51]

In other words, Kant's "principles," understood as "synthetic judgments," must be understood as statements that the categories are *in fact* applicable. As such, they "can never be known *a priori*," but require for their validation two premises: not only that the categories are applicable to "all possible experience" (although Kant usually emphasizes this premise, in terms of which, as definitions of possible experience, they *are* valid a priori), but also that there is in fact experience as so defined. The latter premise is the synthetic one, and for that very reason it is, as Kant recognizes, "altogether contingent"; but once its truth is assumed ("presupposed"), the "principles" become "apodeictically certain"—because, although Kant does not explicitly say so, their truth follows *analytically*.

Are we justified in assuming the truth of such an existential premise? The assumption that "there is experience" may indeed appear to be undeniable if we think of "experience," as philosophical usage often does, in terms of a lowest common denominator—if we mean anything that occurs or exists of which anyone is aware. Such a statement, if not exactly synthetic a priori, might well be called, with much the same effect, analytic a posteriori. It states and is validated by an empirical fact, which is a "contingent" fact; yet the statement adds nothing to our knowledge which the occurrence of the fact itself does not add, but merely points to that occurrence without interpretation, and therefore cannot be mistaken. On the other hand, if we use the term "experience" as Kant uses it, i.e., as designating (by definition) that kind of occurrence that is subject to the categories, there is, up to this point, no reason to assume that any such occurrence must take place, or that all or any occurrences of which we are aware must be of this sort.

There is no doubt that Kant sometimes appears to take advantage of this ambiguity in the term "experience," insofar as its associations in the mind of the reader are concerned; I do not believe that he ever departs in so many words from the usage established by his own definition. Yet, even when we are careful to steer clear of this possible ambiguity, we find that the structure does not collapse; for we all do, of course, know of countless occurrences such as fit Kant's definition of experience. As a matter of empirical fact, we do have consciousness of physical objects, which means experience in terms of the applicability of the categories, which means in turn that something has occurred to which application of the categories is possible. As Kant expresses it, "possible experience" must be "presupposed" for the "principles" (interpreted existentially) to be certain; but the "principles" in turn must be "presupposed" for actual experience to be explained. Thus each of these principles "makes possible the very experience which is its own ground of proof, and . . . in this experience it must always itself be presupposed." [52] The structure, in other words, is circular; yet it is not empty, because it contains within it a valid empirical reference. We do have the kind of experience that it analyzes.

This, however, is not enough for Kant, although it might perhaps be enough for an adequate and important theory of knowledge if we were to stop right here. It is not enough for Kant that "experience continually presents examples of such regularity among appearances"; for how do we know that we shall have such experience in the future? i.e., that we have it "necessarily"? Moreover—and this amounts to the same question in another form—why do we have such experience? The existential content of our experience, after all, is sense impressions, which have nothing to do with logic, and might, on the face of it, just as well not be organizable in terms of the categories. "That objects of sensible intuition must conform . . . to the conditions which the understanding requires for the synthetic unity of thought, is a conclusion the grounds of which are by no means so obvious." [53]

Kant, therefore, finds the "metaphysical deduction" of his categories from the structure of logic insufficient, and goes on to a "transcendental deduction" of them from the structure of consciousness itself. The main point of Kant's involved analysis here is that consciousness is essentially temporal; an instantaneous sensation would be no sensation at all, since we should not have time to be aware of it. Sensory content, however, is a "manifold" as soon as it is more than instantaneous; for the identity of one sensation over a temporal spread, however brief, involves an act of consciousness by which the earlier content is not only apprehended but remembered and identified with the later content. This act must be that of a *continuous* consciousness; I can remember and recognize only my own sensations, not those of some other conscious being. I cannot, on the other hand, perceive any entity to be identified as "consciousness" or "myself," apart from the object of which I am conscious; the continuous, conscious self, the *subject* of consciousness, therefore, is "transcendental," and not existential. It is a logical premise, an explanatory construct which we must supply if we are to explain or understand the possibility of sensory perception such as we in fact have.

We cannot, however, conceive of a subject without an object. For the transcendental subject, then, sense perceptions are not sufficient objects, because we are conscious of relations between sensations also, and because a consciousness merely coextensive with sensation could provide no continuity which sensation alone could not provide. The continuous *object* of consciousness, therefore, must be "presupposed" (i.e., supplied as an explanatory premise) in the same manner in which the continuous self is presupposed. Thus the "transcendental unity of apperception" and the "transcendental object $= x$" are correlative concepts, required for the explanation of conscious sense perception.[54]

The foregoing account of the "transcendental deduction" is based on Kant's first edition, in the belief that his second version is much less readily comprehensible, and not comprehensible at all except in terms of the first. The chief later omission, that of the "transcendental object," appears to me to be unfortunate, and some of the chief later additions appear unnecessary. Kant does add, however, a clarification of the relevance of all this extended analysis of consciousness to the categories which it is supposed to "deduce"; and with this matter we must now concern ourselves.

The concept of a continuous object at which the "transcendental deduction" arrives is precisely the concept whose application to sensory material constitutes the object defined by the categories. This, Kant believes, is as we should expect; for the "synthesis" by which sensations are incorporated in a continuous consciousness contains an intellectual element, which of course performs just those intellectual functions (expressed, in Kant's scheme, by the logical "forms of judgment") of which human minds are capable.[55] Conversely, the intellectual equipment of human beings is just that kind that, by the very nature of its operations, "combines and arranges the material of knowledge, that is, the intuition . . ."[56] Kant attempts to support this view by interpreting the copula "is," which in the type of logic at his disposal is required for any "judgment," as an assertion of an objective relation between "representations";[57] but he himself apparently feels the inadequacy of this argument, concluding after all that

This peculiarity of our understanding, that it can produce *a priori* unity of apperception solely by means of the categories, and only by such and so many, is as little capable of further explanation as why we have just these and no other functions of judgment, or why space and time are the only forms of our possible intuition.[58]

Thus, in terms of the transcendental deduction, the "synthetic a priori" is synthetic in a double sense—not only in its application to given sensory material, but also in its very derivation from the nature of human consciousness. For while the derivation is analytic, the nature of human consciousness is a logically unexplained, contingent fact, which could have been otherwise.

It is at this point that the most serious difficulties arise, both in the interpretation of Kant and in Kant's own development of his position. For we now have two "deductions" of the categories, the "metaphysical deduction" from the structure of logic and the "transcendental deduction" from the structure of consciousness; and it is by no means clear why the two results coincide. Starting with the derivation from logic, we needed a justification for the supposition that *some* existential subject matter of an appropriate kind would be available for the application of the categories so that the latter would be empirically relevant and not empty. With the derivation from the nature of consciousness, however, Kant seems to have established too much; for he has established that *all* existential subject matter available to consciousness (i.e., all sense data) must be subject to the categories. If so, the function of the categories as definitions appears lost (since such definitions would exclude nothing of which we are conscious); and lost with it is the distinction between sensation and experience, the subjective and the objective, which Kant has taken such pains to establish. And then there is a second difficulty. If the categories are derivable from the nature of consciousness, why do we have to derive them from logic at all? Indeed, how *can* we do so and obtain the same set of categories, unless there is a prior relation between logic and consciousness, involving new difficulties which we have not even begun to consider? Is logic to be reduced to psychology, dependent on the human mind? If so, on *what* human mind?

The question of the extent to which the categories must be applicable, i.e., whether they are to be regarded as applicable to all contents of consciousness or only to experience of an objective world, has been widely discussed by Kant's commentators; and a useful summary is provided by Paton. He cites Vaihinger, for instance, as labeling "pre-critical" all statements by Kant that there can be conscious sense impressions without application of the categories; and Kemp Smith as attributing to Kant in his "critical" stage the belief that animals, since they lack concepts, cannot have consciousness. According to Paton himself, however, Kant's alleged later denials of the so-called "pre-critical" view assert merely that "there can be no *knowledge* or *experience* of *objects*—in the strict sense—apart from the categories," not "that no *representations* can exist for *consciousness* apart from the categories." [59] Unfortunately, while Paton lists many passages supporting his view (e.g., Kant's assertion that "appearances can certainly be given in intuition independently of functions of the understanding"),[60] he fails to list the passages to the contrary (e.g., Kant's paragraph heading, "All Sensible Intuitions are subject to the Categories, as Conditions under which alone their Manifold can come together in one Consciousness").[61]

Paton attempts a further reconciliation of the conflicting statements on the grounds that Kant intends merely to make clear a structural distinction; "it is due to our sensibility that we see the red colour, and it is due to our understanding that we see it as the colour of a thing or object . . ." Whether "sensibility" ever occurs without "understanding" is then a question of empirical psychology.[62] This, however, does not answer the fundamental question as to whether the understandable character of the objective world is a matter of selective definition or an actual exclusion of the unintelligible from sense perception. The first alternative is, as Paton reccognizes, both highly original with Kant and highly valuable for subsequent philosophy; but is it Kant's view? There appears to be at least as much evidence to the contrary, especially in the context of the "transcendental deduction."

Nevertheless, Kant does seem to provide himself with the rudiments of a way out of this situation, although he does not pursue the point so far or so consistently as he might. Little emphasized by Kant himself and even less by either Paton or Kemp Smith is the distinction between those categories that admit of "mathematical employment" and those that admit only of "dynamical employment." The categories of quantity and of quality and the corresponding principles of their application (that "All intuitions are extensive magnitudes" [63] and that "In all appearances, the real that is an object of sensation has intensive magnitude, that is, a degree") [64] are "*a priori* conditions of intuition" and therefore "unconditionally necessary." I.e., they are deducible from the nature of rudimentary sensory awareness, and therefore of all consciousness. The categories of relation and modality and the principles of their application, on the other hand, are "*a priori* conditions . . . of the existence of the objects of a possible empirical intuition," and therefore "in themselves only accidental"; they still have, in a sense, "*a priori* necessity, but only under the condition of empirical thought in some experience . . ." [65] I.e., they are deducible only from the nature of our consciousness of an objective world—as indeed the titles of these principles, "analogies of experience" and "postulates of empirical thought," indicate.

Kant is most convincing when he takes this view. It is readily recognizable that there cannot be a sense impression without spatial or temporal extension ("extensive magnitude") or without some qualitative character ("intensive magnitude"); but to argue that causality, for instance, is similarly required for sense impressions, is quite another matter. Thus the "*dynamical* principles" are "merely regulative principles of *intuition*," although "constitutive in respect of *experience*," while the "*mathematical*" principles are constitutive of both.[66] That is, we can have sensations to which the dynamical principles are inapplicable, but—by definition—not "experience" (by which Kant means objective experience). Their application as far as possible (i.e., "regulatively"), however, provides a criterion for sorting *all* sensations into subjective and objective, rooted in the attempt to understand that is part of human consciousness and organized by the transcendental unity of apperception; so that Kant's structure requires fundamental readjustment, but does not break down.

This limitation of the dynamical principles to a regulative function is indispensable for the understanding of illusion and error. Kant sees the difference between true perception of objects on one hand and illusion or error on the other as not sensory but conceptual,

not ascertained by the nature of the representations which are referred to the objects (for they are the same in both cases), but by their connection according to those rules which determine the coherence of the representations in the concept of an object . . .

When, for instance, the paths of the planets appear to the senses as "now progressive, now retrogressive," there is nothing wrong with our senses; but our understanding is not functioning properly if we regard this as "the objective character of their motion," because we are failing to "connect our intuitions . . . in space and in time, according to the rules of the coherence of all knowledge in experience . . ." [67] We are capable, then, of misapplying categories. Besides such "error in judgment," moreover, there may be "delusion of imagination (in dreams)." This, too, is perceptual in content, for "in the absence of perception even imagining and dreaming are not possible"; yet here we do not merely make the wrong connection between our perceptions and a physical object, but rather perceive as an object something that is not actual at all. Here, too, however, the rule holds that *"Whatever is connected with a perception according to empirical laws, is actual."* [68] It is the breakdown of conceptual connections, then, the failure of physical *laws* to be applicable, not any perceivable difference in sensory content, that identifies certain occurrences as dreams, having no actual objects. Here, then, Kant apparently recognizes areas in which some, at least, of the categories are inapplicable.

On the other hand, we may recall Kant's remark in regard to apparent failures of causality, "I should have to regard the succession as a merely subjective play of my fancy; and if I still represented it to myself as something objective, I should have to call it a mere dream." [69] Here a dream is called "objective"; i.e., it is implied that the classification of any sensory content as subjective or illusory is merely tentative, and that when the *correct* rules are found for relating it to the rest of the physical world (e.g., the rules governing the occurrence of dreams, which are just as coherent, although not the same, as the rules governing perception of physical objects), we may properly classify it as objective. Unfortunately, Kant is not particularly interested in the subject of illusion and error, and does not attempt to reach any more definite conclusion in this respect; yet it seems that a clarification on this point would hold the key to the crucial question as to just how universal the applicability of the categories is to be considered.

For a clarification of this kind we shall have to wait for the very relevant and illuminating analysis by Lewis, which proceeds much further along the lines at which Kant merely hints in the last passage quoted. As for Kant himself, meanwhile, it is evident that, on one hand, he attempts to establish the entire categorial structure as necessarily applicable to all the content of consciousness, and that, on the other hand, in distinguishing the "dynamical principles" as merely "regulative" and in defining illusion as sense perception which violates empirical laws, he eliminates some of the content of consciousness (in some sense, at least) from the application of some, if not all, of the categories. It is further evident that the second alternative is the one that maintains the status of the total system of categories as a definition of objective experience, and their applicability to such experience as analytic.

Yet, why this definition and not another? Surely a distinction as fundamental as that between a physical object and a dream is not one which each of us invents arbitrarily for himself. As we have seen, Kant has two answers, one in terms of the structure of logic and the other in terms of the structure of consciousness; and it would not be difficult to jump to the conclusion that, for the sake of consistency, we must get rid of one answer or the other. For those who take this approach, it is usually the metaphysical deduction that falls by the wayside.[70] If, however, we regard Kant's entire enterprise in the first *Critique* as an attempt to explain the applicability of *logical* reasoning to the existential subject matter provided by sense perception, as surely we have seen good reason to do, nothing could be further from the mark than the removal of the metaphysical deduction from the picture. At no point does Kant redefine the categories, or appear to regard them as anything but "forms of thought" or "logical functions of judgment" as applied to perceptual material. The transcendental deduction, which sets out to explain this applicability, may not be entirely successful in doing so, and it may run into some conflict with the metaphysical deduction; yet it would be almost pointless without that deduction.

As to the obsoleteness of the list of forms, it must be remembered that while modern logic has opened up the possibility of a vastly expanded number (perhaps an infinite number) of such forms, it has not rejected the traditional ones. What it has found unacceptable in some traditional *treatments* of them is the assumption of existential implications; and it is this assumption that Kant himself eliminates once and for all. He does, of course, mistakenly assume the completeness of his list; but surely most, if not all, of his categories are still recognizable as relevant to the interpretation of the empirical world; and the increased flexibility of logic means that it should be easier to find logical foundations for such categories, avoiding those of Kant's derivations that appear strained. Moreover, some of the most important of his derivations, e.g., those of substance and causality, do not appear strained at all; and surely a second glance is in order for the derivation of "number." By identifying "number" as "the pure *schema* of magnitude (*quantitatis*), as a concept of the understanding," [71] Kant clearly indicates its derivation from the logical concept of the quantity of judgments, earlier established as the source of the categories of quantity. If Russell's interpretation of the concept of "number" in terms of logic is so much more sophisticated than Kant's as to make the latter seem negligible, the significance of the fact that Kant even attempted such a thing, however crudely, can hardly be overestimated.

The derivation of the categorial system *both* from the structure of logic and, at least to some extent, from the structure of consciousness cannot be eliminated without causing Kant's doctrine to fall hopelessly apart. And this double derivation depends upon the prior assumption that *logic itself is somehow inherent in the nature of consciousness* and derivable from it. Kant nowhere makes this assumption explicit, and it appears as awkward for him as for any logician today. For him as for later logicians, however, it seems more easily denied than replaced.

Kant is very explicit in his assertion that the rules of logic are not composed of "subjective dispositions of thought implanted in us . . . by our Creator," since in that case they would provide "only an arbitrary subjective necessity." [72] Indeed, "pure logic . . . does not, as has sometimes been supposed, borrow anything from psychology, which therefore has no influence whatever on the canon of the understanding." Yet, at the same time, Kant speaks of logic as "the science of the rules of the understanding" or of the "absolutely necessary rules of thought," the "form of thought in general," "laws which the understanding employs . . . in thinking," and the like.[73] It is true that this may entitle logic to be called "objective" in Kantian language, because "Thought is the act which relates given intuition to an object"; [74] but this is a circular kind of objectivity, since the object itself, as we have seen, is "objective" (as distinguished from "subjective" sensations) because the "rules of the understanding" which determine objectivity are applicable to it. There might, moreover, still be a different logic, a different object, a different standard of objectivity for each conscious subject, if there is no further criterion.

This, however, cannot be all there is to objectivity; for "when a judgment agrees with an object, all judgments concerning the same object must likewise agree among themselves . . ." [75] Since sensation may vary with the observer and with various conditions, objectivity in this sense, possession of the character of a *common* object for all observers, a *normal* object, must be provided by the categorial structure, ultimately by the logical structure, which therefore must be the structure not of the variable individual mind but of a *normal or standard human mind*. It should be noted, too, that "objectivity" in the sense of relation to objects, for whatever it may be worth, applies only to the "functions of judgment," not to their logical manipulation. The rule of the syllogism, for example, is regarded by Kant as a principle not of "understanding" but of "pure reason," [76] implying "no relation to any object" and in that sense providing only a "subjective derivation." [77]

The concept of a standard human mind is undoubtedly the key to the situation; for without it, a logic identified as in any way a feature of "the mind" or of "thought" would be deprived of any normative character. As Kant recognizes, logical necessity would then mean "only that I am so constituted that I cannot think this representation otherwise than as thus connected; . . . nor would there be wanting people who would refuse to admit this subjective necessity . . ." [78] Kant, however, distinguishes throughout between "a consciousness in one subject only" and "consciousness in general"; [79] and surely the latter meant to him no such existential, collective super-consciousness as his Hegelian successors made of it, but simply an abstract, definitive, *standard concept* of consciousness, both a descriptive and a normative criterion of what is required for human consciousness to be recognizably as it in fact is. Whatever is "united in consciousness in general" is united "necessarily," [80] because the reference to "consciousness in general" is merely Kant's way of saying that there could not otherwise be consciousness as we know it.

This does not mean that there cannot also be consciousness of some other type; indeed, Kant often speculates about a kind of being that would have "non-sensuous intuition" which the human mind does not have. But all *human* consciousness, to be reasonably identifiable as such, must have a certain minimal conceptual structure in common, just as it must have a sensory "mode of perceiving" which, although "not necessarily shared in by every being," must at least be shared in "by every human being." [81] The "unity of apperception" which is the basis of that structure, then, contains the "ground . . . of the possibility of the understanding, even as regards its logical employment" [82] as well as its employment in application to existential subject matter; both are part of "the peculiar way in which we think," which must be accepted as a self-validating fact because we can think in no other way. For "how this peculiar property . . . itself is possible . . . cannot be further analyzed or answered, because . . . we are in need [of it] for all our answers and for all our thinking . . ." [83]

On the face of it, this view appears too suggestive of existential logic, on the one hand, and a priori psychology, on the other, to avoid the label of rationalism today. Yet here there are qualifications which need to be made. First of all, it is indeed a fact that there is within the field of knowledge a kind of procedure which we call logic. It is also a fact that we cannot have knowledge without taking logic into account. We can and often do *think* irrationally, but we cannot *understand* irrationally; and if the equivalence between understanding and rationality is analytic, an equivalence by definition, it is also to some extent descriptive of understanding in the psychological sense. It would, of course, be fantastic to suppose that the whole system even of Aristotelian logic, not to mention the whole of *Principia Mathematica*, could be derived deductively from a description of the nature of human consciousness, standard or otherwise; and if this is what Kant has in mind, he is surely guilty of exaggeration, to say the least. Yet it is quite otherwise with the assumption that there are some more general and simpler features, perhaps reducible to the one feature of consistency, which distinguish the rational from the irrational, and which make sense both of logic (which is founded on them, however varied its forms may be) and of the empirical world (which is conceptually organized in terms of them in the very process of being observed), to the extent that anything makes sense to us at all. For if rationality indeed has nothing to do with existence, as Kant himself is the first to make clear, surely it would be quite another matter to suppose that it has nothing to do with knowledge.

It should be noted, too, that alternative attempts at explanation of the status of logic involve just as many problems and perhaps solve fewer. We may probably assume without too much arbitrariness that both the Platonic rationalist conception of logic as existentially self-validating and the empiricist conception of logic as derived from sense perception may be regarded as discredited. In that case, what else is there? Is the reduction of logic to tautology, valid as far as it goes, really an answer? That something further is required to explain tautology, and that a psychological element of some sort constantly threatens to intrude, will become evident when we consider Lewis and Reichenbach, both of whom have all the equipment of contemporary logic at their disposal.

As for the associated notion of a standard or normal human mind, quite aside from the rigid structure and formidable array of "faculties" which Kant gratuitously assigns to it (in line with psychological doctrines of his day), surely it is a notion difficult to dispense with entirely. We may well question whether human beings could experience a common world and use common languages, to a sufficient extent for communication with each other, if they had not *some* basic mental apparatus in common. Surely they must share at least the ability to refer their sense perceptions to a common objective world, a world in which all these diverse perceptions fit into a conceptual structure which all can recognize; and this is just what Kant's categories are intended to provide, or rather constitute. They are his formulation of the minimum conceptual basis for an objective world and, consequently, for a *common* objective world. They do not claim to tell us anything about what that world or our experience of it

will contain, but "concern *solely the form of an experience in general
. . .*" [84] I.e., the "transcendental synthesis [framed] from concepts
alone . . . relates only to a thing in general, as defining the conditions under which the perception of it can belong to possible experience." [85]

Kant's fundamental "synthetic a priori" assumption is, then, that
there is experience in the full sense; that human beings generically
have a kind of consciousness which enables them to have sense perceptions; to construct at least rudimentary logical systems which apply to these sense perceptions; and to come out with something systematically similar to the experience of other human beings, to a
sufficient degree for intelligible communication. "Synthetic a priori"
or not, surely this assumption appears justifiable. Actually, it states
an empirical, synthetic, and contingent fact; as we have seen, Kant
himself asserts as much; yet it is also the logical premise upon which
Kant's so-called "a priori synthetic judgments" turn out to be *analytic,* and therefore valid a priori. The same premise may also be
stated as the assumption that these judgments, taken as definitions,
are *applicable to something.*

What Kant gives us, in other words, is an extended analytic definition
of experience, which also purports—as do most definitions worth the
effort of formulation—to describe something actually existing, in this
case the experience which human beings actually do have. As an analytic structure, it is "a priori"; as a descriptive one, it is "synthetic."
This does not justify the term "synthetic a priori," but provides an
opening for its use, in the context of the mathematical and scientific
assumptions of Kant's time. His use of this unfortunate term, however, is less important than the degree of validity, analytic and descriptive, to be found in his definition of experience and his development of that definition; and it has become evident, I hope, that
this degree of validity is very considerable, although of course many
difficulties remain.

There is still required, both for the complete understanding of
Kant's analysis of knowledge and for the full development of its potentialities, the interpretation of actual knowledge in terms of it.
Kant, we may remember, finds both in science and in mathematics
alleged instances of actual a priori synthetic judgments, which (as
we can now see) must therefore be regarded as analytically derivable
from the categorial structure and synthetically applicable. We must

now discover how this interpretation works out, and, in so doing, pin down more specifically Kant's view of science and any relevance that this view may have for the understanding of science today. The central position which this matter occupies in Kant's epistemological structure, however, is already clear; both logically and in fact, the development of that structure brings it back to the explanation of those scientific laws whose assumed synthetic a priori character Kant has originally set out to explain. Nothing could be more ironic than Reichenbach's belief that Kant is obsolete because "philosophical systems have lost their significance and . . . their function has been taken over by the philosophy of science." [86] On the contrary, it is precisely as background for a philosophy of science that Kant's system comes into focus and remains relevant today. It is this aspect that we must now consider.

3

The Synthetic A Priori
& Kant's Interpretation of Science

THE FOUNDATION for Kant's interpretation of scientific laws is laid, of course, by his analysis of the conceptual element in all knowledge of the physical world. Rational structure in things is a product of our way of understanding them, by virtue of which they are constituted as physical objects; but rational structures by themselves are empty and irrelevant to knowledge unless there is sensory subject matter that fits into them. Thus Kant, whatever his inconsistencies in further elaboration on the subject, contributes permanently to the analysis of scientific law the conception that

understanding is itself the source of the laws of nature, and so of its formal unity . . . Certainly, empirical laws, as such, can never derive their origin from pure understanding . . . But all empirical laws are only special determinations of the pure laws of understanding, under which, and according to the norm of which, they first become possible. Through them appearances take on an orderly character . . .[1]

Empirical laws, in other words, derive their existential subject matter from sense perception, but their structure ("formal unity") from logic; and they are particular cases ("special determinations") of applied logic and so of the basic principles according to which logic is applied to sensory material.

Laws, then, are not entities which somehow exist independently of us waiting to be discovered, nor are they a by-product of our senses; we *understand* sensory material by means of them, and we develop them in so doing.

For just as appearances do not exist in themselves but only relatively to the subject in which, so far as it has senses, they inhere, so the laws do not exist in the appearances but only relatively to this same being, so far as it has understanding.[2]

There is no guarantee that everything is understandable; indeed, the bare sensory content of our perceptions, taken in isolation, is not understandable but only "sensible." Physical objects, or nature, however, must be understandable, at least to some extent, because it is through our understanding that they *are* physical objects.

So much is both definite and important. From this point on, however, Kant's interpretation of science divides into two; for he wants to justify a view of Newtonian physics as absolutely valid and certain which he accepts as a scientific premise but which his philosophical premises do not actually justify. In order to do this, he must attempt to derive what he regards as the fundamental laws of science deductively from the very principles by which physical objects are constituted, i.e., from the "principles of pure understanding" by which the categories are applied. Physical objects must be subject *by definition* to these laws, so that we cannot possibly conceive anything as a physical object without conceiving these particular laws of physics, and without conceiving these laws as applicable to the thing in question. On the face of it, however, it seems highly improbable that anything nearly so elaborate can be derived analytically from the rudimentary concept of "physical object"; moreover, it contradicts Kant's own doctrine that only those conceptual features indispensable for coherent experience of a common world are to be presumed applicable whenever we actually have such experience. This Kantian doctrine, indeed, leads to a very different view of scientific law.

On the basis of the first view, Kant takes his interpretation of "empirical laws" as "special determinations" of the categorial principles to mean that they are part of a complete and definite hierarchy of such determinations. We learn them "through experience," of course, "so far as they are objective, and therefore necessarily depend upon the knowledge of the object"; i.e., we learn through experience to what existential subject matter they are relevant. But "they are only special determinations of still higher laws, and the highest of these, under which the others all stand, issue *a priori* from the understanding itself."[3] Therefore, since we have already decided what concepts of "the understanding itself" must be applicable to all physical objects in our experience, it should be theoretically possible to arrive at a complete system of physics deductively. Such a system would, of course, be abstract; Kant never retreats from his recognition that "the existence of any object of the senses cannot be known completely *a priori*."[4] But once we do experience objects of the senses, according to this view, we may be sure that this system of physics will apply to them, and by means of it we may make completely certain inferences from objects actually perceived to objects not actually perceived.

On this basis, a completely integrated "architectonic of all human knowledge" is theoretically and even practically attainable and "would not indeed be difficult." Even here, Kant advances no claim that any science is actually developed on the basis of such a structure; the actual procedure is rather "collection of materials in somewhat random fashion at the suggestion of an idea lying hidden in our minds." Ultimately, however, these materials must be completely systematized if they are to form a science, and the sciences themselves must be "one and all organically united in a system of human knowledge, as members of one whole . . ."[5]

This aspect of Kant's doctrine comes to a head in his efforts actually to work out, on the basis of his categorial principles which define physical objects, an a priori derivation of certain physical laws which, however abstract, are surely synthetic as descriptions of a world which could logically be otherwise. The important point here is the fact that, on his own philosophical premises and in terms of his own conceptual framework, he does not succeed in this attempt.

The law of conservation of matter, for instance, is supposed to be established as valid a priori by identification with the principle of substance. But surely the notion "that even in fire the matter (substance) does not vanish, but only suffers an alteration of form," that by subtracting the weight of ashes from the weight of the wood burnt to produce them we obtain the weight of the smoke, as in Kant's example, does not follow at all from that principle of substance which he has established as part of what we mean by experience. "Matter" as a physical concept, matter as measured by weight and as possessing various other definite properties dealt with in physics, is not at all the same concept as Kant's category of "substance." In regard to the latter, "the proposition, that substance is permanent, is tautological";[6] but the proposition that *matter* is permanent is not tautological, nor is it so regarded by Kant. Similarly challengeable is Kant's attribution of a priori validity to the physical concepts of "action" and "force" as alleged derivatives of causality.[7]

The derivation of the "law of the continuity of all alteration" from the principle of causality is, perhaps, somewhat more successful. If all alterations are the effects of causes, says Kant, they must be continuous; because the causal relation is a relation in time, and time is continuous.[8] Kant seems here to have in mind something on the order of the paradoxes of Zeno, in terms of causality rather than motion, with the continuity of time very aptly offered as the basis of a solution. If the objection is raised today that the phenomena of quantum mechanics have nevertheless nullified causality as a universal principle, it should be noted that they have also, in the same sense, nullified continuity as a universal principle; so that the association between the two is strengthened rather than weakened. On the other hand, the subatomic phenomena of quantum mechanics are not part of our sensory experience, but are introduced conceptually in order to provide *causes* for some rather puzzling observations. Statistical laws and discontinuity are introduced on the conceptual level in order to maintain universal causality (and, in that sense, continuity) on the level of experience. Kant's concept of causality, it would seem, could be revised and expanded to include explanations of this sort, which he certainly could not have anticipated; but for this we shall have to look to Reichenbach in due time. Nevertheless, from causality of this abstract sort (which Kant's identification of causality as a purely conceptual "category" at least suggests), such a principle as *"in mundo non datur hiatus"* [9] would certainly not follow.

Kant, indeed, tires in the midst of his attempt to derive all of the basic scientific laws of his day from his a priori principles, remarking that he could "easily" do so but will leave this task to the reader! [10] On occasion, moreover, he seems to go so far as to allow scientific principles to stand as synthetic a priori entirely on their own. Newton's law of inverse squares, for example, is true a priori because "no other law of attraction . . . can be imagined as fit for a cosmical system." Interestingly enough, however, when Kant goes on to explain *why* this law is so pre-eminently "fit for a cosmical system," his reasons are thoroughly pragmatic ones—that the law in question is based on "simple" foundations, and that "its consequences are so valuable with regard to the variety and simplicity of their agreement . . ." [11]

As an attempt to establish the contents of Newtonian physics as a description of the actual world on an a priori basis, then, Kant's philosophy proves to be less than successful. Kant does, of course, establish *something* about a universal, a priori system of law and order in the world; but it is something quite different from what we should today call "physics." The "physical system" which Kant genuinely establishes, on his own philosophical premises, as universal and necessary, is something extremely general and abstract, not to be identified with the Newtonian or any other theory formulated in scientific physical terms. Indeed, we come closer to Kant's conception when we think in terms of a *logic of physics* rather than of physics itself; and this logic is provided by the system of categorial principles. The "formal conditions of all judgments in general . . . offered in logic . . . constitute a logical system"; the categories "grounded thereupon" constitute a "transcendental system"; and "the principles, by means of which all phenomena are subsumed under these concepts, constitute a physical system . . . which precedes all empirical knowledge of nature, and makes it possible." [12] The conceptual system which enables us to have that coherent consciousness of an objective world that Kant calls "experience," as we have seen, consists of the application of those concepts which enable us to think logically about, or understand, the sensory material of which we are aware; and it is this same conceptual system, or an expansion of it, that lies at the logical foundation of physical science. Such a system is not, however, itself physics in the ordinary sense.

In principle, when not distracted by consideration of the scientific structure which he accepts and tries to justify, Kant himself is fully aware of this distinction between the definition of a physical world and a specific system of physical laws. "Pure understanding," he states clearly, making a point that can hardly be overemphasized,

is not . . . in a position, through mere categories, to prescribe to appearances any *a priori* laws other than those which are involved in a *nature in general,* that is, in the conformity to law of all appearances in space and time. Special laws, as concerning those appearances which are empirically determined, cannot in their specific character be *derived* from the categories, although they are one and all subject to them. To obtain any knowledge whatsoever of these special laws, we must resort to experience . . .[13]

I.e., just as physical objects are defined by the categories, so is "nature," which is the sum of all physical objects. The categories, therefore, in guaranteeing the applicability of logic to physical objects, guarantee at the same time that *some* science applies to them. Science, then, is "subject to" the categories; it cannot violate the principles of their application without becoming irrelevant to the physical objects which they define. It cannot, nevertheless, be deduced from them.

Indeed, Kant on occasion recognizes even some of the concepts of the so-called "universal science of nature" itself as empirical concepts, including motion, impenetrability, and inertia, and leaves only a few very general principles, such as those of substance and causality, as "actually universal laws of nature, which hold completely *a priori*." [14] This does not mean, moreover, that any specific causal law is valid a priori.

If . . . wax, which was formerly hard, melts, I can know *a priori* that *something* must have preceded, . . . upon which the melting has followed according to a fixed law, although *a priori*, independently of experience, I could not determine, *in any specific manner*, either the cause from the effect, or the effect from the cause. [15]

Thus the only "laws" valid a priori for all of nature are those which are valid by definition and thereby "make nature possible"; indeed, we may note that the principles both of substance and of causality, which Kant gives as examples here, are among his fundamental "principles of pure understanding" which directly apply the categories in defining an objective world. We know a priori not the "many laws of nature which we can know only by means of experience; but conformity to law in the connection of appearances . . ." [16] This is a clear statement that we cannot derive the foundations of physics from logic via the categories (although we have seen Kant attempt just that and claim success); we can derive in this way only the minimal principles which define physical objects and the objective world ("nature"). In short, *these principles tell us that there must be laws that apply, but not what these laws are.*

How, then, do we establish what these laws are? One of the rare instances in which Kant provides a concrete illustration of his analysis concerns this very question. [17] We sometimes find "in perception," says Kant, "that a certain appearance is constantly followed by another (though not conversely); . . . for instance, . . . if the sun shines long enough upon a body it grows warm." Here, in this very statement of the facts as perceived, we are applying a "conditional judgment," or "hypothetical judgment," the "form" of which is "first given *a priori*, by means of logic." This form is applied whenever "we have one cognition given as antecedent and another as consequent." It does not itself provide any "necessity of connection or concept of cause," but merely a "rule of relation." (As we might say in logical terms today, this statement does not express any deductive relation between antecedent and consequent, but merely a general material implication, a relation determined entirely by whatever facts happen to exist empirically.)

Kant now considers how we may transform "this proposition, which is merely a subjective connection of perceptions," into "a proposition of experience." We shall, of course, see nothing "subjective" about it in the first place unless we remember Kant's own definition of experience; for it is in contrast with "experience" that he speaks here of a "subjective connection of perceptions." Kant surely does not mean that either the sun or the body on which it shines is "subjective"; for in identifying them as the sun and as a body we apply to them the categories which define objects and the laws which define these particular kinds of objects. But the relation which we have noted between them, however generally it may be stated, represents a mere observation of past cases; and since we have no *reason* for this relation, we can neither understand it nor assume that it must hold for future cases. Indeed, we cannot—and this amounts to the same thing—call it a relation between the objective sun and objective body, but merely a relation between our "perceptions" of them; it has no place in the logical structure of the objective world.

To acquire such a place, i.e., to be "considered as a law," the relation in question "must be seen as necessary and universally valid. Such a proposition would be that the sun is by its light the cause of heat." There is no difference whatever, we may note, between the empirical data (in terms of sense perception) of the "subjective" statement and those of the "objective" statement; the difference, consisting of the designation of a cause, is conceptual. It is this conceptual difference that belongs to the "form of experience" and determines objectivity; and "the concept of cause denotes a condition not at all belonging to things, but to experience." [18] (Here, obviously, Kant uses the term "things" to mean "things in themselves," existents independent of our consciousness of them, not physical objects as objects of experience.)

This explanation may seem rather incomplete. Can we make something a law of nature merely by saying so? Can *any* relation we choose be "seen as necessary and universally valid," merely by our decision to see it in this way? Unfortunately, Kant is not explicit here, but there are clues. First of all, while the law relating the sun and heat is not deducible from the general principle of causality, it is deducible from a more general law about light; and when that law is assumed as a premise, it therefore becomes "necessary"—analytically. Thus Kant includes in the objective causal law the information that the sun is *by its light* the cause of heat. We cannot infer a priori the existence either of the sun or of the body warmed, or indeed of any light at all; but *if* the antecedent is true, the consequent must necessarily be true also, since the relation is deductively necessary in terms of a more general law of which it is (in Kant's phrase) a "special determination." It is helpful here to recall the clearer modern statement of such a view by Feigl, the assertion, already mentioned, that the necessity involved in scientific laws is the logical necessity of "the *implication* underlying the inference from assumptions to conclusion." [19] Kant's analysis is not quite so explicit in expression, or perhaps even in his own mind; but once we have Feigl's statement before us, the similarity is readily apparent.

But how do we know that the assumptions themselves, the more general laws from which the laws in question are deducible, are necessary or applicable? However comprehensive or intricate our structure becomes, there is still this same question. Kant has still been able to show no deducibility from the general principle of causality or from any other categorial principle, and in his most lucid moments he has recognized that it is impossible to do so. Yet our laws do *follow the pattern* of such principles (as a "norm," [20] we may remember) in applying logic to experience; and so long as we *do* regard any statement as a law, it is part of the definition of experience of a particular kind. Thus Kant adds to his account of the law under discussion,

For experience can be nothing but objectively valid knowledge of appearances and of their succession, only so far as the earlier can be conjoined with the later according to the rule of hypothetical judgments.[21]

Presumably, then, if we find that we cannot similarly relate this kind of earlier and later "appearance" on some other occasion, we relegate the discordant part of the experience to the field of illusion.

But suppose we cannot do so without violating too many other accepted laws? Or suppose we find so many exceptions that we can no longer apply our "law" at all? Kant does not appear to reflect very much about these obvious questions; presumably he is not especially interested in what happens when we have the wrong law, because he assumes that such a situation can never arise for any important law of Newtonian physics. This is, however, the crucial question involved in the transformation of the "subjective" statement of past observations into an "objective" law. Even assuming that experience must be subject to *some* laws or cease to be experience, how do we know that *this* statement can be "seen as" a law without hopeless confusion? Kant comes entirely too close to the circular argument that the statement is a law because it is universal and necessary, while it is universal and necessary because it is a law.

At another point, however, Kant does discuss precisely this question, the validity of the step from past observations to a universal law; i.e., induction, although he does not use the term. Logical reasoning, the process of "deducing the particular from the universal," he points out, will lead to conclusions which are certain only if the premises are certain. Besides such "apodeictic use," however, such reasoning has also a "hypothetical use," in which conclusions are deduced although "the universal is admitted as *problematic* only." Under these circumstances, the deductive inference is still performed; indeed, it is implicitly repeated each time we add a particular case in that accumulation of such cases that constitutes the most obviously distinctive feature of induction. As Kant puts it,

Several particular instances, which are one and all certain, are scrutinised in view of the rule, to see whether they follow from it. If it then appears that all particular instances which can be cited follow from the rule, we argue to its universality, and from this again to all particular instances, even to those which are not themselves given.

(That the "particular instances" must be "certain" is questionable, of course, but irrelevant to Kant's point.) This is not a strict proof, Kant continues, since we cannot know "all the possible consequences" of a rule. The purpose of induction, therefore, is "regulative only;

its sole aim is, so far as may be possible, to bring unity into the body of our detailed knowledge, and thereby to *approximate* the rule to universality." [22] Thus, although Kant is not particularly interested in induction and does not discuss it often, he is apparently well aware of its role. When he does discuss it, moreover, his analysis is a radical departure from the Humean and earlier views of induction, which attempted to proceed in simple empirical terms exclusively. The reasoning process involved, we may observe, is a deductive one and therefore certain; the scientific law used as a premise is universal in *form* but uncertain as to its *applicability* (i.e., empirical relevance) in the future. Thus the law may indeed be "seen as" universally valid, as a hypothesis; it must then *be* universally valid to be valid at all, although future experience may compel us to reject it as invalid. In other words, it is universally valid in a "regulative" sense; we set it up as a hypothesis so that it may help us to objectify and understand the physical world, and we maintain it so long as empirical facts permit.

In this discussion of induction and of scientific laws established by it, however, we are no longer in the field which Kant assigns to "understanding," but in the field which he assigns to "reason." It is difficult to determine just where we have crossed the boundary; for the analysis of the scientific law relating the heat of the sun to the warming of the stone is carried out by Kant on the basis of "understanding," and surely there is very little relevant distinction to be found. Yet we must pursue the point further; for Kant regards the principles of reason as entirely regulative, and it is in the exposition of reason that the concept of a regulative law is fully developed.

Kant's own summary of the distinction between understanding and reason is as follows:

Understanding may be regarded as a faculty which secures the unity of appearances by means of rules, and reason as being the faculty which secures the unity of the rules of understanding under principles. Accordingly, reason never applies itself directly to experience or to any object, but to understanding, in order to give to the manifold knowledge of the latter an *a priori* unity by means of concepts . . .[23]

We need not, of course, be thrown off by the language of the "faculty" psychology of Kant's time; distinctions between different kinds of mental processes or methods of procedure are still legitimate and relevant. Fundamentally, Kant seems to be saying that the term "reason" designates operations on a higher level of abstraction than those of "understanding." Just as we establish coherence among our sensations by applying the categories to them and thus interpreting them in terms of physical objects, so we establish a further coherence among these results by applying further conceptualization to them in terms of more abstract systems; and the "principles of pure reason" are concepts which point in the direction of an all-inclusive unifying system.

This would seem to mean that "understanding" deals with sense perceptions, providing only that degree of unification involved in organizing our sense perceptions into physical objects; while "reason" deals with physical objects, providing an indefinite degree of further unification by organizing physical objects under scientific laws. Thus it is "understanding" that "makes experience possible" (when experience is defined in terms of a physical object world) and whose applicability is analytically necessary once the synthetic assertion is made that we do have experience as so defined. Reason, on the other hand, would provide knowledge *about* physical objects, knowledge required not for our basic experience of a physical world but for our coherent understanding of that world. Kant's statement that "reason never applies itself directly to experience or to any object, but to understanding," must be taken to mean merely that the conceptual and not the sensory element within experience is the subject matter of further conceptual organization; Kant certainly does not mean to deny all relevance of reason to experience. Although reason "does not . . . *create* concepts (of objects)," nevertheless it "*orders* them . . . Just as the understanding unifies the manifold in the object by means of concepts, so reason unifies the manifold of concepts by means of ideas . . ." [24] It would seem, then, that science would fall within the purview of reason, while ordinary cognition of physical objects, those objects of experience which science assumes and takes as its empirical data, would be assigned to understanding. Science would thus take on the regulative character of reason—a view highly acceptable today.

We cannot correctly say, however, that this and nothing else is Kant's meaning, since it is obvious that he often treats science as a product of understanding. This he does, obviously, in his attempt to establish an absolute physics as an inference from the definition of physical objects; and his characterization of understanding as "the *faculty of rules*" [25] fits in with this attempt. Nevertheless, even in this context the kind of "rules" ordinarily regarded as part of science would be applications of the "dynamical" categories, and therefore would share in the regulative character which Kant attributes in some sense to these categories though more emphatically to reason. Indeed, as an attempt to reserve a field for an absolute and complete physical science while recognizing the regulative character of the system of knowledge as a whole and of various features within it, the rigid distinction between understanding and reason is self-defeating, perhaps even self-contradictory; for when reason is invoked "with a view to making experience systematically coherent," [26] it is surely implied that experience is not already "completely coherent" on the level of understanding,[27] as Kant sometimes indicates.

Kant himself appears troubled by this ambiguous relationship between reason and understanding (which is really the ambiguity involved in his two conflicting views of science). Reason tries "to secure coherence in every possible way." But can we, in spite of the purely regulative character of such coherence, "in a certain measure postulate this unity *a priori*"? Does "knowledge of the understanding" actually *have* such unity, "common principles from which all its various modes can, in spite of their diversity, be deduced"? Only if an affirmative answer could be given, would "systematic unity" be a "*transcendental* principle" and "necessary . . . objectively"; i.e., only in this way would it be, like the categorial principles, prerequisite for any experience and therefore automatically applicable to every experience. If not, why is it applicable at all?

This question Kant appears unable to decide. He considers several examples from the methodology of science; but in each case "It is, indeed, difficult to understand how there can be a logical principle by which reason prescribes the unity of rules, unless we also presuppose a transcendental principle whereby such a systematic unity is *a priori* assumed to be necessarily inherent in the objects"; [28] for how can reason propose aims "inconsistent with the constitution of nature"? And without such a logical principle "we should have no reason at all" and therefore not even empirical knowledge. The problem, in other words, is again that of the applicability of logic to the empirical world.

Kant seems to conclude that there must be *some* basis in nature for our assumption of the applicability of logical structure, but that the *extent* to which the structural elements are capable of unification in the direction of one total system is "undetermined." The requisite foundation in nature is, of course, provided by the categorial structure constitutive of our experience of objects; but how can this insure the applicability of the principles of reason, which are not so constitutive? Kant vacillates between the view that it cannot (which explains why the area of applicability of the principles, not being necessarily coextensive with experience, is "undetermined"),[29] and the view that these principles are rules for possible experience after all, in the sense that they have "given rise to all that is systematic in our knowledge of nature" [30] (i.e., made possible the "understanding" which in turn makes experience possible). In the latter view, they would be constitutive of experience "mediately"; [31] but does this make them less necessarily coextensive with all experience than they would be if they were constitutive "immediately"? Obviously floundering for a compromise position, Kant gives some grounds for Kemp Smith's assertion that he entertains two conflicting views of the status of the "fundamental Idea of Reason, that of the unconditioned"; although it is not true that his "transcendental" interpretation ever goes so far as to assert the possibility of a "transcendental deduction" for such an idea (a possibility which he expressly denies),[32] nor that his alternative interpretation regards the "Ideas" as deriving "their entire authority . . . from experience." [33]

Still less is it true that Kant fails to provide at least the rudiments of a solution. These appear when he himself overlooks the rigid distinction between understanding and reason in favor of a continuous structure of knowledge, with each subordinate level frankly incomplete and the final level of completion just as frankly unattainable. At no point does reason, as Kant describes it, require a fundamentally distinctive type of cognitive equipment, in the sense in which understanding is different from sensibility; indeed, when he sets out in the *Dialectic* to determine what the regulative principles of reason are, they turn out to be merely extensions of the categorial principles themselves beyond the systematization *in* objects to the systematization *of* objects, with complete and final unification as its ideal limit. As Kant summarizes this structure, the "mathematical principles of understanding" are constitutive for intuition, the "dynamical" ones are constitutive for empirical concepts (experience) though not for intuition, and the "principles of pure reason" are not constitutive for either [34]—although, as he might well have added, they are constitutive for our understanding of (or knowledge about) experience. That is, Kant here distinguishes a rudimentary conceptual apparatus inseparable from any occurrence of human consciousness; a further conceptualization inseparable (by definition) from objective experience, by which we organize and understand such occurrences; and a still further conceptualization, proceeding indefinitely further and further into abstraction and unification, by which we understand that experience.

Thus, in the sense of applicability to an indeterminate field of subject matter, to be extended as far as possible, both understanding and reason are regulative; there may be sensation that we cannot objectify in a physical object, just as there may be experience of physical objects that we cannot systematize by definite laws. But in the sense of determining a field of knowledge, both are constitutive; without a rudimentary conceptual structure there is no objective experience, and without a law explaining such experience there is no rational understanding of it. The only difference is, that we obviously do in fact have objective experience, in this sense, and can with empirical validity assert that we have, whenever we meaningfully assert anything at all; while rational understanding of that experience, since by definition it is not confined to one particular level of conceptualization but includes all the infinite number of subsequent levels, is something that we never have completely. The regulative, empirically non-universal character of the latter is therefore more clearly and constantly in evidence; although either function may be interpreted regulatively.

In contrasting understanding and reason, Kant points out that knowledge obtained through the former, "in so far as it is synthetic, . . . does not depend on thought alone, nor contain in itself a universal obtained from concepts," since it must be "supported by pure intuition (in mathematics), or by conditions of a possible experience in general." [35] In other words, the synthetic element is the element of empirical applicability, as we have seen. In the field of reason, then, the universal *is* obtained from concepts (i.e., independently of experience); but Kant warns that we are actually "misled" [36] if we regard the resulting synthetic a priori principles as expressing a *truth* that is synthetic a priori. Actually, they express no truth at all (since truth is "agreement of knowledge with its object," [37] i.e., with experience) but merely tell us how to advance our understanding of experience. Thus Kant appears to acknowledge clearly, at this point, that his so-called "a priori synthetic judgments" are either (in the case of understanding) not a priori in respect to their synthetic feature, or (in the case of reason) not judgments at all, although stated in the form of judgments.

To understand this, we must understand Kant's account of the manner in which reason operates. It is the function of "reason, in its logical employment," Kant says, to supply logical grounds ("the universal condition") for our conclusions. In terms of "pure reason" (which, as distinguished from the "logical employment," means the application of logic *to experience* by reason) this means that we supply logical grounds *for the facts of experience*. The attempt to do this is equivalent to the assumption that there *are* such grounds; and this in turn involves "our assuming that . . . the whole series of conditions, subordinated to one another—a series which is therefore itself unconditioned— . . . is contained in the object and its connection." [38] That is, the only complete explanation is an ultimate ground that is self-explanatory ("unconditioned"). Moreover, since we are trying to explain existential subject matter, and since logic alone cannot supply grounds for the existence of anything, complete explanation would require an *existential* ultimate ground, or "necessary being," which Kant calls "the ideal of pure reason." [39]

The assertion that there is in fact such a being, or that we can by any method of reasoning (e.g., by tracing back events in time, causes, etc.) reach an "unconditioned" or ultimate explanation, would of course be genuinely synthetic a priori—synthetic because "the conditioned is analytically related to some condition but not to the unconditioned," [40] and a priori because it would be asserted on no empirical evidence, but solely to complete a logical structure. Kant does not, however, make any such assertion. He insists, on the contrary, that it cannot properly be made, thereby accepting the consequence that completeness of knowledge is "a completeness which is never, of course, obtainable." [41] He does not mean merely that it is practically unobtainable but rather that it is not even theoretically possible. For "an absolute whole of experience is impossible," [42] even logically; while an absolute whole transcending experience, although logically conceivable, does not have that "real possibility" which, for

Kant, means agreement with "the formal conditions of experience" [43] or inferability from actual experience by means of law; [44] and consequently "we have no right . . . even to assume the possibility of such an hypothesis." [45] A complete system of *knowledge,* on the other hand, as distinct from a system of existence, is a hypothetically possible notion; but it is an empty one nevertheless, as we have no means of knowing whether our actual world would fit into any such system.

Thus the system of all possible knowledge is not a logically determinate structure having some sort of abstract or ideal reality to which we come closer although we cannot reach it; much less is it a structure inherent in our understanding, as Kant supposes when he is thinking in terms of Newtonian physics. It is rather ". . . a *focus imaginarius,* from which . . . the concepts of the understanding do not in reality proceed . . ." In other words, it is a unity projected from the knowledge that we already have, a direction in which our knowledge points, a "goal upon which the routes marked out by all its rules converge . . ." [46] It is not a ready-made premise waiting to be discovered.

Thus the concept of an ultimate "ideal of pure reason" is significant merely as *a means of pointing the direction of progress in knowledge.* I.e., it functions as a "logical precept," though a precept definitive of knowledge itself, directing us "to advance towards completeness by an ascent to ever higher conditions . . ." [47] There is no question of truth involved at all; and surely there is no question as to the legitimacy of setting up a methodological "precept" which may be called, by an extension of the meaning of the term, "synthetic a priori"—synthetic because we use it to organize empirical data, a priori because it is conceptual in origin, and applicable to experience so far as any rational knowledge of the physical world is possible (i.e., "transcendental") because it underlies the actual structure of such knowledge.

There may be some question, however, as to the *value* of a methodological "precept" of this kind. Assuming that it is regulative in character, *how* does it "regulate" knowledge? What, in specific terms, do we *do* when we adopt the recommended goal?

First of all, the pursuit of such a goal is the pursuit of systematic unity in knowledge. It sets before us "the Idea of a whole of knowledge," which "must impart to our knowledge a peculiar kind of unity, that of a system." [48] Kant explains what that kind of unity is. By "*systematization*," he means

to exhibit the connection of . . . parts in conformity with a single principle. This unity of reason always presupposes an idea, namely, that of the form of a whole of knowledge—a whole which is prior to the determinate knowledge of the parts and which contains the conditions that determine *a priori* for every part its position and relation to the other parts. [49]

In other words, knowledge of any empirical event cannot be "determinate" (i.e., logically determined, capable of logical treatment) unless it is assigned a place in a logical structure—a structure in which all parts are logically deducible from the premises ("conditions") of the structure as a whole. Since this structure is itself "determinate," in this sense, only if these premises in turn are "determinate" (or "systematized"), knowledge of any experienced event would be complete and final only if all knowledge were incorporated in and deducible from one logical structure. There is in fact no such structure; the function of knowledge is, however, to create as close an approximation to one as possible.

Secondly, the "regulative principle" implies that the method by which we attempt to systematize knowledge is an *explanatory* one; "the task of reason" is a "search for unity of the grounds of explanation." [50] It is by the construction of more and more inclusive hypothetical explanations of the knowledge already at hand (starting, we may recall, from experience) that we aim toward one ultimate *most* inclusive system. The relation of each new hypothesis to the subject matter to be explained is that of logical "grounds"; but the hypothesis itself is constructed on the basis of the subject matter to be deducible from it, and not vice versa. Once constructed, it is *logically* prior to (i.e., a premise for) the subject matter, and thus logically "determines" it; and it is in this sense, and no other, that an assumed total system of all knowledge must be assumed as "prior to the determinate knowledge of the parts." [51] We cannot by logic or any other means establish the ultimate explanation or premise first and derive the intermediate ones; for, as we have seen, there *is* no such ultimate explanation. The "ideal of pure reason" is an *ideal limit* of explanation; it does not itself explain anything but points the direction of explanation, which is toward "unity." I.e., knowledge advances not by finding a separate explanation for each fact but by finding one explanation for many facts—or for many other explanations—and so on indefinitely. It is in this manner that "the routes marked out by all its rules converge."

Third, the logical structures of knowledge must have empirical relevance; for an explanation that does not explain *something* is no explanation at all. Since "The principle of reason is . . . a *rule*, prescribing a regress in the series of the conditions of given appearances," [52] it has no application (as Kant would say, it is "empty") apart from such "given appearances." The unity which it seeks to establish is "unity in the connection of things," and therefore it succeeds "only in proportion as we are in a position to verify such unity in empirical fashion . . ."; [53] for empirical data supply the only "things" available for our laws to connect. Empirically irrelevant hypotheses, therefore, do not lead us toward the ideal system which Kant has in mind, and are not knowledge.

Finally, all of these requirements of "reason" taken together mean that knowledge must move in the direction at once of increasing logical coherence and increasing empirical comprehensiveness; or, as Kant puts it, toward "the greatest [possible] unity combined with the greatest [possible] extension." [54] For the greatest possible unity we must seek ever wider laws, more inclusive "conditions" (premises); for the greatest possible extension we must bring more and more empirical facts into the scope of the system. Thus the laws of science at once proceed in the direction of "an imagined ultimate ground" and make possible continual "further derivation" of one empirical fact from another.[55] These are the two directions of scientific advance which, when misinterpreted as indicative of ultimate ontological facts, split up into the mutually contradictory theses and antitheses, respectively, of Kant's antinomies. As methodological principles, however, they are not contradictory but become aspects of one process. In terms of causality, for instance, we cannot regard one empirical event as the cause of another without assuming a causal law relating the two events, i.e., explaining *why* one is the cause of the other; and we cannot set up such a law if we cannot find empirical events for it to relate.

Thus Kant makes us aware of the futility of, on one hand, merely pursuing an endless chain of causes further and further back into the past or, on the other hand, constructing a chain of more and more abstract explanatory hypotheses without thereby incorporating any further empirical material. Those facts that enable us to construct new and broader hypotheses, as well as those hypotheses that enable us to interpret more facts, are those that are relevant to the advance of knowledge. In Kant's terms, "the *ultimate* causality" is also "the *highest* causality"; if the series of events could be traced back to a first cause, and if the series of hypotheses could be extended to an all-inclusive explanation, both processes would have to lead to the same "being which contains primordially in itself the sufficient ground of every possible effect . . ." [56] This cannot, of course, be done; but the interpretation of the concept of such a being as a regulative principle clearly means to Kant the requirement that knowledge move in both of these directions simultaneously. His ideal of "systematic unity" implies as much; it is, indeed, an alternative statement of the same principle; but the dual direction of knowledge is made clearer when the principle is split into two as a result of the antinomies. Recognition of this dual direction, moreover, establishes a "regulative principle" which has lost none of its force today, when the interdependence of the empirical and the deductive elements in science, as well as their independence, is recognized as never before.

In the context of Kant's interpretation of "reason," then, the status of the so-called synthetic a priori laws of science, or of "nature," is quite different from the status implied when Kant attempts to assign them to "understanding." He is no longer in a position to say that "all events in the sensible world stand in thorough-going connection in accordance with unchangeable laws of nature"; [57] on the contrary, his treatment of the "ideal of pure reason" seems explicitly to deny the legitimacy of such an assertion unless we interpret it in a "regulative" sense. Indeed, the very fact that knowledge is one system even in intent (although not actually) makes it inevitable that the status of its logical foundation—that of a "logical precept" which reason merely "postulates"—be transmitted to the subordinate structures, the laws of science.

Kant himself, notwithstanding his preconceived notion of an absolute science, takes full note of this implication of his own philosophical doctrine. Reason, he now says, "postulates a complete unity in the knowledge obtained by the understanding, by which this knowledge is to be not a mere contingent aggregate, but a system connected according to necessary laws." [58] The necessity of the laws, in other words, is a logical, *analytic* necessity, deriving from the wider logical structures from which the laws are deducible and ultimately from the assumed structure of the whole of knowledge. The latter, however, is merely *postulated, in order* to provide logical necessity for scientific laws; it is postulated because knowledge "is to be" a necessary system; Kant, as we have seen, does not here say that knowledge *is* such a system. In actual fact, there is always some point at which the hypothetical structures of science stop short, although that point may always be pushed back. Consequently, it is at least clearly implied, if not quite explicitly stated, that the necessity of scientific laws itself is a postulated or regulative necessity, analytic within the established structure of science itself but merely assumed in regard to both the validity of its premises and the applicability of its conclusions. It is in this sense that "Hume was . . . in error in inferring from the contingency of our determination *in accordance with the law* the contingency of the *law* itself." [59] It is the law that is a priori, in other words, and its application that is synthetic and contingent. Whether experience is such that the law can be applied to it, can be determined only by that experience; but the law itself is analytic within its hypothetical explanatory structure.

Scientific laws are not, then, deducible from the actual structure of the understanding, as Kant has elsewhere asserted, although they may be deducible from other scientific laws. The *form* of scientific laws, however, the assumption (that of a universal system) in line with which science advances, is derived from the actual structure of reason, although only as its ideal limit. Thus the laws are not arbitrary; those laws are to be regarded as valid that *most* advance that structure in the direction of (unattainable) completeness, besides being empirically applicable. In short, the factual assertion of *the uniformity of nature*, since it cannot be justified, is supplanted by the ideal goal of *the unification of knowledge*, as a basis for the justification of scientific laws.

Can we say the same for mathematical laws? Not in terms of the views which Kant actually held; for there was no doubt in his mind as to the synthetic character of mathematics, and all his special notions about mathematics—his analysis of it in terms of "construction," his close association of it with the experience of space and time, his doctrine of "a priori intuition"—are devices for maintaining that synthetic character. Indeed, the mere fact that he does *not* find these devices necessary in regard to the categories is a good indication that he does not really think of the latter as synthetic; it is the idea that a mathematical concept must be synthetic "in itself" and not merely in its application to empirical subject matter that makes the difference. For "an *a priori* concept . . . either already includes in itself a pure intuition (and if so, it can be constructed), or it includes nothing but the synthesis of possible intuitions which are not given *a priori*." [60] These two alternatives, of course, apply to mathematical concepts and the categories respectively.

Without this preconceived notion of mathematics, however, Kant would certainly have no reason to place mathematical concepts anywhere else in his scheme than among the products of understanding. Indeed, two of his four groups of categories are designated as "mathematical" in any event; and in the very process of identifying "number" with the temporal act of counting, Kant identifies it also as the "schema," or temporal rule, for the application of the categories of "quantity," which are themselves nontemporal and conceptual, belonging entirely to the understanding.[61] It is here that Kant comes astonishingly close to the derivation of mathematics from logic, with "number" as its distinctive concept.

Moreover, Kant himself finds his "a priori intuition" inadequate to explain either the conceptual structure or the applicability of mathematics. Asking whether a geometrical law concerning the properties of a circle, for example, is to be found "in the circle or in the understanding," he answers that "When we follow the proofs of this law, we soon perceive that it can only be derived from the condition on which the understanding founds the construction of this figure, namely, the concept of the equality of the radii." [62] Here the construction has no important role; it is the conceptual definition (in accordance with which a figure *may* be constructed) that is the basis of proof. "Even the judgments of pure mathematics," Kant recognizes, must be "subsumed" under a "pure concept of the understanding." [63] Nor is the problem of objective applicability solved by a "pure intuition" which gives us only the "form" of intuition; for "whether there can be things which must be intuited in this form, is still left undecided." To decide this question we need "empirical intuitions." [64] Moreover, we need those criteria by which the objectivity of these intuitions is determined, i.e., the categories; and more specifically, the categorial principle of "extensive magnitude" which "alone can make pure mathematics . . . applicable to objects of experience." [65] The only function actually left to "a priori intuition," then, in respect to mathematics, is preservation of the "synthetic" character of the latter.

There is still, of course, the function of "a priori intuition" in respect to space and time; for it is by means of such intuition, according to Kant, that space and time are presented to us. Such a doctrine, however, is far more convincing when the mathematical element is removed from it. For it is quite true that all of our sense perceptions have both temporal duration and spatial location, and could not otherwise have the kind of sensory character that they do in fact have. Space in this sense, however, is not the space of physics, which is a conceptual structure intended and assumed to be *applicable* to our perceptions in their sensory-spatial character, just as any other system of physical laws is intended and assumed to be applicable.

Thus the situation is considerably clarified by an incidental footnote by Lewis. Modern geometry, he declares, does *not* demonstrate the falsity of Kant's views on space "as *arguments concerning the certainty of our knowledge of the phenomenal world*, i.e. as a metaphysics of space." Modern geometry shows that synthetic principles are unnecessary for *mathematics*. "But . . . Kant's account is concerned with the source of our certainty about the *world of nature*," Lewis continues, while

the abstractness of modern geometry comes about through definitely renouncing . . . the certainty of its applicability to our space. When geometry becomes abstract, the content of the science of space splits into two distinct subjects: (1) geometry, and (2) the metaphysics of space, which is concerned with the *application* of geometry.

Kant's arguments, Lewis adds, can be "rehabilitated" for the latter.[66]

In other words, Kant has a great deal to offer as to the nature of perceptual space and time and their role in consciousness, if we divorce all of this from mathematics—as, indeed, modern mathematicians do in any event. His arguments as to the "required" nature of space (and also of time) do demonstrate the spatiality (and temporality) of sensory consciousness; and therefore they demonstrate also that, to the extent that such sensory subject matter is to be conceptually organizable (i.e., capable of incorporation in objective experience in the Kantian sense), *some* systematic geometry must be applicable to it. It is in regard to the nature of such a system (i.e., of mathematics, and of space as a mathematical concept) that Kant goes astray. For if such a system is conceptual in origin and logical in its validation, it is indeed an a priori structure; but for that very reason, we cannot determine a priori the applicability of any particular system of this kind; just as, in Kant's view, we can determine a priori that the physical world is to have laws, but not that any particular law will be empirically valid.

Thus the interpretation of geometry as entirely abstract is directly connected with the recognition of alternative geometries, as in the modern view. It is because of Kant's belief, on the basis of the mathematics available to him, that only one system of geometry is possible, that he infers its nonconceptual origin (correctly enough, on his premises) and attempts to base mathematics directly on the nature of perceptual space and time. For Kant even recognizes that a non-Euclidean geometry is *logically* possible; "there is no contradiction in the concept of a figure which is enclosed within two straight lines . . . The impossibility arises not from the concept in itself, but in connection with its construction in space . . ." [67] The problem, then, is one that Kant himself solves in respect to scientific laws, explaining them as conceptual and a priori in construction and synthetic in application; and it is only the assumption that the construction of mathematical *laws as such* must be "construction in space," imaginatively if not physically, that prevents him from reaching a similar solution for them. It is by this assumption that he can maintain the view that there is only one possible mathematics; whereas the view that there is only one possible science, as we have seen, meets with many vicissitudes and in fact breaks down in his hands. And indeed, the synthetic assumption about mathematics involved in the view of geometry as "construction in space" (i.e., in perceptual space) is already weakened by Kant himself in his view of algebra, where he is obliged to regard the element of "construction" as "symbolic" only.[68]

Surprisingly enough, then, it is in the context of the science and mathematics of the twentieth century, and not of the eighteenth, that the fundamental structure of Kant's philosophy is divested of inconsistent and unworkable appendages and takes on its full significance. This, indeed, may not be so surprising, after all; for it is Kant's own distinction between the logical or analytic and the existential or synthetic that provides the philosophical basis and interpretation of much of the change in these fields. Divested of the alleged a priori physics and synthetic mathematics which Kant vainly tried to justify in his own terms, his so-called "a priori synthetic judgments" become applications of the a priori to the synthetic—applications of the definitive or hypothetical or analytic to the existential and empirical. We make such application in objective experience because that is what we mean by objective experience, and in knowledge *about* the experienced world because that is what we mean by knowledge; and the "necessity" of these applications derives analytically from these definitions, but the *fact* that there *is* experience and knowledge in terms of these definitions is a contingent fact, dependent at least in part on the nature of our cognitive equipment and its manner of dealing with the material presented to it.

Thus Kant's alleged "rationalism"—and, aside from ontological questions concerning "things in themselves," with which we have not yet dealt, his idealism also—may be seen to reduce to the recognition that *what* we know, out of everything that may be available, is determined by *how* we know, and that *how* we know is explainable in terms of the application of conceptual systems (ultimately, of logic) to the bare subject matter provided by our senses. If this is rationalism or idealism at all, it is epistemological only, and not ontological; for in all this analysis "the question is not how things in themselves but how . . . knowledge of things is determined." [69] And even within knowledge, Kant says of the rational and the empirical factors that "To neither of these powers may a preference be given over the other. Without sensibility no object would be given to us, without understanding no object would be thought." [70]

Beyond this, of course, lies the rationalistic assumption that all human minds function in precisely the same way, employing (aside from individual variations which may be regarded as errors) one unchangeable, relatively simple system of logic; and the related rationalistic assumption that science consists exclusively of universal and necessary laws. In regard to the latter assumption, we have seen that Kant's *explanation* of the elements of necessity and universality is not rationalistic but rather recognizes these elements as definitive, analytic, and regulative; yet the limitation of science to the scope of such an assumption appears unduly restrictive in terms of the science of a later time. There is, however, inherent in Kant's approach and fundamental doctrine, no reason why these rigid limitations must be maintained. Separated from obsolete science and mathematics and its attempts to justify them, the main structure of Kant's thought shows itself adaptable—perhaps more adaptable—for the justification of the more flexible science of our own time; and it is interesting to see that this adaptation has indeed been accomplished. Reichenbach's accomplishment in this respect is all the more interesting, perhaps, in the light of his own apparent failure to recognize the Kantian origin of his approach. The loosening of the categorial structure from the mental, conceptual side is a more difficult matter, since both logic and psychology are involved, as well as the highly elusive and perplexing relation between them; yet this, too, has been accomplished with very considerable success; and Lewis, in so doing, does make due reference to Kant.

To say this is not to attribute to Kant himself the developments which belong—and which can only belong—to a much later period; these are very large expansions of his system, and can in no sense be found within it. It is the original groundwork for these developments that must be attributed to Kant; and it is the capacity to support such expansion that indicates, more impressively than anything else, the essential soundness of that groundwork.

4

Kant and Lewis

To GRASP the adaptability of the fundamental Kantian scheme to the demands of logic and science in the twentieth century, and to see the chief changes needed for such an adaptation, we need only turn to the work of Clarence Irving Lewis. It is extremely interesting, as a starting point toward the understanding of this aspect of Lewis's achievement, to see how far we can go into his epistemological structure without departing in any significant respect from the Kantian scheme. This preparation will enable us to understand all the more clearly the meaning and the extreme importance of his departures from and additions to that fundamental scheme.

For Lewis as for Kant, the analysis of knowledge must begin with recognition of its two distinct and indispensable components: "the concept, which is the product of the activity of thought, and the sensuously given, which is independent of such activity." Of these two, "the concept gives rise to the a priori." [1] Still very similarly to Kant, Lewis defines the a priori as "knowledge whose correctness can be assured without reference to any particular experience of sense . . . ; that which requires to be determined by sense experience being called *a posteriori.*" Lewis also emphasizes the distinction between analytic statements, "which can be certified by reference exclusively to defined or definable meanings," and synthetic statements, which cannot be so certified. He asserts not only, like Kant, that all analytic statements must obviously be true a priori, but also that, conversely, all a priori statements must be analytic. The second of these assertions he regards as less obvious, although true, pointing out that it has been denied by many people, pre-eminently by Kant. When we keep in mind, however, the understanding of Kant's view at which we have just arrived, and interpret his "synthetic a priori" as expressing the applicability of the a priori to the synthetic, it remains to be seen how far Lewis's own ideas diverge from that view. Certainly Kant would agree with him that whatever knowledge is not derived from experience (and thus is a priori) must be derived from concepts (i.e., in Lewis's terms, from "intended meanings"), since these are the only two sources of knowledge; [2] and that no "relation of meanings" (or concepts) can "require either the existence or the non-existence of any thinkable thing." [3]

The two sources of cognition, however, both contribute to empirical knowledge, which Lewis, like Kant, identifies not with the merely given but with "conceptual interpretation of the given." Indeed, "There is no knowledge merely by direct awareness," [4] since the "data of sense (not excluding the illusory)" *are* just what is immediately apprehended and therefore permit of no error, while Lewis classifies as knowledge only that which can be erroneous and can therefore claim correctness.[5] In the "presented experience" which is the content of our direct awareness, moreover, there is no distinction between the subjective and the objective; for Lewis, much as for Kant, the recognition of an objective world is "an achievement of intelligence expressed in our categorial distinctions." [6]

To understand this view in Lewis's terms, it is best to begin with his analysis of empirical knowledge, which he, like Kant, finds typified in the knowledge of physical objects. Empirical knowledge, Lewis asserts, is analyzable into statements of three types. These are: *1*] "expressive statements" of the immediately given and unmistakable contents of experience, not themselves classifiable as knowledge; *2*] "terminating judgments," or predictions (still in "expressive" terms) as to the content of experience that will follow if certain conditions are fulfilled; and *3*] "non-terminating" or objective judgments about real things existing independently of experience but known by means of experience. An objective judgment is empirically equivalent to an infinite (i.e., "non-terminating") series of terminating judgments, since our belief in the existence of an object is a belief that, if we should take certain actions, certain specific experiences would follow, and since the number of such possible causal sequences is unlimited.[7]

The belief in an objective world, then, is a belief in the existence of *"things* which are now given in experience and now not, and which when given are still thicker than our experience of them," a belief that there is more to the world than our own actual experience—that much is "experientially possible" which is not "experientially now actual." [8] In other words, the continued existence of a physical object "*means* the continued possibility of verifying it if appropriate routines of action be followed . . ." In illustration, Lewis uses Kant's analysis of our successive views of the sides of a house,[9] and his comparison of them with our successive views of a boat traveling downstream. In the two cases, our *actual* views are equally successive; it is because of the *possibility* of reversing the order in the case of the house, although not in the case of the boat, that we regard the house as objectively existing in the same location even while we are no longer looking at it, and the boat as objectively changing its location.[10] Lewis, then, in thorough agreement with Kant but perhaps more clearly, presents the interpretation of *nature as possible experience*, the view that "what an objective fact *means* is certain possibilities of experience which are open to realization through our action." [11]

Under the influence of pragmatism, Lewis emphasizes more than Kant the importance of the element of action involved, the fact that a being incapable of action and of choice among possible actions could not have any conception of possibilities other than the actual content of his experience.[12] Like Kant, however, he emphasizes also the importance of the conceptual element involved. We must learn empirically from the sequences found in experience, what sense perceptions signalize the possibility of what other sense perceptions under what perceived conditions; but the interpretation of this sequence in terms of a physical object, the understanding of it as a *consequence* of the existence of such an object (i.e., as representing a necessary objective "connection"), the concept in terms of which some sense perceptions *do* signalize the occurrence of others, is "contained in the objective belief itself." [13] This conceptual part of our knowledge determines what we know about the object *analytically*, i.e., by definition and by the logical implications of our definition, or, as Kant would say, a priori; "we know this in knowing what we mean by our affirmation of objective fact"; [14] and in no other way can we distinguish an objective world or understand our empirical data as revealing such a world. Thus Lewis's diagnosis of Hume's difficulties is the same as Kant's.

Hume's scepticism results, not from the absence of necessary connections of empirical particulars, but from failure to observe the ways in which the necessary connections of *ideas* are pertinent to the interpretation of the empirically given and hence are antecedent determinations of *reality*.[15]

It is evident that this a priori structure with empirical applicability is the structure of scientific law as applied in the identification of physical objects and their sense-perceptible properties; so that, for Lewis as for Kant, an objective world is a world of physical law by definition, and "a world without law must likewise be a world without recognizable things." [16] Statements that particular kinds of things have certain objective properties are laws; and when we make the "assumption" that there are in fact the "uniformities of possible experience requisite to the existence of things," we assume thereby that there are "uniformities of the type of law." To assume that there is an objective world, that "such correlations, *things in general,* exist" in an objective sense, we need not assume that any *particular* law of science is valid, but we do need the "general assumption that *there are* laws" which are empirically applicable.[17] To find out what particular law is applicable, we must observe the empirical facts to which we wish to apply a law; but Lewis, like Kant, reminds us that we must have a question to put to nature if we are to find an answer there.

We cannot even interrogate experience without a network of categories and definitive concepts . . . We must first be in possession of criteria which tell us what experience would answer what questions, and how, before observation or experiment could tell us anything.[18]

It is interesting, too, to observe the extent to which the *kinds* of laws thus required for the existence of objective things, in Lewis's view, fall into line with Kant's "dynamical categories," those categories which are "regulative" (i.e., to be applied as far as possible but not guaranteed applicable in all cases) in relation to sense impressions but required for all objective experience. It is already clear that, in terms of the objective world as a world of "possible experience," physical laws must be of a kind that will imply (analytically and thus necessarily) an inference from the actual occurrence of some empirical data to the possible occurrence of others; so that the role of Kant's three "modal" categories is obvious. We have already noted, too, the part played in the establishment of such laws by sequences which Kant identifies as causal, sequences repeated in experience and logically necessitated by the concept which we apply whenever there is another such repetition.

The concept of substance, too, enters the picture in a very Kantian manner. Since the concept of an objective thing involves temporal sequences, Lewis points out, there cannot be a "merely momentary" thing; the changes which occur must be incorporated into the concept of a permanent object. A change that is predictable, i.e., subject to law, may be "brought within the concept and made essential," becoming "a 'transformation,' internal to the nature of some conceivable 'thing.'" (As Kant puts it, all changes become "alterations" in something permanent.) Lewis, like Kant, regards this concept as *explanatory* of the existence of *things*. When we can predict a change, e.g., the freezing of water if we conceive water in terms of its chemical properties, we call the change a transformation; but when we cannot, e.g., in the case of the freezing of water if we conceive water as a "potable liquid," we say that the original thing has disappeared—which means that "we cannot understand it." [19] The concept of substance, then, as well as the concept of causality, is a means of understanding properties and the changes among them.

Thus, for Lewis just as for Kant, it is scientific laws that determine what we are to regard as a particular kind of physical object; and it is the application of the concepts of substance, causality, and the modal categories that distinguishes the world of physical objects from the subjective content of consciousness. Of Kant's categories which specifically perform this function, only "reciprocity" is lacking; and surely this may be interpreted as a form of causality.

Turning to the actual application of the concepts or laws to sense data, we find a further parallel with Kant, which Lewis himself points out—a parallel between the Kantian "schemata" and Lewis's distinctive doctrine of "sense meaning" as a means of bridging the gap between abstract concepts and the actual experienced data. For Kant, there is special difficulty with highly abstract concepts like the categories, which are not directly descriptive of sense impressions. We cannot point to anything that is visibly an instance of causality, for instance, as a round plate is visibly an instance of circularity (with roundness "intuited" in the plate and "contained" in the geometrical concept). Therefore, in order to "subsume" sense perceptions under the categories, we need as intermediary "some third thing . . .

homogeneous" with both, "intellectual" in one respect and "sensible" in another.[20]

For Lewis the difficulty does not take quite this form, because for him concepts are not "represented" by objects but rather refer to or *mean* objects. The problem, then, is that of explaining how *any* concept can mean something concrete and empirical. A concept can be defined only in terms of other concepts; for the means of definition is language, which (as it appears in the dictionary) is an abstract conceptual system. There must be, therefore, according to Lewis, a nonverbal *"criterion in mind,* by reference to which one is able to apply or refuse to apply the expression in question"; and this criterion must consist of "sense-presentable characters" by which we can identify sense perceptions as the kind meant.

Both Kant and Lewis see that an exercise of "imagination" is required because we must have the sensory criterion prior to the sensations to be identified. This is not a denial that we need sensory experience first to derive an image; but until we derive it and attach a conceptual label to it, we do not have a meaningful term to refer to subsequent experiences. In many cases, however, sense meaning is too complex to be adequately represented in an image, and in no case can the meaning of a general concept be exhausted by any particular image; so we substitute a "schema" which can be filled out in a series of images—"a rule or prescribed routine and an imagined result of it." Thus we cannot form a precise image of a "chiliagon," nor any image of all possible chiliagons; but we can "imagine counting the sides of a polygon and getting a thousand." This explanation of a schema closely follows that of Kant, to whom Lewis accords full credit.

For both Kant and Lewis, then, the image is empirical, a reproduction of past experience, while the schema, through which the image becomes part of a criterion of empirical meaning, is a priori in its role as a definition of the experience to be interpreted by it. Kant, however, argues that for a *"pure* concept" (i.e., one derived directly from our means of understanding, like the categories or mathematical concepts) there is *only* a schema, and no image; so that the use of imagination involved in such concepts is confined to that "pure a priori imagination" which is surely one of the most obscure of the Kantian "faculties." Lewis, on the other hand, retains the notion of empirical imagery as implied by *all* schematic meanings; we must be able to form images of the test routines, if not of the experience which they identify, if our concepts are to have empirical meaning at all. Thus his conception of sense meaning, modeled on Kant's conception of schemata, may be more effective in bringing our abstract concepts into contact with the empirical world to which they are to be applied.[21]

For all empirically relevant concepts, then, from the most immediate to the most abstract, Lewis retains a type of meaning *both* conceptual and empirically interpretable if appropriate experience should occur (in Kant's terms, both "intellectual" and "sensible"). Sense meaning, with all the empirically acquired imagery that it includes, is a priori meaning; for, as a criterion of identification, it is logically and psychologically prior to the identification of any experience as the one—or the kind—that we mean. It is not itself the experience; i.e., it is to be distinguished from denotation. Indeed, a term may have sense meaning even if its denotation is zero (i.e., if there is nothing to which it can correctly be applied); for sense meaning is not dependent on the existence of anything.[22] Thus it is part of the intensional meaning of the term (in Kantian language, part of the "concept"), by which the denotation is "limited but not fixed"; and the denotation, thus "limited," is "fixed" by "what happens to exist." [23] The validity and usefulness of this distinction will become clear when we come to the fundamental question of the applicability of the categories, where we can make good use of the fact that sense meaning is a priori and denotation is synthetic.

The indispensability of the temporal element in all this is as impressive to Lewis as to Kant and provides another important point of contact between them, a point from which the "transcendental unity of apperception" is not far removed. "If concepts are to be articulate and meaningful, then the application of them must be something verifiable; which means that what they denote must have a temporal spread." [24] No physical object, therefore, can be perceived as such instantaneously; in identifying any sense perception as experience of a physical object, we imply predictions about future experience and believe them on the basis of past experience; and our present experience becomes past before any present predictions are verified. Thus memory is a necessary part of all experience, through that continuity of consciousness which makes present empirical knowledge possible.

Our sense of a cumulative temporal experience, mnemically presented within the epistemological present, or in Kant's phrase, in the transcendental unity of apperception, not only is something of which we cannot divest ourselves; it is constitutive of our sense of the only reality by reference to which empirical judgments could have either truth or falsity or any meaning at all.[25]

Although the "transcendental unity of apperception," as Kant conceives it, is not, strictly speaking, our "sense" of continuous experience but rather the logical condition or "presupposition" of such continuity, the important point here is the fact that we could not experience the "epistemological present," i.e., we could not have *any* consciousness amenable to the application of concepts, without that peculiar continuity which is not itself an experience but which distinguishes all of one's own experience from the experience of others.

It must be observed, too, that this requirement of continuity through a "temporal spread" is not confined to objective experience; that Lewis, like Kant, sees it as belonging to the nature of consciousness itself. "Even the 'stream of consciousness' itself," he points out, "is a highly conceptual construction, requiring, amongst other items, the category of objective time as the order of that change which is irreversible by the 'if' of any altered mode of action." [26] For Lewis as for Kant, time acquires a peculiarly fundamental position by this inextricable involvement with the "transcendental unity of apperception," even though Lewis, free from Kant's preconceptions requiring a synthetic mathematics, can at the same time classify it as a category. Thus time (since Lewis never mentions the "other items" to which he so enigmatically refers in this connection) may be regarded as a peculiarly fundamental category, applicable to all awareness.

Finally, Lewis agrees with Kant that knowledge is a system. He, too, regards "the whole body of our conceptual interpretations" as forming "a sort of hierarchy or pyramid"—not, however, a completely deductive one, of the kind which, as we have seen, Kant envisages but cannot quite fit into his own epistemological structure and often seems to reject. What Lewis has in mind is rather a pyramid in terms of degrees of abstractness and generality, with "the most comprehensive concepts, "such as those of logic, at the top, and the least general, such as 'swans,' etc., at the bottom . . ." [27] The most important logical relation in terms of which the structure is built up is the relation of "congruence," whose role conforms closely to that of Kant's concept of the unification of knowledge as a regulative principle.

Congruence, as Lewis analyzes it, is a relation among "*a set of supposed facts asserted*" such that "*the antecedent probability of any one of them will be increased if the remainder of the set can be assumed as given premises.*" [28] It is this relation, he notes, by which mutual agreement among independent accounts by several unreliable witnesses can provide a very high degree of confirmation of these accounts. It is through this same relation of congruence that conjoint confirmations of a hypothesis may increase the probability of the hypothesis much more than the sum of these confirmations taken separately.[29]

Congruence is particularly important, for Lewis, in connection with memory, whose significant role in all empirical knowledge is already clear. The data of memory, Lewis points out, do not, like present sense data, themselves constitute our experience of the facts under consideration; moreover, their reliability cannot be established inductively without a further appeal to memory.[30] We cannot confirm some data of memory by others if none are reliable; however, if some are, it will be the congruent set of them that are highly probable, while those that do not fit in will be discarded. Thus, if we are to have knowledge at all, we must *assume* that the data of memory have some degree of reliability; [31] but, for that initial assumption in respect to any particular data, congruence with other memories can provide a very high degree of confirmation or disconfirmation.[32]

An important factor, then, in the acceptance not only of memory but of any empirical statement is "congruence . . . with our antecedent beliefs and with what has already some degree of confirmation"; in other words, participation of the new item of knowledge in "the 'systematic unity' of any extensive body of acceptable empirical beliefs . . . concomitantly credible." Such a unified body of knowledge is always in the background as a tacitly assumed premise; when we derive the consequences of a hypothesis, Lewis points out, we usually have a number of "collateral suppositions" among our premises. Every science contains such assumptions; and if we examine the foundation of these in turn, we may be "unable to stop short of the whole body of accepted principles of that science." [33] Just as a physical object can be identified as such with assurance only if it fits into the physical world as already known, so a scientific law, to be accepted with assurance, must not only be verified by empirical observations, but must also fit into the broader structure of science. Indeed, empirical observations could not be verifications of scientific laws if they were not related to those laws in terms of the structure of science—ultimately, in terms of the logical structure which determines what observations will confirm what laws. Lewis's analysis of congruence, then, is an analysis of the manner in which knowledge is a system.

Here the same question arises for Lewis as for Kant. How complete must this system be? Indeed, how complete *can* it be? In this respect, Lewis seems occasionally to go further than he intends. "All the facts of reality undoubtedly form a congruent set," he declares,[34] seeming thereby to claim systematic character not only for knowledge but for existence. Kant, we may remember, takes particular pains to avoid any such claim. Lewis appears to go even further, virtually claiming not mere congruence but a full-fledged deductive relation, when he finds it "quite plausible that 'the whole of the truth' is such a tight-locked system that every particular fact in it is completely fixed by other facts in it" and "totally implausible that the whole of the truth should fail to have such systematic structure." [35] It may, of course, be argued that "reality" and "truth," as conceptual structures, may be of any type we choose, e.g., congruent or even deductive, with their empirical content limited to such sensory material as can fit in. If this is what Lewis means, however, his manner of statement in these passages is misleading. A fundamental question, moreover, as Kant sees particularly in connection with his antinomies, is whether there can be any such thing as "all the facts of reality" or "the whole of the truth" in any determinate sense; and Lewis himself inserts into his reflections in this connection the proviso, "supposing that the phrase 'whole of the truth' means anything." [36]

In any event, we cannot start with abstract knowledge of any such system and derive the particular facts from it. Any number of congruent sets are logically possible, and we must "rely upon experience" to find out *which* such set constitutes "this world we live in," [37] even if we assume, with Lewis, that *some* such set does. Thus the coherence theory of truth is invalid; neither congruence nor any other logical relation is an indication of the truth or even the probability of empirical statements so related, unless the system contains some statements deriving antecedent credibility from some relation to experience.[38] In other words, it is not mere internal congruence, but congruence with facts, that counts. And for initial facts, or some credible notion of them, sense data are needed but are not enough; we must resort also to the assumptions "that mnemic presentation constitutes a *prima facie* probability of past actuality," and "that coincidence in past experience must be a probability-index of the future." These assumptions we must merely "accept," because "we have no alternative"—because they are "indispensable to our having any criterion of the empirically real . . ." [39] Here again, we find that the systematic structure is *regulative* in relation to its empirical subject matter; that we make the assumptions required for building such a structure (because this is what we mean by knowledge) and apply them as far as possible.

This means that we must "approach particular experiences and attempt to fit them, somewhere and somehow, into its preformed patterns." [40] It does not mean, of course, that we shall not have to change those "preformed patterns" if too many experiences fail to fit into them in spite of our efforts; but it does mean that we shall make such changes, if required, rather than admit any particular discrepancy as final. It would be difficult to devise a clearer statement of Lewis's view (or of Kant's, for that matter, in its most consistent form) than the following:

. . . the dictum "There must be some order in any given area of reality" takes on the character of a regulative principle, not particularly different in significance from, "If at first you don't succeed; try, try again." . . . A certain minimal order is prescribed a priori in the recognition of the real. It is a regulative maxim of reason to seek further uniformities which may be stated in principles finally of maximal comprehensiveness and simplicity. But there neither is nor can be any prescription of the specific type of uniformity or correlation which is demanded in this interest of further intelligibility.[41]

We may note here the Kantian distinction between the "minimal order" of objective reality under the categories and the "maximal comprehensiveness and simplicity" sought by reason through science. The degree of orderliness, of conceptual coherence, of which we are analytically assured for real physical objects by definition (i.e., "in the recognition of the real") is not that of one completely unified system of all objects, but it does provide the foundation of a structure which, if carried further, will develop in the direction of such a system; and the pursuit of intelligibility demands that we carry this development as far as possible.

Moreover, since "the set of statements in a deductive system may be thought of as an 'ideal' instance of congruence, to which other congruent sets approximate in some degree," [42] a complete deductive structure is very definitely the ideal limit toward which the development of knowledge in terms of congruence inherently points. "The methodological postulate of all science is that the problem of understanding the process of reality, to which it addresses itself, is essentially capable of solution . . ." [43] This is quite precisely the Kantian regulative ideal. We do not *know* that "the process of reality" is understandable, beyond the analytic "minimal order" mentioned above; but knowledge itself is an attempt to understand, i.e., to fit an increasing body of subject matter into a system in which the parts will mutually support each other and the assumed premises will lead logically to the empirical verifications.

Here, however, we must ask the same question that we asked of Kant. Why should we expect that such an attempt will be successful to any extent at all? Even as to the "minimal order" required for physical objects by definition, this question holds; for there is no guarantee that any presumed physical object will turn out actually to be a physical object in terms of our definition. Indeed, for all we know so far, there may be no given subject matter that can fit into our definition at all. The difficulty is not only that "no substantive conception, determined a priori, is able to confine particular experiences within its conceptual embrace with absolute assurance"; [44] we may wonder why we should have *any* such assurance, however tentative and uncertain. The difficulty, as Lewis sees it, is precisely the one that Kant has made familiar. "Concepts are of the mind," while "the content of experience is independent of the mind" and "cannot be dictated by the knower"; yet "All knowledge is in terms of concepts, and the possibility of it depends upon their applicability to experience." [45] Moreover, *future* applicability is involved, even in the employment of so simple a concept as that of a physical object; for "there is no knowledge of external reality without the anticipation of future experience." Lewis, therefore, sees Hume's problem as fundamental. "Are there any *necessary* connections in experience? Can conceptual order, which is of the mind, be imposed upon a content of experience which is independent and not yet given." Such a connection is something which neither our conceptual structure, whose "necessary" character is analytic, nor our actually given experience, which simply presents itself and implies nothing as to any other experience, can provide. As Lewis concludes, "This is the problem of the a priori." [46]

For the applicability of more complicated concepts on higher levels of abstraction, the problem is essentially the same. Lewis has not the same need as Kant to figure this out for himself; he is squarely confronted by a mathematics admittedly based on abstract definitions and postulates (not on "the principles of intuitive construction which, for Kant, assured a basis of application to all possible experience") and by a physical science in which "abstractness and systematic precision go together," providing "no corresponding certainty about empirical nature." [47] Thus

. . . it becomes a matter of doubt whether the structure science builds is solidly based upon the earth, or is a mansion in some Platonic heaven, or is only a kind of castle in the air . . . the outstanding questions concern the nature of our abstract concepts, such as those which figure in mathematics and theoretical physics, and the relation of them to concrete experience and to reality.[48]

The "problem of the a priori," then, is the problem of the seemingly *synthetic* a priori which cannot be regarded as synthetic in any terms in which the a priori can be understood today; and this problem may also be expressed as that of the empirical applicability of conceptual systems.

This is the problem which both Kant and Lewis recognize as fundamental, and which both recognize as requiring solution if we are to explain the possibility not only of science but even of any experience of an objective physical world; for both analyze the difference between an objective physical world and a mere given sensory content of consciousness as a matter of conceptual structure. In the working out of this analysis, as we have seen, other similarities appear. It is in the attempt to solve the problem thus raised, to explain why and how far the given sensory content of our consciousness *does in fact* fit into such a conceptual structure, that a fundamental divergence occurs. It is in the attempt to avoid the requirement, or any semblance of the requirement, of *any* "synthetic a priori" assumption (even the assumption that there is in fact intelligible experience or that we do in fact have a type of consciousness that provides adequate material for such experience) that Lewis carries out a thorough re-interpretation of the categorial structure. He does, at one point, accept as "a fact" the existence of "*some* discoverable correlation between presented quality and relational context," not explaining it in a Kantian or any other manner but regarding it as "simply the miracle that an intelligible world exists." [49] Nevertheless, Lewis's entire enterprise is an attempt to do better than this in explaining the applicability of the a priori to the synthetic.

At this point, in spite of the far-reaching Kantian element which we have followed in Lewis's thought, we have reached an area which he approaches in conscious opposition to Kant. It will be best, therefore, to examine his explicit criticisms of Kant in this connection, in order to understand just where the divergence lies. We may distinguish several Kantian doctrines which are explicitly criticized: *1*] the justification of the a priori principles as "presuppositions" of knowledge, *2*] the concept of a priori principles as synthetic, *3*] the identification of experience with the phenomenally real, *4*] the doctrine that there are conceptual limitations upon sense perception itself, and *5*] the concept of the a priori structure of mind as absolute and inflexible. We shall find, I think, that the first criticism can be met; that the second and third are reinterpretations more than criticisms, urging in supposed opposition to Kant views which the latter would himself accept; and that the fourth and fifth, in spite of a very erroneous manner in which the last is stated, raise genuine problems for Lewis as well as for Kant—problems, then, for which Lewis himself must attempt to provide better answers. It is in so doing that he makes a contribution of unique significance.

In objection to the notion that there are synthetic a priori principles which are "presuppositions" of knowledge, Lewis argues, first, that Kant does not even make clear what he means by "presuppositions," and second, that whatever he means, his assumptions are not validated thereby. According to Lewis's analysis, "presuppositions" must mean either logical premises, logical consequences, or axioms. Logical premises, however, which Kant would most readily appear to have in mind, are sufficient but not necessary conditions of the consequences deducible from them; so that the categorial principles, regarded as logical premises of experience or of knowledge, would not be necessary a priori. Logical consequences of experience, on the other hand, would be its necessary conditions; but then they are as contingent as experience itself and necessary only relatively to experience. Axioms, finally, are premises, but more specifically the premises of Euclidean geometry, which in Kant's day were regarded as self-evident and therefore certain. Lewis surmises that Kant's notion of "presuppositions" is founded on an analogy with the Euclidean axioms. Today, however, these are recognized not to be self-evident at all. Whatever Kant means by "presuppositions of experience," then, such presuppositions are not established as certain.[50]

We may eliminate the third alternative at once, since Kant obviously does not regard the principles as "self-evident." On the contrary, he regards them as requiring lengthy and intricate justification. Since he often refers to them as "necessary conditions of experience," we must look again at Lewis's second alternative, the only one which logically establishes them as such. Are the principles the logical consequences of experience? That this makes them as contingent as experience, and necessary only relatively to experience, is no obstacle. Indeed, this is precisely the status which Kant accords to them, requiring only that the necessity be relative to experience generically rather than to any particular experience. I.e., the categories are a priori consequences of the *definition* of experience, and the principles of their application are necessarily fulfilled if and only if experience occurs.

Nevertheless, Lewis's first alternative seems to persist in raising its claims also. One cannot help absorbing a general impression that Kant thinks of his "presuppositions" as in some sense *prior* to experience, in some sense premises of experience rather than conclusions from it. This status, I think, is one which Kant attributes to them *in the structure of experience itself*, as distinguished from their status in the structure of the argument by which their validity is established. They are the most general features of experience, so that every experience is a particular application of them; in any reasoning about any particular experience, they are assumed as premises. If they are not assumed as premises, we cannot reason about any experience at all. It is true that this does not in itself make them "necessary"; logically, there may be other principles that might be sufficient for the same purpose. But if there are, we do not know what they are, much less do we in fact use them; and if we did find and use such principles, our experience would be completely transformed; it would not be what it in fact is. Accepting the nature of our actual experience as a premise, therefore, we establish the operation of these principles as logically necessary consequences of that premise.

Kant seems to mean by "presuppositions of experience," then, principles which we *actually* assume as *premises* whenever we interpret our sense impressions in terms of coherent experience of an objective world. They are such general and pervasive premises, however, that any adequate and relevant definition of such experience must include them; thus Kant means further, by "presuppositions of experience," logical *consequences* of any such definition, *necessary* as long as there is experience to which such a definition applies.

Definition of the status of the categorial principles as "presuppositions," however, does not reach the bottom of the question as to their alleged synthetic a priori character. It is in direct consideration of this question that Lewis advances his chief concentrated criticism of Kant. Fundamental to his approach is the hard and fast assertion that "There are no synthetic statements which can be known true *a priori* . . ." Some a priori statements may *seem* to be synthetic, but only through "failure to elicit by analysis the criteria operative in the . . . application of terms in question, or some failure to recognize implications . . ."; [51] i.e., through failure to grasp thoroughly the concepts by virtue of which these statements are really analytic. On this basis, Lewis offers a detailed analysis of the kind of principles that Kant identifies as synthetic a priori. This analysis, unfortunately, although it employs the mechanisms of extreme precision, turns out upon examination to be unexpectedly confused; yet it contains some very illuminating insights which will repay disentanglement.

Lewis argues that each of Kant's categorial terms, such as "substance" or "cause," has both a "broader" and a "narrower" meaning. The "broader meaning" is "purely conceptual" and "not limited to objects of our possible experience," and therefore does not entail any spatial or temporal character; nor is it limited by the conditions of our "capacity to receive sense-impressions." The "narrower meaning" of the categories is their "sense meaning, which is further limited by a schematism of our possible application of them to empirical objects." (Lewis makes much of the fact that the broader meaning is supposed to include possible application to "supersensible" objects, and goes into the difficulties of such a view; but surely this view is quite irrelevant here, aside from the questionableness of attributing it to Kant. It is, on the contrary, the *abstract* character of the concept, as contrasted with *any* application of it, that is relevant here.)

Lewis then goes on to point out that the "wider" concept, since it is not limited to experience and therefore does not entail the conditions of experience, is applied *synthetically* to experience; but for that very reason, such application is not necessary or a priori. The "narrrower" concept, on the other hand, that of "phenomenal" substance or cause, does entail the conditions of experience, i.e., "whatever is involved in that schematism by which alone we can give the term empirical application"; and therefore the so-called synthetic a priori principles, understood in their "phenomenal" meaning, are *analytic*. Regarding them as statements of the form "All *A* is *B*," we may see in them "a fallacy of four terms"; for "the conceptual signification of '*A*' does not entail the conceptual signification of '*B*,' but . . . the representation or schema of empirical application of '*A*' does entail '*B*.' " Thus only the first version is synthetic, and only the second version, in which we mean "phenomenal A," is a priori.[52]

As we shall see in a moment, Lewis is driving at something very important; but his argument up to this point is fallacious. There is *no* meaning for the categories, in Kant's view, except their meaning as concepts referring to experience. Lewis himself points out Kant's statements to this effect,[53] but attempts to reconcile with them the notion of a conceptual, purely abstract significance as well. But the "broader" or "conceptual" meaning which Lewis finds for "cause," "that in the absence of which a thing could not be," appears rather to be a definition in terms of Kant's categories of modality; while the "conceptual" definition which Lewis finds for "substance," "that which is subject and cannot be predicate," is Kant's definition of the *logical relation* on which the category of substance is based, not of the category of substance itself. When we make a subject-predicate statement *about a physical object,* we think in terms of a continuous, identifiable thing and its properties. Thus the broader, more abstract meaning which Lewis attributes to the Kantian categories is rather, for Kant, that of the logical "forms" on which the categories are based and which they translate into experiential terms; while the "narrower" or "sense meaning," the meaning in experiential terms, which Lewis also attributes to them, is their *only* meaning in the Kantian scheme. The distinction and relation between the two types of concept are valid and important, but do not fall where Lewis has placed them; nor does Kant ever confuse them.

Thus there is no ambiguity in the meaning of the categories. Lewis is quite right in pointing out that the application of the logical concept is synthetic and not necessary or a priori; but so is the application of the category, even if we recognize that the qualification "phenomenal" is *always* intended. For that matter, so is the application of any other concept. For although the meaning of the category includes applicability to experience, and therefore entails the conditions of experience, it cannot entail any guarantee of the actual occurrence of anything that will meet those conditions—anything to which the category can be applied. The category is the kind of concept that can be applied to a certain type of sensory material *if* such material is available; it is applicable if and only if the conditions of experience are fulfilled; but the occurrence and identification of suitable material is empirical, and any statement of such occurrence and identification is synthetic.

Here some of Lewis's own terms are of particular value in clearing up an ambiguity in the concept of "applicability." The sense in which the category *entails* applicability to experience, while the logical concept does not, is that of "sense meaning." It has a meaning in terms of experiential criteria, while logical concepts as such (as long as they are uninterpreted) have only linguistic meaning in terms of each other. If by "applicability" we mean "denotation," something actual to which application is possible, we mean something that cannot be entailed by any concept whatsoever. Denotation, we may remember, is "limited" by the meaning of the concept, but can be "fixed" only by empirical fact. Thus the categories entail sense meanings as part of their intensions; but they do not entail denotations any more than the concepts of logic do. Their applicability in terms of denotation is still synthetic, although their applicability in terms of sense meaning is analytic.

Moreover, what the categories do or do not entail is not really the point at issue. Although the term "phenomenal or natural substance," to take Lewis's example, does entail the complete definition of "phenomenal" (and consequently the formulation of the conditions of experience), this entailment does not yield analytically any statement about "all experience," but merely a statement about *some* experience or about all (phenomenal) *substance*. Kant's allegedly "synthetic a priori" principles, however, are about *all experience* (or, equivalently, about "all appearances," the content of experience, as, e.g., in the principle "that in all appearances there is something permanent").[54] We are interested, therefore, in finding out what is entailed in the concept of experience, or in the concept of appearance, not in the categories. We know, for whatever it may be worth, that such concepts as "substance" and "cause" do mean, as Lewis asserts, "phenomenal" substance and cause, and do imply experience analytically; but we want to know whether *experience* implies substance, cause, and the rest of the categories, and, if so, whether it implies them analytically or synthetically, a priori or empirically.

Lewis himself shifts his argument to precisely this question, although without any apparent awareness of a shift. When he sets out to demonstrate the ambiguity of "All *A* is *B*," on the grounds that "*A*" may or may not mean "phenomenal *A*," he has led us to assume that "*A*" stands for a category, e.g., substance or cause, and that "*B*" stands for experience, which is entailed only if "*A*" is phenomenal. When he goes on to a detailed example, however, he analyzes the proposition, "Whatever happens has a cause," in which "All *A*" would be identified with "Whatever happens," i.e., with experience, and "*B*" with the category, and the latter is quite clearly and unambiguously phenomenal because we are talking only about the cause of "Whatever happens." It is here, at last, that Lewis's argument becomes relevant to the categorial principles which are Kant's proffered examples of "a priori synthetic judgments."

The real crux of the matter, therefore, is the following:

For example, if "whatever happens" connotes temporality of what is spoken of, and if being a temporal happening entails being caused, then "Whatever happens has a cause" is an analytic proposition. But if temporality is not here connoted, or if being a temporal event does not entail being caused, then no ground for holding this proposition to be *a priori* is revealed.

Kant, Lewis supposes, recognizes some sort of entailment here, but does not regard it as a *logical* entailment, because he does not regard it as implied by the *definitions* of "temporal event" and "cause." To this possible view, however, Lewis replies that "A definition which does not entail logically all characters essential to what is defined, is faulty." If there are characters necessary for all spatial and temporal things, we must include them in our definition of these things.[55] In other words, as we have already seen in examining Kant himself, the categorial principles are a priori because they are *analytic*.

Lewis's argument, then, does not merely become relevant at this point; it also becomes valid. For if there is any Kantian term whose ambiguity might be said to lead to the kind of fallacy that Lewis has attempted to explain, that term is "experience"—as well as terms like "event" and "object" which refer to the content of experience. If these terms *mean* sensory material as organized by the categories, the so-called "synthetic a priori principles" (which state that the categories apply to all experience) are analytic; while if these terms mean merely the given sensory material itself, the principles applying the categories are synthetic but cannot be a priori. Here, at last, Lewis is altogether right; but Kant himself, as we have seen, except in the persistent use of the term "synthetic a priori," seems fundamentally to agree with him. It is as an interpretation—an extremely important and illuminating interpretation—rather than as a criticism of Kant, that Lewis's point is well taken. The Kantian structure is consistent and comprehensible if we interpret the so-called "a priori synthetic judgments" as analytic judgments empirically applicable, or —to be still more precise, with Lewis's help—as analytic judgments with sense meaning, to which we add the synthetic assumption that they have empirical denotation.

For Kant, as we have seen, does *not* use such terms as "experience" ambiguously in the manner indicated; it is rather Lewis's own usage that conflicts with Kant's. Thus still another criticism of Kant by Lewis is answered, the criticism which asserts that "reality and the content of experience are not directly synonymous," and that "It is reality, not experience, which must be orderly." [56] Here Lewis uses the term "reality" as Kant does, but not the term "experience"; in the Kantian scheme, it is the contents of *consciousness*, the data provided by "sensibility," that are not synonymous with either; and the fact that Lewis, quite permissibly, uses the term "experience" for the latter has nothing to do with Kant. When Lewis complans that Kant uses "the term 'experience' as if experience and the phenomenally real coincide," he goes on to ask, "Did the sage of Konigsberg have no dreams!" [57] Actually, Kant does use the term "experience" in just this way; he does not, however, thereby deny the occurrence of dreams, but rather, as we have seen, excludes them from "experience" just as he excludes them from the "phenomenally real." Lewis recognizes this after all, when he declares that Kant

uses the term "experience" to mean "objective experience," "valid experience," . . . even though he does not make this quite explicit. He certainly does not mean that the categories are requisite to the experience of a buzzing blooming confusion.

Thus it is part of Kant's argument "that the only alternative to a categorized and orderly experience is a meaningless flux of mere *schwarmerei* (*sic*)." [58] This aspect of Kant's doctrine, as we shall see, is one which Lewis greatly amplifies and clarifies, even though he does not always recognize it as part of Kant's own intention.

Lewis criticizes Kant, further, for the view that there is no such "meaningless flux" within the content of consciousness, because all of that content is subject to conditions set by the mind for admission to consciousness itself. The doctrine here attributed to Kant is identified by Lewis as the view that the categories are "valid of experience in general" because

That which cannot validly be thought under the categories cannot be given in intuition . . . The limitations of thinking are also the limitations of sensing; the possibility of knowledge is assured by the fact that experience is not of the independent real but of phenomena already informed by our receptivity.[59]

As we have seen, Kant's own adherence to this view is somewhat ambiguous and inconsistent, but some residue of it remains even after all allowances to the contrary are made. We have also seen, however, that Lewis himself regards even the subjective "stream of consciousness" as having conceptual structure. The significant difference, therefore, seems to turn upon the point of whether this conformity of the sensory to the conceptual constitutes a "limitation" upon the sensory by the conceptual. Lewis's argument that the mind could not recognize limitations imposed by itself upon the given unless there were also areas of the given to which these limitations did *not* apply, that we should regard them—if we noticed them at all—as limitations of the given itself,[60] does not seem conclusive. Kant offers the theory of the conceptual origin of these limitations as an *explanation* of the amenability of sense perceptions to conceptual structure, not as an identification of something directly observed; and that amenability is discovered, by Lewis as well as by Kant, through *analysis* of experience into its component factors and not through comparison of experience where it is present with experience where it is altogether absent. That we do not *need* Kant's explanation, that we can explain the amenability of all the contents of consciousness to a minimum, at least, of conceptual structure without the concept of prior mental limitations upon it,[61] is quite another argument; and we must examine Lewis's own positive doctrine to find out whether he can indeed offer a more readily acceptable explanation than Kant's.

Lewis does not deny, in any event, but rather affirms explicitly and confidently, that the a priori is a "contribution of the mind to knowledge"; but he qualifies this affirmation, apparently as an intended further criticism of Kant, to the effect that this mind need not therefore be "universal, absolute, or of a reality of a higher order than the object of its knowledge." The categories are not "the inscrutable legislation of a transcendent mind," nor is the mind an "ultimate reality" as distinguished from "its object which is not thus ultimate." [62] The view here denied, however, while full of Kantian language and fragmentary Kantian concepts, is certainly not Kant's view. The transcendental (not "transcendent") mind which Kant conceives as the source of a priori concepts is "universal" only for human beings; it is "absolute" (a better term would be "necessary") only within the field of human experience, and therefore may as easily be described as relative to such experience; and it is not a "reality" at all, "ultimate" or not, but rather an abstract construction having reality only through the reality of the experience which it systematizes, or understands. In other words, mind in the Kantian "transcendental" sense *is* the a priori—the available a priori conceptual system found embedded in human knowledge, interpreted as implying and applying a continuity of consciousness without which no conceptual system could be available at all. Lewis here surprisingly confuses this concept with that of mind as an ontological entity, a "thing in itself," which—in the sense that Kant admits it at all—has nothing to do with knowledge or the a priori. Of course there is, nevertheless, in Kant's system of a priori categories, a certain rigidity ("absoluteness" in a loose sense) in regard to which Lewis's criticism has a very considerable point. Here, again, it is important to see how far and in what manner he himself can remedy the situation.

We are left, then, with two substantial criticisms of the Kantian view. Essentially, they are objections to the requirements that the structure of mind must be of a specified character and that the structure of the rudimentary sense perception which supplies the content of that mind must be of a specified character. Thus both objections together constitute an objection to the fundamental assumption which may be regarded as the one "synthetic a priori" that Kant does not ultimately explain away—the assumption that there *is* experience of a kind defined by the categories. They are also objections to a rigidity of structure which, encouraged or even required by the logic and science of Kant's time, is discouraged and revealed as arbitrary by the logic and science of our own time.

Lewis, working in the twentieth century, operates in the framework of a greatly expanded conception of logic, which accepts as admissible to the field of logic *any* consistent conceptual system that may be devised; and so long as the categories constitute such a system and define areas of experience, they may be regarded as principles of the empirical application of logic, without being derived from a ready-made logic specified (largely by Aristotle) in advance. In other words, Kant's "metaphysical deduction of the categories" is automatically eliminated as a mechanical procedure, but its significance in terms of the relation of the categories to logic, its implications as to the status and function of the categories, are preserved.

Moreover, the categories need not be such as to render deducible a ready-made science specified in advance and supposed to be valid deductively as well as empirically. Thus they are not caught, as are Kant's categories, between predetermined logical premises and predetermined physical conclusions; and Lewis is provided with the opportunity to avoid precisely those faults which he finds in Kant, faults which indeed are partly identifiable with and partly attributable to the rigidity of the logic and science by which Kant is inevitably bound. It remains to be seen, then, how Lewis adapts the Kantian approach —which, as we have seen, he shares to a very great extent—to this new situation. It remains to be seen, specifically, whether in this new framework the synthetic a priori assumption (that there is, in fact, intelligible experience) can be eliminated. For this purpose, we must turn to Lewis's own doctrine of the categories, in which his reinterpretation of and departure from the Kantian doctrine are embodied.

Lewis and the Applicability
of the A Priori

W HAT LEWIS means by "categories" is stated with considerable
clarity. Since they are a particular kind of concepts, we are first
told what he means by concepts. The mind, he says, "confronted with
the chaos of the given," seeks some means of "adaptation and control." It seeks, therefore, orderly patterns "through which distinguishable items may become the signs of future possibilities. Those
patterns . . . are our concepts," which must be fixed in advance of
any particular experience if that experience is to be interpreted in
terms of them. Concepts, then, are the source of all a priori truth,
which arises from them in one of two ways. First, there is "elaboration of concepts in the abstract, without reference to any particular
application to experience," as in pure mathematics.

Second, the concept in its application to the given exhibits the predetermined principles of interpretation, the criteria of our distinguishing and
relating, of classification, and hence the criteria of reality of any sort. This
is most clearly evident in the case of those basic concepts, determining
major classes of the real, which may be called the categories, though in
less important ways it holds true of concepts in general.[1]

In a sense, then, all concepts are abstract; but some are *merely*
abstract, to be understood only in terms of other concepts in a system,
while others have a definite empirical reference, and are to be interpreted in terms of sense data, actual or predicted. The categories
are the broadest, most general concepts with empirical reference,
indicating the *kinds* of concepts that are to be applied and the cri-

teria of their application. Lewis does not enumerate them; and indeed, as we shall see, he cannot maintain a rigid division between the
categories and other broad, general concepts. It becomes apparent,
however, that he has in mind such "major classes of the real" as
physical objects, illusions, etc., and such "criteria" as conformity to
laws of various kinds.

The categories are intermediate between the abstractions of logic
and mathematics and the empirical concepts of science and of daily
life;

. . . beyond such principles as those of logic and pure mathematics whose
permanent stability seems attested, there must be further and more particular criteria of the real prior to any investigation of nature. Such definitions, fundamental principles and criteria the mind itself must supply before experience can even begin to be intelligible.[2]

Both in their function of determining "the concept in its application
to the given" and in their position in the scheme of knowledge between logic and physical science, Lewis's categories may be regarded
as principles for the empirical application of logic. On the whole,
then, Lewis means by "categories" just about what Kant means.

There is, however, a fundamental difference. It results directly
from the fact that Lewis, not being constrained by the requirements
of a fixed science and a fixed logic, can see that the categories are
not bound by their extremely fundamental and general character to
be forever unchangeable. Although they "must . . . be prior to the
particular experience," they might be changed in adaptation to some
extremely far-reaching change in the given content of experience as
a whole, which could ultimately render some of them irrelevant or
inadequate (though not actually false). The categories

represent . . . deep-lying attitudes, which the human mind has taken in
the light of its total experience up to date. But a newer and wider experience may bring about some alteration of these attitudes even though . . .
no experience can conceivably prove them invalid.[3]

Their a priori character is absolute in an abstract sense, in that they
cannot be falsified by experience; like purely logical concepts, they
are abstractly valid in terms of mutual consistency alone, i.e., analytically. It is their empirical relevance, their suitability as means
of interpretation and organization of experience, that depends upon

the nature of experience. Thus "Categories and concepts do not literally change; they are simply given up and replaced by new ones"; [4] but it is important to note that categories, like other concepts (although under much rarer circumstances), *may* be "given up and replaced" for empirical reasons.

Once this possibility is admitted, the way is opened to new and valuable developments in the doctrine of categories. First, in explanation of the a priori character which the categories must nevertheless retain, we shall find an emphasis on their status as definitions, and on the consequent analytic nature of their "necessary" validity. Although we have already discerned this view in Kant, Lewis maintains it with such an increase in explicitness, consistency, and clarity as to constitute in effect a reinterpretation; and he also attempts to carry it further so as to solve some aspects of the problem of applicability for whose solution Kant must resort directly to the nature of consciousness. Second, in further explanation of the empirical applicability of the categories, we shall find Lewis introducing a genetic analysis of the manner in which our construction of a categorial system (though not its logical validity) is determined by the development of human experience as a whole. Finally, we shall find also a clarification of the status of scientific law and its relation to empirical fact on one hand and to the categories on the other, in the light of this reinterpretation of the latter.

Lewis continually reminds us, in much more precise terms than Kant (or at least in language conveying a much more precise meaning today), that a priori truth, whether dealing in pure uninterpreted abstractions or in concepts having empirical reference, *"is not a material truth . . . but is definitive or analytic in its nature . . . a* truth about our own interpretative attitude." [5] The fact that the mind "legislates for reality" does not contradict the fact that it "prescribes *nothing* to the content of experience"; for it legislates merely by "determining its own interpretations." It "anticipates the character of the *real*" only because "The real . . . is not the given as such, but the given categorially interpreted." [6] The categories which it sets up are explicitly definitions; in regard to "experience of the physical," for instance, "The formulation of our deliberately taken, and consistently adhered to, attitude of interpretation constitutes a categorial *definition* of the 'physical.'" Such a definition "forbids nothing in the way of experience; . . . neither illusion nor senseless dream"; nor can it be invalidated by the occurrence of such nonconforming events. Instead, "what would be exceptional is at once thrown out of court"; by definition, "no experience of the physical can fail to bear those marks the absence of which would bar the given content of experience from interpretation as physical reality." [7] The categories are valid without exception for all physical facts, only because all exceptions are excluded as nonphysical by definition.

The fact that principles applying the categories may be expressed as "universal propositions," then, does not automatically make them applicable to all experience. For "Amongst universal propositions which refer to nature, we must distinguish between empirical generalizations which are synthetic . . . and analytic principles which exhibit the consequences of our concepts . . ." [8] Any "universal proposition the subject of which denotes a class of *objects*" is an "empirical generalization," not a definition, and therefore contingent. It asserts "a limitation of nature and of experience" and therefore requires verification by experience and can be falsified by experience; while a definition asserts no such limitation. The categories appear to limit nature, but "only because *'nature' is itself a category*"; they still do not limit the given content of experience.[9] Thus Lewis makes clear the important point which Kant recognizes but sometimes obscures by his language and perhaps sometimes forgets—that the categorial principles as statements about all reality do not imply that there *is* reality in the sense which they define; that the synthetic assumption that there is in fact such a reality is not included in their a priori (analytic) meaning.

The applicability of the categories to all reality in this sense, then, cannot tell us that any particular item of the given is interpretable in terms of a specified category, or even in terms of the categorial system (i.e., that this item is "real"). "Our subsumption of the given under concepts is, thus, always contingent upon future experience, and the a priori knowledge of universal principles does not secure any a priori knowledge of empirical particulars." [10] Any concept has analytic, a priori consequences, which are themselves conceptual and which constitute "*criteria of its applicability*"; and "to determine its applicability" in fact, we need "some orderly sequence in experience" which meets these criteria. Whether any given item is part of such a sequence can be determined only empirically, over a period of time, and is therefore "verifiable only approximately . . ." [11] The "bringing . . . together" of our concepts and "the chaos of given experience," even when the concepts involved are the fundamental categories of all of our knowledge, "is that empirical and material truth which is never more than probable . . ." [12]

Thus there is an a priori (definitive or analytic) element and a synthetic (empirical) element even in so simple a statement as "This is round"; but the two elements are sharply distinguishable and do not add up to a synthetic a priori. They are, according to Lewis,

(1) "If this is round, then further experience of it will be thus and so (the empirical criteria of objective roundness)" and (2) "This present given is such that further experience (probably) *will be* thus and so." The first of these is a priori; the second is our statement of the probable empirical truth about the given object. [13]

That is, the a priori element is a set of "If . . . then" statements. We do not know all such statements that would be valid, because they are too numerous; but those that we do know, we know a priori, i.e., analytically. [14] (We may recall Kant's interpretation of objectivity in terms of conformity to a causal law, which is a hypothetical judgment in form and is applied to temporal sequences.) The second element, the statement of probable empirical truth, is a generalization from past experience; but it is about "the *presentation itself* (or the class of such)," not about "the *object*." [15] (Here we recall Kant's characterization of the mere perceived recurring sequence, as distinguished from the sequence seen as necessary in terms of a law, as "subjective.") The a priori structure is analytic; the statement that it is applicable to a given case is empirical, descriptive of the perceptual data concerned.

At this point we may easily be perplexed by Lewis's assertions to the effect that "the application of any particular concept to particular given experience is hypothetical . . ." Has he not just said that it is empirical? We must note, however, as does Lewis, that "empirical truth is never more than probable"; [16] what we think is a round object may turn out not to be round, or not to be an object, on the basis of future data. When we say "This is round," however, i.e., when we apply a concept to an item of experience, we overlook the element of doubtfulness and assume, pending any empirical reason to change our minds, that the statement is true. Indeed, we *must* do this, in a very important sense; for, even to find out whether a concept *probably* applies, we must try it out as a hypothesis. It is the hypothesis (in Kant's language, the "presupposition," the "regulative" element) that brings together the abstract concept and the actual and anticipated (probable) empirical data; *if* the concept applies to the data, its necessary consequences are empirically true. The relation between the analytic, synthetic, and hypothetical elements now becomes clear. Definitions and the implications analytically derived from them

are a priori and certain; but their a priori certainty is either that of abstract conceptual systems, or when they are given denotation and application, it is hypothetical, and when mention of the hypothesis is omitted, they are not certain but are merely probable.[17]

Direct comparison of this statement with Kant's equivalent one, quoted on p. 37, is extremely illuminating.

Obviously, then, since the categories are definitions, all categories are not necessarily applicable to all given subject matter; there may always be something left over. Indeed, everything may be left over; for we still have no guarantee that the categories will be applicable at all. Kant, we may remember, seems to be attempting a solution of this problem when he views the given material excluded by the "dynamical" categories, which are "regulative" in relation to sense perception, as at least included by the "mathematical" categories, which are "constitutive" of sense perception because inherent in the nature of all human consciousness. Yet, although this is in some respects an enlightening analysis, it is not a solution. There is still no guarantee that the "dynamical" principles, which are to be applied as far as possible, will apply to anything at all merely because the "mathematical" ones do; while the latter, since they apply to everything in consciousness without distinction, cannot perform the function of definitions. Lewis, moreover, aims to eliminate any a priori requirements as to the nature of consciousness. He therefore attempts to establish some sense in which the categorial system as a whole is applicable to *all* experience, *whatever it may be* (i.e., without any "limitation" upon it), and therefore *applicable on analytic grounds*.

One such attempt, put forward tentatively in an appendix, is based on the view that any conceptual system can be applied, by sufficient elaboration, to any subject matter. On the grounds that many of the conceptual structures of science introduce distinctions where none exist in their empirical interpretations, thereby adapting themselves to these interpretations, he concludes (not very confidently) that "It is unsafe to say that *any* concept *could not* be applied to any empirical content." [18] On the other hand, in an equally detailed discussion, he concludes that there are two minimum requirements that must be met by the actual world if concepts are to be applicable and knowledge possible. First, "It must be false that every identifiable unity in experience is equally associated with every other." [19] Second, in any area of experience where there are no given entities so correlated as to satisfy the first principle, we can find—by analysis, organization, or abstraction—"other entities, systematically connected with the former," which are so correlated.

Lewis attempts to demonstrate that these requirements are not "limitations upon the actual," i.e., synthetic a priori. One attempt is based on the concept of randomness. Where we can find no correlation at all among data, Lewis argues, we find randomness, which is the best possible "basis for statistical generalization"; and any departure from randomness is a correlation also "subject to generalization of some sort." This is impressive; but one is led to ask whether there cannot, then, be random departures from statistical randomness, and indeed, whether randomness does not otherwise lose its distinctive meaning and become just another exact law.

On a more general basis, Lewis argues that his two principles must be valid because no alternative is conceivable.

That conception *in general* should be invalid, is quite impossible. The attempt to envisage an experience or state of affairs such that *every* attempt to discover stabilities must fail, is the attempt to conceive the inconceivable . . . The experience or reality which should be incompatible with conception, *ipso facto* cannot be conceived.[20]

Here, however, Lewis begs the question by assuming that the logically impossible is existentially impossible. The inconceivable cannot be conceived, and Lewis argues that "If this . . . statement is a tautology, then at least it must be true"; [21] but the question is not whether the inconceivable can be conceived, but whether it can occur; whether any, or indeed all, of our experience may fail to be conceptually understandable. That some of it *is* conceptually understandable is irrelevant; for Lewis intends to dispense with synthetic assumptions and to establish the possibility of knowledge analytically.

Indeed, Lewis here engages in a venture more rationalistic than any of Kant's; for he tries to establish a priori that nothing can exist without meeting the conditions of conceivability. There is, however, a second, more significant approach by which Lewis attempts to insure the applicability of the categories on analytic grounds, one which imposes no "conditions" because it reserves a place for anything that fails to meet the very conditions which it sets up as criteria of rational experience.

While individual categories are definitive, thus including some empirical data and excluding others, the categorial system as a whole, in Lewis's scheme, is not definitive but *logically exhaustive*, thus automatically including all data; "whatever does not conform to the principles of a particular category will conform to the principles of some other which is co-ordinate." [22] This is always possible, as "any set of co-ordinate categories is simply a method for exhausting the possibilities"; whatever violates the precise categories can fit into one which is their negation, the category of the "unreal."

The "unreal" is a temporary pigeon-hole for what requires to be sorted or analyzed in some further fashion. The unsatisfactoriness of such a scrap-basket category merely reflects this desirability of a further understanding of its content. But to be able to classify what is presented as "unreal" or "illusion," though it may represent only superficial understanding, means nevertheless a very important understanding, precisely because it means that this content of experience is not relevant in the present connection, that it cannot figure as a negative instance of an empirical generalization and so on . . . The only question is, *how much* of experience will be reality, and how much illusion . . . this depends, in part, at least, upon the intellectual ingenuity of the knower . . .[23]

Thus not only is each category valid for *all relevant* experience (because all contrary material is excluded as irrelevant by definition), but the system of categories as a whole is valid for *all* experience (because all material contrary to other categories is included by definition in the category of the unreal). The function of defining the real world, performed in Kant's most consistent view by the total system of categories, is performed for Lewis by the total system of all categories except that of the unreal; but the addition of this category provides universal applicability for the total system on analytic grounds.

At first glance, this seems to be a complete solution of the problem of the applicability of the categories. They are applicable to the given content of our experience—indeed, to *all* of it—because they exclude nothing, but classify whatever we have. Certainly this explanation clarifies an important sense in which the categories are universally valid a priori. Yet, as Lewis himself points out, there is still the question of "how *much* of experience will be reality, and how much illusion." A system of categories of which all except the category of the "unreal" should be empirically irrelevant, so that all experience should be regarded as unreal, would hardly contribute to our understanding of anything. And so, in a significant sense, the "unreal" turns out to be a sort of pseudo-category, designating an incompleteness in the positive categorial structure or in its applicability; and we are confronted by our old problem in new terms. Lewis must now explain why anything is "real" in his sense.

That the category of the "unreal" is unsatisfactory to Lewis himself is further attested, not only by his reference to it as "transitory," but by his analysis of "the adjective 'real' " as "systematically ambiguous." [24] "There is no such thing," he points out, "as reality in general; to be real, a thing must be a particular sort of real." [25] His development of this point sheds important light on the relation between the exhaustiveness of the categories and their definitive character. When we call anything "real," Lewis asserts, we mean to assign it to some specific category of reality, such as "material reality," "psychic reality," "mathematical reality." Thus

whatever is real in one such sense will be unreal in others. Conversely, every given content of experience is a reality of some sort or other; so that the problem of distinguishing real from unreal . . . is always a problem of right understanding, of referring the given experience to its proper category. The mirage, for example, though not real trees and water, is a real state of atmosphere and light . . . The content of every experience is real when it is correctly understood, and is that kind of reality which it is then interpreted to be. Metaphysics is concerned to reveal just that set of major classifications . . . by which the whole array of given experience may be set in order and each item (ideally) assigned to its intelligible and unambiguous place.[26]

This analysis merits attention in several respects. Aside from its bearing on the points which here concern us, it is an important and illuminating explanation of the difficult concept of "reality," solving the perplexing problem of how the term can signify a meaningful distinction while at the same time everything is real. Some interest attaches also to the use of the term "metaphysics" to mean, just as for Kant, systematic epistemology. A still more significant Kantian feature is the identification of the real with the understandable, which in Lewis's context is greatly clarified. (We may recall Kant's assertion that a violation of causality must be regarded as "a merely subjective play of my fancy," or, if it is to be regarded as "objective," as "a mere dream." [27] Lewis's analysis makes clear what Kant apparently had in mind somewhat obscurely—that a dream is "objective" as meeting definite criteria; it is a real dream, though its contents are not real physical objects.) At the present juncture, however, the main point to be noted is Lewis's assumption that "ideally" *all* the contents of experience can be regarded as real, i.e., can be understood; that by some set of categories "the whole array of given experience may be set in order" and the "scrap-basket category" of the "unreal" emptied of content.

We must note that complete understanding or systematization, synonymous with the complete "reality" of experience, is to be sought "ideally"; no claim is made as to its attainability in fact. Kant's "ideal of pure reason," maintained as a "regulative principle," confronts us once more, but with a genuine addition to our comprehension of it. The category of the "unreal," then, however unsatisfactory, must be retained as a repository for whatever can *not* be understood, to make the system logically exhaustive and therefore universally applicable on analytic grounds.

That some, at least, of the given subject matter of experience will in fact be capable of incorporation in our categorial structure as *reality* of one kind or another, that the ideal goal can be advanced at all, must still be established. Moreover, it must still be recognized as a fact about the nature of human experience, not to be explained by analytic means alone; and it must still be recognized as a fact about the experience of all human beings, sufficient in scope to provide the applicable conceptual basis for a common world. It need not, however, be an unchanging fact, since, as we have seen, the categories themselves need not bridge over from a fixed logic to a fixed science. Lewis, therefore, can introduce *a genetic account of the categorial structure* of reality, explaining at one stroke both the applicability of that structure to empirical data and the inherence of the same structure in all human minds.

Human beings, according to Lewis, must have something in common at the outset, if they are to be capable of communication in terms of a common world. Like Kant, he recognizes that "the hope of agreement between minds . . . must rest upon the presumption that this accord somehow exists already," i.e., that human minds share a common conceptual structure applicable to the given experience of all. Lewis hastens to add, however, that such a structure need not therefore be based on "some universal pattern of human reason." [28] We cannot assume "an initial community of categories, as a psychologically identical and miraculous endowment," [29] established for all times and places and without reference to empirical fact; for "Our common world is very largely a social achievement . . ." [30]

Is this circular? In a sense it is, and quite properly so; for the building up of a common world is a cumulative process, one in which past progress makes possible future progress. Thus there is an obvious sense in which social achievement is impossible without a *prior* common world, i.e., without means of communication, although development of the means of communication is itself social. On the conceptual level, too, "Most . . . identifications of meaning will, of course, be based upon previous identification of *other* and related meanings"; [31] thus our common categories and the common world which they define seem mutually interdependent.

Yet there must be, as Lewis makes clear, a preconceptual, rudimentary form of social activity which is genetically prior and out of which the full-fledged common world, the world of meaningful communication in terms of both concepts and action, is developed.

The coincidence of our fundamental criteria and principles is the combined result of the similarity of human animals, and of their primal interests, and the similarities of the experience with which they have to deal . . . Our common understanding and our common world may be, in part, created in response to our need to act together and to comprehend one another. [32]

Because "we are creatures fundamentally alike" in interests, needs, and powers, and because "we are confronted by a common reality, mediated to us in sense-experience which is comparable," we have in common "certain very fundamental tendencies to action" whose "formal or relational" aspect will be expressible and communicable in terms of common categories. [33]

It will be noted that these primitive patterns develop in response to a "need to act together," and, in general, in response to the need of each organism for adaptation to the environment (of which other, similar organisms are a part). Thus, on this very primitive level of the formation of concepts, there is easily recognizable a pragmatic element which is the basis of the "pragmatism" in Lewis's analysis of more advanced stages of knowledge. The social development of categories and thereby of a "common world" involves a continuing common effort [34] to build up and apply the conceptual system which best "serves our interests of reducing experience to order and securing control." [35] This remains true when our "interests" have become more complex, and when accordingly the notions of "order" and "control" may be interpreted in terms of "the achievement of intelligible order amongst the phenomena in question" and may be said to include also "such criteria as intellectual simplicity, economy, and comprehensiveness of principle." [36]

The relation of this pragmatic factor to the other elements in knowledge is made clear in a discussion extremely illuminating as to the sense in which Lewis calls himself a "pragmatist." The analytic element, the "truth about" our abstract concepts and their implications, "answers only to the criteria of consistency and adequacy," and is "absolute." Equally "absolute" is the purely empirical element, "the brute-fact of given experience"; once it occurs, it is a determinate fact which our concepts cannot alter. The relation between these two elements, therefore, is absolute also, once the concepts have been assigned an empirical meaning; in any particular case either that meaning is in fact exemplified or the application of the concept is false; "it is . . . given experience which determines the truths of nature." [37] (In all of this, of course, Lewis is in essential agreement with Kant—and with most others who do not, like Lewis, call themselves "pragmatists." Whether he is in agreement with most others who do call themselves "pragmatists" is more doubtful.)

The hypothetical element, as we have seen, is the assumption that a concept or conceptual system is empirically applicable. If there are implied predictions which are falsified by events, the hypothesis is *false* (although the system is still analytically valid). Sometimes it may be possible to assign the events to some other category and retain the hypothesis; but if the system is thus rendered irrelevant too often, some other may be more adequate to take all the facts into account. Then the hypothesis will be given up; the conceptual system will be abandoned (not internally changed) and replaced by a new one.[38] It is here that the pragmatic element lies; "the *choice* of an abstract conceptual system" is "determined by pragmatic considerations." [39]

This does not mean that each of us consciously makes such choices, certainly not in regard to our basic categories, which are built up by the long social process which Lewis describes and transmitted to each of us largely ready-made (primarily, one would suppose, although Lewis does not go into this aspect of the matter, as part of the transmission of language). Yet any social process must consist of the activities of individuals, however interrelated and cumulative these activities may be. It is quite possible, moreover, that individuals may entertain concepts which are not standard human equipment. Because of the need to co-operate, however, Lewis points out, there is a psychological process whereby "the importance of those concepts which are framed in terms of distinctions and relations which *are* common, is enhanced, and of those which should be in terms of what some only can discriminate, is diminished." As for the latter, "no socially current concept will be framed in terms of them"; there will be no language to express them. Consequently, they may "largely pass unnoticed by the individual himself"; or, if he does notice them, he will regard them as "subjective." [40]

It would have been interesting and important if Lewis had similarly considered the process by which an already established category may be abandoned. Any instance where this has occurred, of course, has probably been obliterated by that very abandonment. What happens, however, when the status of a long-established category is at least threatened, may be observed by means of an example currently available—the threat to the concept of universal causality created by the development of quantum mechanics. An interesting and relevant point is the confusion as to whether or not the offending phenomena are to be regarded as physical objects, or even as "real." Here a decision is being made between relegation of certain data to the realm of the "unreal" (i.e., the incomprehensible) and revision of the categorial system by which the "real" is defined; and the issue will be decided by criteria which Lewis calls "pragmatic," i.e., in favor of that set of concepts which interprets as many data as possible, as intelligibly as possible, with as little disturbance to the established categorial system as possible. Another interesting feature of the situation is the wide gap between the conscious, deliberate development of the new concepts in science and the continued automatic assumption of the traditional causal concept in the ordinary life, language, and thought of human beings, including scientists in their non-technical activities. Only if the new concepts become established and disseminated sufficiently to enter into the language transmitted to human beings in infancy, i.e., only by a social process making these concepts part of the human mind, can they become also part of the common world; and no such process has yet occurred. Both points fully support Lewis's views.

The adaptation of categories to empirical data is still further assured, according to Lewis, by the operation of a similar social process in respect to the data themselves. What is now our "instant mental reaction to experience" can be seen to "reflect millennia of nature's work to the end that we may grasp whatever in experience is clue to some uniformity of the sort which intelligibility requires," while everything else that may be "given" in experience "slides off the surface of the mind." [41] Thus, in this unexpected context, we find Lewis maintaining the view that the given content of experience conforms to our concepts because it is limited by our conceptual requirements, the very view which he finds so objectionable in Kant. Lewis, however, accounts for this limitation genetically and psychologically, rather than as a "presupposition" alone.

How complete is this limitation? As we have seen earlier, Lewis speaks of *some* concepts—"the category of objective time" and unspecified "other items"—as requisite even for the "stream of consciousness" itself; [42] yet he speaks also of "those evanescent appearances and puzzling transitions of experience which it baffles us to understand," [43] implying, it would seem, that there are data which fit into no determinate category and cannot be conceptualized. (There seems to be no reason, however, why these cannot be assigned to the category of the unreal.) On the question "Whether consciousness of pure immediacy without conceptual interpretation would be below the level of awareness altogether," Lewis expresses indecision.[44] It seems, however, that if conceptually unassimilable material is eliminated simply because it "slides off the surface of the mind," the elimination is not likely to be rigid or complete; nor does Lewis's doctrine require it to be.

In terms of the genetic account, then, we may conclude that both the limitation of experience by concepts and the structure of the concepts themselves acquire a flexibility which they lack in Kant's version. Yet the limitation is there, with new justification, and performs essentially the same function as in Kant's analysis; it insures that a substantial part (not quite all, as Kant sometimes assumes) of the given subject matter of experience will fit somewhere into the categorial structure of "reality," and so also into that common world which a common categorial structure makes possible.

Turning now to Lewis's interpretation of scientific law, we find something very similar to his interpretation of the categories. For all existentially meaningful concepts and laws are, from a genetic point of view, empirical, their applicability having at some point been assumed on the basis of generalization from experience; while on the other hand, just as all terms are abstract in a sense, so all laws are a priori in a sense, functioning as definitions and therefore valid analytically wherever they are relevant. As Lewis puts it,

. . . principles of the order of natural law are reached by some generalization from experience—that is, from *veridical* experience . . . But what experience is *veridical*, is determined by the criterion of law. What is first, then . . . ? The answer is that the law is first precisely so long as and so far as we are prepared to maintain it as criterion of the real.

For "not real" means "not really this very specific sort of thing," whether we are dealing with a narrowly limited class or with the very broad class of physical objects; and "all concepts, and not simply those we should call 'categories,' function as criteria of reality." [45] Thus Lewis shares and clarifies Kant's view that an empirical generalization becomes a scientific law when it is "seen as necessary" (i.e., when we regard it as a definition, or criterion of reality, and therefore employ it in an a priori manner). [46] Empirical generalization is inductive; but when it exhibits the properties of anything in "systematic interconnections" (i.e., in such correlation that they can be incorporated in a deductive system), the generalization may be adopted as a "definition." Further induction then becomes unnecessary, although the relevance of any particular item of experience must always be determined empirically and is always merely probable; the deductive system itself must be worked out analytically, and all its implications hold for the field of reality that it defines. [47] There is a difference among laws, however, as to the extent to which we are "prepared to maintain" them as definitions, or criteria of reality; and Lewis finds it

inappropriate to characterize as a priori a law which we are prepared to alter in the light of further experience even though in an isolated case we should discard as non-veridical any experience which failed to conform.[48]

Any scientific law is a priori in relation to the "isolated case"; but if a sufficient (unspecified) number of cases fail to conform, too many cases for us to explain away without disturbing the structure of science, we drop the law as empirically inapplicable. The procedure here is that of "hypothesis and verification," and the test is "simple conformity with experience." In the case of "the *terms* in which hypothesis and law are framed," however, concepts so fundamental that we dismiss nonconforming instances from reality, the test is rather "achievement of intelligible order," whether we are dealing with "the uniformities of common sense comprehension" or with the "further reach" of these in the "uniformities . . . of a high order" sought by science.[49] In other words, the question here is one of choice between conceptual systems, and the criteria are to that extent pragmatic.

Unquestionably, these fundamental concepts include the categories. Just what else they include, if anything, is more difficult to pin down. Lewis makes an attempt to include the concepts of geometry, on the grounds that we reject any empirical violation of them as a "mistake," and that we should deny the Euclidean character of space rather than abandon them. In contrast, he calls the law of gravitation "a posteriori," on the grounds that we shall give it up if experience fails to verify it. This distinction, however, does not seem entirely valid; for the law of gravitation is very similar in status to the laws of *physical* geometry, and would be abandoned under very much the same circumstances as the Euclidean conception of space. (Indeed, the same circumstances *have* led to the abandonment of both in relativity theory.) When Lewis asserts that we should never "abandon . . . the meaning of 'Euclidean triangle,'" what he has in mind must be merely the fact that we retain our interest in geometry as an analytic system even if it does not apply where we thought it would; while the abstract conceptual system of Newtonian gravitation theory, though just as valid analytically, would be of no further interest if it were empirically inapplicable.[50]

Another difference between gravitational theory and physical geometry concerns the manner in which they have been built up. It is a difference which Lewis makes clear when he says that science can be regarded "as the discovery of empirical laws sufficiently comprehensive to constitute a systematic whole, or as the selection of an abstract system which will be applicable to the facts." Lewis himself emphasizes, however, that the same scientific issues may be regarded in both ways.[51]

It is relevant to note, here, that Kant himself maintains such distinctions much less precisely than he intends. We may recall, in this connection, his attempt to derive some laws of physics directly from the categories in order to distinguish them from empirical laws, while on the other hand maintaining "necessity" as a criterion of any law whatsoever; his difficulty in keeping "understanding" and "reason" strictly apart; and the conflict between an absolute and a "regulative" science in his doctrine.

For Lewis, however, a rigidly compartmentalized structure of knowledge is not only unnecessary but obviously impossible; and he is mistaken in any attempt to specify one set of concepts as a priori and another as a posteriori. The difference, in terms of his own doctrine taken as a whole, is one of degree rather than of kind; and there is a merging at the boundaries, a shifting of any particular concept from one status to another. We may begin to use a successful empirical generalization as a definition without quite realizing it; and "the determination of what belongs to the deductive elaboration of concepts and what to empirical generalization from experience, depends . . . upon our modes of conception themselves." [52] Just when our "modes of conception" are general enough and stable enough to be regarded as categories is still more difficult to determine. As for the difference between "hypothesis and verification" on one hand and the pragmatic criteria for fundamental concepts on the other, it is obvious that the selection of a hypothesis for verification is itself a choice between conceptual systems, while even the categories themselves would be abandoned if the hypothesis that they are applicable to experience were empirically disconfirmed on a large scale.

Naturally, we may suppose that a very narrow definition, or "criterion of the real," will be abandoned more readily than a very comprehensive one, as the consequent disruption of the system of knowledge will be less drastic. But between the generalizations that one failure of expected applicability will upset and the categories that only a vast change in human experience can alter, there are innumerable gradations. Just what concept is to be modified or abandoned, or just what experience is to be regarded as unveridical in what respect, in any given situation where something of the sort is required, must be determined in the context of the total system of knowledge, as an adjustment of that system to include as intelligibly as possible the empirical subject matter that presents itself. Thus, as Lewis puts it, *"The determination of reality, the classification of phenomena, and the discovery of law, all grow up together."* [53]

Seeing Lewis's doctrine of categories in the context of its Kantian foundation, we can now understand the full magnitude of its achievement. We can see how greatly Lewis has clarified the status of the categorial system as a definition of physical reality, and consequently the analytic nature of Kant's so-called synthetic a priori principles, which state the applicability of the categories to objective experience. Lewis's extensive debt to Kant on this score amply repays itself; for one must wonder whether this aspect of Kant's doctrine would be clearly discernible today—indeed, whether Kant would be genuinely comprehensible today—without the clue provided by Lewis's more explicit and unequivocal formulation in modern terms.

As important as the clarified restatement of this doctrine is its disentanglement from the obsolete logic and science which encumber it in Kant's version. Lewis shows us that the basic categories can be logical in their structure and interrelation, thus constituting a mechanism for the application of logical reasoning to those areas of experience which they define, without following the precisely specified structure of a ready-made logic; and that they can be applicable to the physical world, thus providing basic "modes of conception" for scientific laws, without serving as deductive premises for a ready-made science. And since they need not meet such requirements, Lewis can introduce his highly significant genetic explanation of why we have those categories that we do in fact have, thus introducing a much-needed flexibility into the structure of mind in place of the arbitrary rigidity so unconvincing today.

Lewis shows us, then, that it is quite possible to eliminate Kant's obsolete and untenable assumptions in regard to logic, psychology, and physics, and still retain his fundamental epistemological scheme —the two sources and types of cognition (the conceptual or a priori and the sensory or empirical); their conjunction in coherent, understandable experience, which is identifiable with experience of a common world; their interrelation (i.e., the *application* of the a priori to the synthetic) by means of categories (i.e., concepts which order experience and *define* the objective world) in accordance with the "pragmatic" ("regulative") criterion of maximum intelligibility. We find, indeed, that the arbitrary elements *are* largely eliminated when this Kantian structure is maintained, as Lewis maintains it, in the context of the logic and science of the twentieth century.

Does this mean that *no* limitations of a synthetic a priori character, either on mind or on the content of experience, are required? Let us review the difficulties involved here, as Kant left them, and see what Lewis has done about them.

Kant, we may remember, demonstrates that the conceptual structure of experience is derived from logic and therefore a priori; that this structure, by defining objective experience in logical terms, constitutes an application of logic to experience and to its sensory content. To show that there must be in fact sensory content to which these terms apply, so that we can have experience as so defined, he derives this same conceptual structure from the nature of consciousness itself. This leaves us with the question as to why—and how far—the two deductions of the categories produce the same results; why—and how far —the categories, as definitions, define the contents of consciousness. To explain the coincidence of the conclusions otherwise than as a fortunate accident, we must assume the coincidence of the premises; since the categorial systems derived from them coincide, the structure of logic and the structure of consciousness must be the same.

One explanation offered by Kant is the view that the logical requirements of our minds limit the sensory content of consciousness. Then, however, what becomes of the function of the categorial system as a definition of objective experience as distinguished from subjective sensation? And what becomes of the "regulative" function of reason, if all the contents of consciousness are systematized at the outset? A second explanation offered by Kant, probably with the intention of reconciling the contradictory notions, is the view that some categories apply to all the contents of consciousness, by virtue of the structure of consciousness itself, while others apply only, by definition, to the contents of objective experience. This view, as we have seen, may successfully make room for both interpretations of the categories, but retains some difficulties of both. Kant's third answer, then, appears most harmonious both with his own approach and with the requirements of the science and mathematics of our own time, though not of his. The categorial system, as a definition of an objective world, is part of a rational ideal to be applied "regulatively," i.e., as far as possible, to the sensory content of consciousness; and the nature of consciousness *is in fact such* that we can apply this definition at least far enough for a common, reasonably stable objective world.

This fact may appear somewhat arbitrary, but Kant has no further explanation for it; that is why it must remain a synthetic a priori presupposition of knowledge. It is synthetic, and could logically be otherwise; but we accept it a priori in knowing anything at all, as it could *not* logically be otherwise if any knowledge is possible.

This unexplained premise, then, which Kant leaves at the foundation of the explanation of knowledge, may be seen to involve the following arbitrary assumptions: *1*] The sensory content of consciousness is amenable to definition and organization in terms of the categories. (Whether all of that content is equally amenable, and whether amenable to all of the categories equally, is inconclusively answered, although the most consistent answer in both cases is negative.) *2*] This circumstance exists, more or less uniformly, in the minds of all human beings. *3*] Since the categorial structure is an application of the structure of logic, all of this means also that the structure of logic is part of the nature of human consciousness, reflected in its sensory content as well as in its conceptual organization. This last item is not an independent assumption, but rather an unwelcome consequence of the other two, involving difficulties of its own.

To an extraordinary extent, Lewis succeeds in removing the arbitrariness of these assumptions. The sensory content of consciousness is amenable to categorial treatment because our categories have been evolved so as to bring about this situation. No inapplicable category would be established in the first place, and any subject matter incapable of being categorized at all is banished to the fringes of consciousness by a perfectly comprehensible psychological process. The question as to how much of the content of consciousness is subject to how many of the categories can also be answered. The aim of systematizing *all* conscious content can be fulfilled in that the categorial system is logically exhaustive; but some categories governing one kind of reality do not govern another, and some experience cannot be identified in terms of any except the catch-all category of the "unreal." We have, then, a flexible structure, in which the classification of various kinds of reality (plus the "unreal") is the most fundamental level, and in which maximum coherence and minimum relegation to the "unreal" comprise the aim and direction of progress. In pursuit of this aim, empirical generalizations may become laws, laws may become categories, and categories may ultimately be relinquished.

The assumption that a *common* conceptual structure exists for all human beings, too, loses its arbitrariness when Lewis calls attention to the fact that the structure has been developed by human beings in the process of common activity, as a basis for communication with each other. Thus the same genetic explanation accounts both for the approximate suitability of the conceptual structure to its sensory material and for its approximately identical character in all human minds.

The assumption, then, that the categories are empirically applicable and common to all, i.e., that knowledge—interpretation of the empirical in terms of the a priori in a communicable form—is in fact possible, is not really "synthetic a priori" at all. It must indeed be accepted a priori by the individual, since the categorial structure which it justifies is a basic part of his mental equipment, without which he has no means of thinking; to that extent it may be said to function in a synthetic a priori manner in the individual mind. At the same time, it is not an a priori assumption in the context of the development of human knowledge as a whole, but genetically explainable in empirical terms.

The fact that all empirical knowledge *combines* synthetic and a priori elements, however, is not denied; rather, it is explained and reinforced. In any particular instance of such knowledge, the application of a priori conceptual structures to empirical data is hypothetical (in Kant's language, "regulative"); but the hypothesis is justifiable as such, in advance of the application (i.e., it can be "presupposed"), because of the character of knowledge itself, *genetically explained* as being a suitable basis for such justification. At the same time, and for the same reason, the hypothesis justifiable in terms of empirical validity will be justifiable also in terms of its furtherance of the goal of knowledge, in pursuit of which it has been selected in the first place. This latter type of justification, which Lewis calls "pragmatic," is one which Kant could with equal validity call "rational"; for the goal guiding the process, we may remember, is the establishment of a conceptual structure "by which the whole array of given experience may be set in order and each item (ideally) assigned to its intelligible and unambiguous place." [54]

Thus the "synthetic a priori" assumption that knowledge is possible, i.e., that the a priori can be applied to the synthetic, is not a "judgment" at all, but a hypothesis selected on pragmatic grounds, as Kant obscurely recognizes when he regards it as "regulative" in application and as based on a "regulative ideal." And although it must be accepted a priori by the individual in the very act of knowing, we can nevertheless find empirical justification for it, and for its interpretation in terms of a common world, in the development of knowledge by the human race throughout its history.

We are still confronted, then, with the third problem left over by Kant, that of the implied identification of logic with the structure of the human mind. For the categories are still so identified, and Lewis believes as firmly as Kant that "Categories and precise concepts are logical structures," [55] with logical interrelations and implications. The flexibility of modern as contrasted with Aristotelian logic removes the most awkward implications as to the nature of mind; and surely *some* standardization of the human mind, sufficient to coincide with the normative character of a flexible logic, is implied by the recognition of a common world and explained by the genetic development of such a world. But what about the awkward implications as to the nature of logic? Must we accept the view that logic itself, not merely the categorial structure which applies it, is inherent in the nature of human consciousness, that it evolves with that consciousness and ultimately changes with the content of our common world?

Our consideration of this difficult question must be not only incomplete but indecisive. We shall find that Lewis himself is indecisive. This very confusion, however, even if we find no adequate way out of it, may call attention to important aspects of the problem.

Lewis, we have seen, clearly regards the conceptual element in knowledge as supplied by the mind. Indeed, "the relation of the a priori to the mind, is really of prime importance" for him in immunizing the a priori from empirical determination; for "Whatever experience may bring, the mind will be there . . ." And here Lewis means by "the a priori" not only the categories as definitions but the logic which they apply; "logic" is specified as having "its roots in the human mind." Yet, on the same page, he objects to the "confusion of logical and psychological," which he attributes to "rationalist conceptions," probably with Kant in mind. (Kant, however, we may recall, raises the same objection, although he, too, may seem self-contradictory in doing so.) Moreover, Lewis asserts on one hand that "Some logic is true, and hence some logical principles are necessary" and on the other hand that "the stamp of mind's creation . . . is not inevitability but exactly its opposite, the absence of impulsion and the presence of at least conceivable alternatives." [56]

The crucial question, of course, concerns the meaning of "Some logic is true" and the reason why "some logical principles are necessary." In his earlier work as a logician, Lewis starts with the conviction that "there are certain ways of reasoning which are correct and valid, as opposed to certain other ways which are incorrect or invalid." What these are, however, is difficult to demonstrate, because there is no criterion of a "proper" logic except that logic itself; for logic is circular, using its postulates and theorems "not only as premises *from which* further theorems are deduced, but also as rules of inference *by which* the deductions are made." Thus we must assume that the "proper" meaning of implication, the meaning that leads us to use this relation for "valid inference," is clear to everyone "in denotation"—i.e., that we can recognize it when we see it. For "If two persons should really disagree about 'implies'—should have different 'logical sense'—there would be nothing to hope for from their argument." [57] A valid logic, then, is one based on this "proper" meaning of implication, thus providing "that canon and critique of deductive inference which is the desideratum of logical investigation"; [58] but for the ultimate criterion, for assurance that our "canon" is indeed "proper," we must resort to a "logical sense" inherent in the human mind.

Lewis does not intend to deny here the analytic or tautological nature of logic. His own logic of "strict implication" (the "proper" kind) is a tautological system. Moreover, the statement "p strictly implies q," expressing the fundamental relation of that system, is applicable, he tells us, when the statement "p implies q" is a tautology; [59] so that his logic turns out to be an analysis of tautology, an attempt to show us in logical terms what we mean by analytic truth. If this attempt is entirely successful, "logical sense" may seem to be superseded.

In *Mind and the World-Order*, however, Lewis becomes perplexed by the fact that a "bad," or "false," or "pseudo-logic" may also be tautological and self-consistent. What, then, does he regard as wrong with such logics, and by what criterion? Unfortunately, he seems to have in mind two different criteria, which he is here unable either to relate or to differentiate clearly.

One criterion is involved in Lewis's argument that the a priori (including logic) "has its origin in an act of mind; it has in some sense the character of fiat and is in some respects like deliberate choice." The difference between a "good" and a "bad" logic is not "*imposed* upon the human mind" (here Lewis tries to get away from the theory of "logical sense" and logical "self-evidence"). If the a priori were so imposed, "it would have just that brute-fact character which distinguishes the given." Rather, it is imposed *by* the mind—which means that the mind must have available to it alternatives from which to choose.[60] The "mind," then, reappears more actively than ever; but on the other hand, the element of choice appearing with it suggests that Lewis is now thinking of the *pragmatic selection* of conceptual systems for *application*, and no longer of criteria of *analytic* truth within the systems themselves. And his further discussion shows this to be the case.

Lewis has, however, at least at the beginning of the discussion, a second criterion simultaneously in mind. When he asserts that "Some logic is true," in a sense in which "the truths of logic are not proved" by internal consistency alone (since such consistency "begs the question" of the truth of the system itself),[61] he seems to have in mind some criterion that has indeed "that brute-fact character which distinguishes the given." It is this fact of validity of inference that his own system of logic is supposed to analyze; but since, like any logic, it is itself circular, it merely carries the operations of analytic reasoning one step further and does not thereby help us to understand their nature in terms of *knowledge*. We must still ask why Lewis's own logic is valid; or rather, what is meant by calling it valid. Thus what we need is an epistemological description of the nature of analytic truth, which Lewis provides in *An Analysis of Knowledge and Valuation*. It is there that we must find out whether analytic truth can be defined and accounted for without being regarded as "mental" in any sense.

There Lewis definitely recognizes "such a fact as the logical deducibility of one proposition from another . . ." Cognition of such a "fact" is one sort of a priori knowledge, while the other sort is "Correct understanding of what is intended by the use of a term—of its defined or definable meaning . . ." The first is "logic" in a strict sense, but there is an "essential connection" between logic and definition; [62] for the fact of deducibility is a fact about meanings and their relations. Analytic statements, since they cannot state facts of experience, must state "such facts as are . . . capable of being known with certainty merely through clear and cogent thinking"—which can only be "facts of intensional meaning." [63]

One might perhaps suppose that an analytic statement states no "facts" at all. But what, then, does it state? Lewis rejects the view that it is purely conventional or stipulative, although elements of both types are involved. Symbols and assignment of meanings to them are conventional, and "what meanings" shall be "entertained" is "subject to decision." Yet,

the meanings entertained are as they are and not otherwise, whether they should be entertained or not. And a relation of meanings, once these meanings themselves are fixed, is something which no decision of ours and no mode of symbolization can affect.[64]

Even the analytic statements of logic itself, which are "formal" (i.e., contain variables) and therefore do not depend on *specified* meanings for certain of their terms, Lewis declares, are "analytically true" because of "precisely that element of their meaning which is non-formal and specific" (i.e., the specified logical relations between variables). These relations may be expressed by "rules," but *"the only final test of the validity of logical rules, is the test of them as analytically true statements."* Thus analytic truth is logically prior to rules; indeed, Lewis believes that we should not need rules of logic if we understood meanings infallibly and fully.[65]

Whatever the questions that may suggest themselves in regard to logical rules in this respect (and Lewis himself, despite his views on *logical* rules, mentions an uninterpreted *mathematical* system as a "case of symbolic convention"),[66] there is no doubt that these rules must have meaning in terms of operations which they prescribe; otherwise, we should have an aggregation of symbols, but no system. And this meaning is part of a system whose *total* structure is analytic—which is all that Lewis need maintain to prove his point. For it is because of what the rules mean, because of what we do with logical symbols in accordance with them, that the resulting propositions of a logical system are tautologies; and tautology is equivalence of *meaning*, to which the application of the rules has contributed. Thus the interpretation of logic and analytic truth generally in terms of meaning is an extremely impressive one.

We shall now want to see, of course, whether or not "meaning," in turn, can be interpreted without the psychological element which the term normally suggests. To do so, we must consider the type of meaning on which Lewis bases analytic truth, "the intension of propositions." Lewis defines "intension" as "the conjunction of all other terms each of which must be applicable to anything to which the given term would be correctly applicable." [67] This is the simplest, everyday meaning of "meaning," he says, in which "what we mean by '*A*' is what we have in mind in using '*A*' "; in other words, "the *concept of A*." [68] Thus the intension of a proposition "comprises whatever the proposition entails"; for the logical consequences of any proposition are the other propositions which must be applicable whenever the given proposition is applicable.[69] Logical entailment, then, is a relation between meanings, "fixed when the meanings themselves are fixed." [70]

Two types of question now arise. First, does not this concept of "meaning" contain a latent ambiguity? We have seen Lewis refer to "meaning" as something which we "have in mind" and also as something which has a determinate character "whether . . . entertained or not." Can there be, in any comprehensible sense, a meaning which no one means? And second, how can one meaning require another? Why *must* certain "other propositions . . . be applicable whenever the given proposition is applicable"? We shall find that the answers to both difficulties, as far as there are answers, converge toward one central point, the reappearance of a psychological factor —the same psychological factor on which Lewis bases his concept of a common world.

The first question, of course, concerns the extent to which such a factor is inherent in the concept of meaning. If meanings "are as they are . . . whether . . . entertained or not," this self-subsistent character may as readily be assigned to logic itself, in the Platonic manner, and the interpretation in terms of meaning is superfluous. If, on the other hand, "the intension of a term represents our intention in the use of it . . . the *criterion in mind* by which it is determined whether the term in question applies or fails to apply in any particular instance," [71] we have a psychological criterion with its attendant problems. Must we not ask *whose* intention, *whose* mind Lewis means? Suppose I do *not* intend, in making a statement, to affirm some other statement which Lewis tells me is its logical consequence; why is his logic right and mine wrong?

Surely Lewis does not wish to attribute to logic either a Platonic existential character or a subjective character varying with the individual mind, although he implies both on different occasions. The only alternative, then, is in terms of a *standard or normal human mind*, with standard or normal criteria of meaning. Meanings as interpreted by logic are what we must mean if other human beings are to understand us and be convinced by our reasoning; and the "fixed" relations among meanings are the ways in which human beings relate them in communicating with each other in terms of a common world.

The second question, as to how one proposition requires another by virtue of its meaning, is the question of the "necessary" character of logic. Lewis takes two approaches. Primarily, he relies on the concept of "any possible world"; thus "the intension of a proposition comprises whatever must be true of any possible world in order that this proposition should be true of or apply to it." [72] Similarly, an analytic proposition, since it expresses a relation of meanings only and nothing existential, "would apply to or hold of every possible world . . ." It "does not distinguish this actual world from any other which is consistently thinkable," or "impose any restriction . . . which could conceivably be absent." [73] But what does Lewis mean by "any possible world"? To say "*logically* possible" would beg the question; and his equivalent use of the terms "consistently thinkable" and "conceivable" raises the question, "Thinkable or conceivable by whom?" Again we must answer, thinkable or conceivable by a standard human mind.

Lewis also attempts an explanation more directly in terms of meaning. The meaning of one term (or proposition) may "include" the meaning of another, he says, just as my plan for a trip to Chicago may include a plan for a visit to Niagara Falls. Such an explanation makes sense and justifies the use of the concept of "meaning" in interpreting logic. But how can I fail to recognize that the plan includes Niagara, as long as I have that plan in mind (and not some other that I mistake for it)? This very difficulty plagues Lewis. Since errors in logic are obviously possible, he must assert that "We are capable of failing to observe what is involved in our own intentions and of mistaking our own meanings through inconsistency"; [74] but he provides no further explanation of this decidedly paradoxical notion of meaning. Again the concept of the standard human mind comes to the rescue; for then there is a possible discrepancy between what the individual erroneously means by a statement, and what he means by the same statement when he is thinking in such a manner that other human beings can understand his reasoning.

On this basis, while there is a sense in which we always mean just what we think we mean, there is also a sense in which, as Lewis asserts, there are "relations which . . . meanings themselves have or fail to have" [75] whether or not we recognize these relations (*not* however, whether or not anyone "entertains" the meanings). For these relations are *part* of the meanings, not only "fixed when the meanings themselves are fixed," but evolved *in the same manner* as the meanings themselves, the manner in which "Meanings are identified by the relational pattern which speech and behavior in general are capable of conveying." [76] We are brought back, therefore, to the possession by human beings of a common structural pattern of thought, genetically explainable, in terms of which communication of meanings is possible to the extent that it is possible at all.

The interpretation of logic as psychological in any sense at all is commonly regarded as objectionable by philosophers, who, however, often accuse each other of such interpretation while regarding themselves as immune to it. We have seen Lewis object to "confusion of the logical and psychological," apparently oblivious of such confusion in his own analysis; and we have seen Kant, whom Lewis undoubtedly includes in his complaint, raising the same objection. Yet, if logic is to be regarded neither as empirically established nor as metaphysically self-subsistent, what other alternative is there? The interpretation of logic as tautology is, as we have seen, a supplement and not an alternative; it does not answer the same question. Yet, since tautology is equivalence of *meaning*, it is a feature of logic which points directly toward the interpretation of logic in terms of meaning. There are difficulties in all the alternatives; but of them all, Lewis's type of psychological interpretation, in terms of the analysis of "meaning"—essentially a modernized and greatly amplified successor to Kant's interpretation in terms of the analysis of "concepts"—may well be the least unsatisfactory.

It should be observed, too, that if logic is "psychological" in such a sense, it is not thereby either synthetic or subjective, as one might at first suppose. Indeed, some such interpretation is the only kind that shows logic to be analytic and nevertheless accords to it something of the character of "truth" as this term is ordinarily understood in connection with objective empirical statements. In Kant's framework, the propositions of logic can be seen as "objective" in precisely the sense in which empirical statements are "objective," i.e., by virtue of applicability to physical objects (although the propositions of logic have abstract validity also).

In Lewis's framework, a parallel situation is demonstrated, but we can be even more precise about it. Relevant here is his analysis of truth in terms of extension. "Every statement asserts a proposition and attributes a state of affairs to the actual world." Thus the extension of every true proposition is the actual world (i.e., it has "universal extension"), while every false proposition has "zero extension" (i.e., it applies to nothing actual).[77] Analytic propositions, imposing no "limitation on the actual" in order to be applicable, and thus carrying no restriction as to their extension, must have "universal extension." [78] In other words, they must be *true;* like true empirical propositions, they denote or apply to the actual world (although, unlike empirical propositions, they apply to every other conceivable world also). That the actual world *is* a "conceivable" world, of course, cannot be taken for granted, although Lewis appears to do so in discussing logic; but that the actual world is in large measure, at least, a conceivable world is assured, as Lewis shows us, by the definitive application to it of a categorial structure developed for that purpose.

May we conclude, then, that the problem of the applicability of scientific law, of the categories, ultimately of logic, to sensory subject matter, has now been solved? Kant thought he had solved it along these lines; and Lewis, as we have seen, has adapted Kant's solution to modern logic and science and reached a high degree of success in meeting the chief difficulties. It will now appear, however, that the gap is not yet quite closed. That Lewis is able to take the final step in closing it is an achievement whose magnitude has too rarely been observed. Indeed, it is rather puzzling that Lewis himself seems to accord to this step much less emphasis than its importance warrants.

Kant, we may remember, defines "judgment" (i.e., the application of logic to experience) as "the faculty of subsuming under rules." Formal logic cannot tell us "how . . . to distinguish whether something does or does not come under" a particular rule; for that we must depend on "so-called mother-wit; and its lack no school can make good." Transcendental logic, on the other hand, can "specify *a priori* the instance to which the rule is to be applied"; for its categories, and logic through them, are applicable to *all* experience, and so we know that they are applicable to *this particular* experience.[79] Nevertheless, if this universality is that of a definition only, we must still determine whether a particular sense perception *is* an instance of "experience" in the sense defined; and Kant implicitly recognizes this situation in introducing the schemata which are supposed to state the "formal conditions of sensibility" under which each category is applicable.[80] Yet the schemata are still general, or "formal," and recognition of a concrete case is a different matter. Our situation, then, is no different than in the application of formal logic; in the end we must still "subsume." Thus the analytic interpretation of the categories, as Kant does not always seem to realize, throws us back upon unexplained "mother-wit" after all for the final step from concept to content.

Lewis, however, sees that there are two separate difficulties here, only one of which—the gap between abstract concepts and concrete things—can be solved in terms of "sense meaning" (his successor to Kant's "schemata"). There is a further difficulty in the analytic character of logical systems. This difficulty affects not only the principles of application of the categories but also the laws of science, and even the identification of physical objects, since the concept of such an object (as we shall see more clearly when we examine the problem of "things" in greater detail) is also a logical system definitive in character. Analytic propositions, and so also analytic systems of propositions, imply nothing, require nothing, *mean nothing* as to the facts of existence; how, then, can we "subsume" under them anything whatsoever of a factual nature? Indeed, what can we *mean* by their applicability to experience, however *hypothetical* that applicability may be? It is this type of question that Lewis answers by his theory of *holophrastic and analytic meaning*.

We have seen that all analytic propositions have "universal exten-sion" (i.e., denote everything actual) because their truth requires nothing as to the actual world. This lack of requirement as to the actual may also be expressed by the statement that analytic proposi-tions have "zero intension." This does not mean, Lewis points out, that they have *no* intension; that would make them nonsense locu-tions. They do have intension, i.e., implications, but do not imply the *existence* of anything; for their implications, too, are analytic, and require nothing actual.[81] The difficulty is, however, that all ana-lytic propositions now appear to have the *same* intension and the *same* extension. (They are therefore the same, also, in respect to other "modes of meaning" which enter into Lewis's complete analy-sis but which need not be discussed here.) This seems to indicate that all analytic statements must have the same meaning—which is, as Lewis says, "disconcerting." [82]

We may note, here, that the "zero intension" of analytic proposi-tions is the feature more often indicated by their characterization as "tautological" or "empty"; and the sense in which these propositions must be shown nevertheless to differ from each other in some sort of meaning is the sense in which formal procedures can make a con-tribution to knowledge. But language is meaningful because it is language *about* something, as Lewis's discussion of "sense meaning" has made clear. What, then, can be the meaning of statements which are about nothing?

The foundation of Lewis's solution is his distinction between "ana-lytic meaning" (meaning as constituted by the component parts of an expression and their syntax) [83] and "holophrastic meaning" (the meaning of "a whole expression" as a unit).[84] For the purpose of exhibiting analytic meaning, any statement can be analyzed into a series of "elementary expressions," each of which "has no symbolized constituent, the intension of which is a constituent of the intension of the expression in question itself." That is, they are neither elements of meaning which are not separately expressed (such as "feline" and "animal" as elements of the meaning of "cat"), nor elements of expression which have no separate meanings (such as letters of the alphabet). The division need not, however, correspond throughout with the division into words, since words with prefixes or suffixes are often complex.[85] In other words, the elementary constituents are the smallest actually appearing units of intensional expression.

The importance of such analysis lies in the fact that the constituents retain their own meanings while at the same time combining to produce the meaning of the whole statement. If the meanings of elementary expressions were changed by every new context, we should have no way of knowing what they meant either individually or in combination.[86] On the other hand, the meaning of the whole expression (or holophrastic meaning) is not the *same* as the meaning of the constituents taken separately (analytic meaning).

This explains why analytic statements may all have zero intension and in that sense "say the same thing" and "say nothing," while in another sense "they say different things, and what they say is significantly factual." In analytic statements, it is the constituent expressions that refer to empirical facts, thus rendering the complete statement "significant," [87] while the constituents in syntactical order say that their intensions are so related as to result in an intension equal to zero; and a formally analytic statement (one which explicitly purports to be analytic) is false, i.e., not analytic at all, if these intensions are *not* so related. Thus analytic truth is truth about meanings, while meanings are about empirical facts. This theory establishes, Lewis notes, the mutually independent character of analytic truth on one hand and empirical truth on the other—the fact that these two kinds of truth "can have no effect upon each other" (because the analytic validity of a statement is a matter of holophrastic intension, while the empirical reference is a matter of analytic intension—the meaning of the constituents).[88]

This conclusion, however, although unquestionably important, is readily established by other means as well, and widely recognized since Kant. The really tremendous significance of Lewis's contribution to this subject is rather to be found in the opposite aspect of his analysis—the demonstration of the manner in which these two kinds of truth which are totally independent in their validity and totally different in character are nevertheless *related in knowledge.*

The doctrine of holophrastic and analytic meaning is a demonstration that analytic statements, although they analyze meanings only, nevertheless refer to the actual world insofar as the meanings which they analyze are meanings about the actual world. Although they do not determine experience, the relations among meanings (expressed by analytic statements) do determine "the manner in which we may consistently think about whatever experience presents." [89]

The doctrine is a demonstration also that empirical facts, although they cannot prevent us from meaning whatever we choose, play a part in determining whether our meanings are consistent with each other, insofar as empirical facts are denoted by what we mean. Holophrastic zero intension is itself "constituted by a significant relation—one which obtains sometimes only—amongst constituents which are themselves specific and are significant in the sense of sometimes applying and sometimes not." [90]

We see, then, that "the manner in which we may consistently think about whatever experience presents" is determined *both* by whatever experience does actually present and by the manner in which we may consistently think. And the *actual* process of thinking consistently about whatever experience presents, as we have seen, is the process which makes possible and creates our common human world. Thus the Kantian conception of the objective world as an interrelation of the conceptual and the sensory finds its culminating justification; for the perplexing logical relation of the a priori to the synthetic is resolved as a relation of holophrastic to analytic meaning.

This explains why, with adequate empirical premises, we can make logical inferences about the existent world—why logic can be *applied* with results of value to our knowledge. Lewis mentions this only in passing, but by means of an illustration of extraordinary clarity. Showing how such expressions as "the day following Monday" and "the day preceding Wednesday," identical in holophrastic intension, differ in respect to the meaning of their constituents, "following" and "preceding," "Monday" and "Wednesday," he points out that this difference is responsible for the fact that the statement "The day following Monday is the day preceding Wednesday" has more point than "Tuesday is Tuesday." And he adds that "this is the *only* kind of point which deductive demonstration, such as the mathematical, has." [91] This kind of point, however, is obviously a very considerable kind.

Kant and Reichenbach

W ITH LEWIS'S reinterpretation of the Kantian structure in terms of his own doctrine of categories and completion of it by means of his theory of holophrastic and analytic meaning, we reach a point where the importance of that structure for dealing with the most urgent of current philosophical issues is thoroughly clear. The understanding of the so-called "synthetic a priori" as standing for the applicability of the a priori or analytic to the empirical or synthetic makes possible the adaptation of Kant to modern logic, mathematics, and science, and to the philosophical foundations on which they rest, foundations which Kant himself has provided—the analytic character of logic and synthetic character of existential knowledge, and the importance of the conceptual element in all knowledge. In terms of this understanding of the "synthetic a priori," too, it has become possible to remove from Kant's scheme the rationalistic assumptions, drawn from the intellectual equipment of his time, with which it was encumbered—the rigid, absolute structure attributed to logic and to mind, and the rigid, absolute structure attributed to science. Lewis has shown us, by means of his genetic and pragmatic account of human concepts, how to loosen the structure of logic and mind within the Kantian framework; and, to the extent that the structure of science depends upon and reflects that of logic and mind, how to loosen that structure also. It is this last step, however, the loosening of the Kantian scientific structure so as to adapt that doctrine to the science now current, that is here still incomplete.

The aspect of science explained by the developments examined up to this point is the deductive and therefore "necessary" aspect. It is the conceptual structure which, as Lewis has shown, is a product of the human mind as it evolves in the human environment and may be partially or entirely superseded on pragmatic grounds, but which nevertheless, as long as it is not thus superseded, is definitive and in that sense universal. That this aspect of science is indeed fundamental and indispensable is demonstrated by the ever-increasing role of mathematics in science today. Increasing at the same time, however, is the role of the probable and indeterminate in science, the area in which scientific concepts and laws themselves—and not merely their empirical application—incorporate the concept of probability. A means must still be sought, therefore, for a further loosening of the Kantian structure to include and explain this aspect of science.

Kant himself, we may recall, recognizes (at one point) a "hypothetical use" of reason in the establishment of scientific laws, by which we merely *"approximate* the rule to universality"; and he analyzes the method of this use of reason in terms unmistakably descriptive of induction.[1] Lewis, as we might expect, goes further, taking note (although without definitely committing himself) of the possibility that all scientific laws are statistical generalizations.[2] He is convinced that some are, in any event; for many laws are hardly distinguishable from those generalizations, used "in common sense and in practice," which persist in spite of past exceptions and "would not be regarded as invalidated by future exceptions." Under these circumstances, the requirement of universality even as a formal feature of scientific laws seems to Lewis to be "possibly, a bit artificial."[3] Does Lewis here reverse his own distinction between empirical and a priori scientific laws, drawn on the grounds that the former are, while the latter (as definitions) are not, upset by exceptions? Not if the permissibility of a somehow limited number of exceptions is, in the former case, *incorporated in the law itself;* so that such occurrences are exceptions not from the law but only from the hypothesis which, according to the law, will "probably" apply under the circumstances in question. In this sense we may understand Lewis's assertion that, in empirical verification of a hypothesis, "consequences of a hypothesis" are to be regarded not as "deductions from it," but rather as statements to which the truth of the hypothesis, "together with other statements which may reasonably be assumed, gives a high probability . . ."[4]

That *a law stating a probability,* however, *is still an abstract conceptual structure which may or may not prove to be empirically ap-*

plicable, is recognized by Lewis when he calls his theory of probability "an a priori theory." A calculation of probability, he asserts, starts from given data and produces a *"valid estimate"* of the frequency with which a specified property will occur among members of a reference class. The validity of the estimate is guaranteed by the data, even though it may turn out to be empirically inapplicable, i.e., even though the actual empirical frequency may turn out to be other than the estimated frequency. Thus the estimate, like the conclusion of a deductive argument, is valid by virtue of its derivation from the given premises by "correct principles of judgment"; i.e., valid a priori.[5] The probable, in other words, does not always happen; but if it does not, we may still correctly say that it *was* probable in terms of the original data, although it is no longer probable in terms of the new data provided when events disappoint our prediction.

Nevertheless, since it is the "objective frequency" of events that is to be validly estimated, and since Lewis himself emphasizes that the purpose of probability judgments is prediction,[6] he has merely postponed the question of why the estimate is valid, why the "correct principles of judgment" are "correct" *for prediction;* i.e., why the estimate applies to events and indicates that an event will *probably occur.* This, of course, is the question of the validity of induction; and Lewis, we may remember, although showing how the initial credibility of any induction may be increased by incorporation in a congruent system, is ultimately compelled to accept that initial credibility itself merely on the grounds that without induction we can have no knowledge at all.[7] In other words, when probability is interpreted as a priori, the problem of its empirical applicability becomes acute. In the assumption that a probability estimate valid in terms of the data and the principles of its derivation will (probably) be valid also as an empirical prediction, we have the apparent synthetic a priori all over again.

We need not here concern ourselves with further details of Lewis's view of probability, as a more complete and enlightening exposition of the problem is provided by Hans Reichenbach. Interestingly enough, although Reichenbach labels his view an "empirical theory of probability," the a priori and empirical elements in it are precisely the same as in Lewis's so-called "a priori theory," although the use of the term "probability" is somewhat different. While Lewis reserves the term for the a priori estimate, as dintinguished from the objective frequency which it estimates, Reichenbach speaks of the probability of events and identifies the estimation of that probability with induction. It is in the latter sense that he regards the determination of probability as "a posteriori"; it is a prediction of empirical events based on other empirical events as data.[8] From both points of view, however, it is the abstract mathematical calculation that is a priori and analytic, and the prediction of events that is empirical and synthetic; and it is the prediction by means of the calculation, the applicability of the a priori to the synthetic, that presents the chief problem. Thus Reichenbach confronts in regard to probability logic the same problem which Kant confronts in regard to deductive logic, the problem of why the logic concerned is applicable to the empirical world.

In view of Reichenbach's selection of Kant's philosophy as the chief foil against which the superiority of "modern" or "scientific" philosophy is displayed, the attempt to treat any part of Reichenbach's own doctrine as an adaptation and expansion of Kant's in a present-day context may appear arbitrary and unwarranted, if not perverse. Reichenbach himself takes pains to deny the validity of any apparent resemblance and so to divest himself of any "unpleasant flavor" that such a resemblance might attach to his own views.[9] Yet the very fact that he finds such a denial necessary may give us pause; and we shall find that a substantial element of Kantian doctrine slips into the very views which he presents as superseding that doctrine.

First of all, Reichenbach definitely and obviously accepts the Kantian distinction between synthetic propositions, which are "informative," and analytic propositions, which are "empty" and "self-explanatory." It is directly from this starting point, moreover, that he finds "amazing" the seeming ability of reason, in geometry, to discover "general properties of physical objects"; and he points out that this is the very problem which Kant saw and tried to solve.[10] Reichenbach accepts also the other fundamental heritage of current philosophy from Kant, the recognition of a conceptual element in our knowledge of a physical world. Although Reichenbach rather carelessly condemns, with the Platonic view in mind, the belief that any "knowledge . . . depends upon the use of other sources than sense perception,"[11] it is obvious that he does not mean exactly what he says when in this polemical mood. It is true that Reichenbach, unlike either Kant or Lewis, speaks of a given "world of immediately existing things" or "concrete objects around us" as "entering into our knowledge without any intellectual operations being performed by us." Nevertheless, the "concrete objects" mentioned here are not physical objects in the full sense, but rather constitute "a world where there is no difference between waking and dreaming; in which everything exists exactly in the form in which it is observed." [12] And when we go on from here to cognition of physical objects properly so called, we do find "intellectual operations being performed by us" after all.

In such cognition, we "construct a net of combining relations between the things" given in consciousness; these relations are "physical laws." When the predictive inferences made on the basis of these laws are contradicted by further "immediate things," we restore order, reducing the contradictions and unsuccessful inferences to a minimum, by identifying such things as "unreal." Thus Reichenbach, like Kant and Lewis, regards physical laws as conceptual constructions, and the identity of physical objects as determined by these laws as definitions. Like Lewis, too, he sees clearly the analytic character (demonstrated but also obscured by Kant) of the identification of physical reality with rational structure.

The laws of nature involve contradictions if we consider the whole immediate world as real—this is the reason that the distinction between the objective and the subjective world is introduced.

And further, again in agreement with an obscure intimation by Kant and a definite clarification by Lewis, he recognizes the manner in which much that is "subjective" in this sense can be incorporated in the objective world by adequate rational explanation.

It is possible to combine both worlds into a single one if we leave the things of waking as they are but interpret the things of the dream in a way quite different from their immediate appearance. [13]

(Of course Reichenbach has already made clear that we do not really "leave the things of waking as they are," but interpret them, too, in terms of a conceptual structure, although a different one from that of dreams. Moreover, he recognizes, like Lewis, "a domain of included predictions" in every identification of a physical object.)

Reichenbach also recognizes a sense in which *all* the contents of consciousness are conceptually organized. It is difficult to conceive anything much closer to the Kantian view of the limitation of sense perception by the structure of consciousness itself than the assertion that

The mechanism of sensation is organized in such a way that it cannot produce a sensation without superimposing upon it a certain description. We do not see things as amorphous but always as if pressed into a certain conceptual frame . . .[14]

Like Lewis, Reichenbach sees the character of this "conceptual frame" as a product of human evolution;[15] like Kant, although by virtue of a rather dubious argument,[16] he sees it as at once psychological and logical in character ("a psychological phenomenon which is connected with the logical structure of the existence concept").[17]

The conceptual frame, moreover, is a unifying factor; in it the series of subjective, intuitive perspectives by which we view the world are combined into one system of objective knowledge. We gradually eliminate their false features and retain their true ones, Reichenbach says, as we

organize all the different pictures . . . into one superior whole . . . it is by a kind of intellectual integration of subjective views that we succeed in constructing a total view of the world, the consistent expansion of which entitles us to ever increasing claims of objectivity.[18]

We may note here the close relation between objectivity and progressive systematic unification which plays so important a role for both Kant and Lewis.

It is interesting, too, that the concepts both of substance and of causality still appear, in Reichenbach's analysis, as important features of this "conceptual frame," both in ordinary cognition of physical objects and in scientific explanation of them, despite his emphatic assertion that these concepts "are no longer recognized by the physics of our day" and that therefore "the Kantian frame of knowledge does break down" in physics.[19] In formulating his own views, Reichenbach does not use the term "substance," but the meaning of that term, very much as Kant conceives it, is reproduced in the concept of "the *normal system*." It is possible, Reichenbach says, to describe the world in terms of the assumption that unobserved objects are identical with observed ones (i.e., that objects are continuous). It is also possible to assume that objects vanish when unobserved. The former assumption is selected, however, because it alone makes possible a "normal system"—one system of laws holding for all objects, observed and unobserved.[20] Thus the continuity of objects is implied by the concept of a coherent physical world, and is taken as a premise in the construction of the laws of such a world. In Kantian language, substance is a presupposition of (objective) experience.

Reichenbach also makes the Kantian connection between substance and causality. "The description of unobserved facts depends on . . . postulates about causality," especially a postulate requiring us "to construct homogeneous causal laws, as far as it is possible." [21] A causal law, for Reichenbach just as for Kant, is a statement of an *"if-then always* relation"; [22] and, as in Kant's example, so impressive to Lewis, of the house and the boat, it is our belief in such a statement (or in a complex of such statements) that tells us where the previously observed object will be if we look again and that therefore makes possible the recognition of an objective world.

Reichenbach acknowledges, too, the element of *necessity* in such causal laws and therefore in the objective world which they determine. Indeed, in his logical treatment of them, he introduces a concept of "physical necessity" which appears astonishingly Kantian in character. Is not "physically necessary" virtually synonymous with "synthetic a priori"? Reichenbach admits as much when he speaks of a natural law as a "synthetic connective implication" (with "connective," in his terminology, meaning "necessary"). The concept is introduced because, as Reichenbach points out, not every general implication ("if-then always" statement) is a natural law; it may be merely a statement which happens to be true of all existing cases but indicates nothing as to future cases. Such a general implication, expressing no causal relation, can be known only by complete enumeration; we know that it is true only because we already know all existing cases. If we are to know a general implication without such enumeration, so that we can make inferences from it about cases *not* previously known, the consequent must follow from the antecedent *necessarily*— either by logical necessity (because the implication is a tautology) or by physical necessity (because the implication is a natural law).[23]

But why and in what sense, then, is the nontautological implication, the natural law, necessary? Denying that we can "reduce the necessity of natural laws to logical necessity by introducing a tautological implication in place of the synthetic connective implication," Reichenbach nevertheless shows us how to do just that. If we choose "a suitable definition," we can "deduce" the law. This, we may notice, is just what Kant does for the categories defining the objective physical world as the understandable world; and it is just what Lewis does more explicitly—explicitly enough to eliminate the apparent synthetic a priori element which Reichenbach's "physical necessity" seems to perpetuate. Strange to say, Reichenbach declines to follow suit, on the grounds that we should never be sure whether a given body fits the definitions, but should need another law, a new "synthetic connective implication," to show that it does.[24] We may remember, however, that neither Kant nor Lewis is at all unaware of the uncertainty as to particular cases; indeed, it is Kant who points out that no law can possibly show that a particular case fits a definition, since we should still have to decide whether the particular case fits the law.[25] There is, of course, a sense in which both would accept the logical necessity of a physical event; but it is a sense in which Reichenbach accepts it also.

The necessity of a particular physical event, Reichenbach points out, is relative to given conditions which are not themselves necessary, and is derived from these conditions by means of laws.[26] This, again, is just what Kant says: "That which in its connection with the actual is determined in accordance with universal conditions of experience, is (that is, exists as) *necessary*." [27] Thus "*q* is physically necessary relative to *p*" means "there is a nomological statement '*n*' such that '*q*' is derivable from '*p·n*.' " ("Nomological statement" is Reichenbach's phrase for "law".) Here again, Reichenbach sees the possibility of interpreting physical necessity in terms of logical necessity; for he points out that this statement may be translated into "*q* is *logically* necessary relative to *p·n*" (i.e., logically derivable from a prior condition or event p plus a natural law n). Yet here again he rejects this alternative, regarding it as "not expedient." It would seem, on the contrary, to be very expedient indeed; for it makes clear that there is *no* necessity but logical (analytic) necessity, and that whatever necessity there is in the physical world is attributable (as Kant saw) to the logical structure which defines that world.

This conclusion is one which Reichenbach accepts. We can never be sure that a particular physical event will occur; its necessity is relative both to a synthetic, factual premise about which we may be mistaken, and to a physical law which—if regarded as "necessary" by definition—may not be applicable. Thus part of the premises, though often unmentioned, is the assertion that the individual event mentioned fulfils the antecedent of the law; and this assertion is, as Reichenbach points out, always "non-nomological." [28] Yet necessity is still involved, because "The conclusion of an inference is tautologically implied by its premises," whatever "the form of the premises." [29] I.e., if they are synthetic and therefore uncertain, the conclusion (asserting the occurrence of a physical event) is not necessary, but the inference from premises to conclusion is. Thus the apparent synthetic a priori, or "physically necessary," is really the applicability of the logically necessary to the empirically real. Reichenbach clearly recognizes this interpretation as valid, even though he so surprisingly rejects it at crucial points as inexpedient and continues to search rather unsuccessfully for a better one. It explains the role of logical deduction in science and necessity in nature, and makes clear that the applicability of logic to experience constitutes the chief problem of knowledge.

So far, then, Reichenbach may be seen to continue, at least in some sense, the Kantian doctrines of the distinction between the analytic and the synthetic, the conceptual element in all objective knowledge and (in a rudimentary way) even in all consciousness, the unifying function of knowledge, and the important role of the continuity of objects, of causality, and of necessity in the conceptual structure of the physical object world. Nevertheless, we must now turn to a series of fundamental and emphatic criticisms which Reichenbach aims against Kant, criticisms which appear to challenge some of these very concepts. We shall find that the "unpleasant flavor" which Reichenbach finds in Kant generally is that of rationalism, and that his more specific criticisms are directed against the concept of the synthetic a priori as the culminating product of that point of view. Rationalism, for Reichenbach, is the supreme antagonist in a philosophical crusade. "The rationalist philosopher is antiscientific from the very roots of his mind," and "has made philosophy an object of derision . . ." [30] Rationalism leads inevitably—since the facts of the empirical world cannot support it—to system-building and idealism, by which "the enemies of science" have "belittled scientific thought and pretended to establish a world of ideal existence" known only to the philosopher. Kant, like all rationalists, has given aid and comfort to these "enemies"; for "his artificial restriction of the powers of reason and his introduction of a metaphysical reality of things in themselves" have played directly into their hands.[31]

The doctrine of "things in themselves," relatively extraneous to the present discussion, must be reserved for later consideration. As for the "artificial restriction of the powers of reason," it is obvious that human reason differs from the mental processes of fish, for instance, and must obviously have some definite characteristics, which must restrict its scope; we can understand only what is understandable in terms of our mental processes, just as we can see only what is visible to our eyes. Reichenbach's objection, then, like Lewis's, must be aimed primarily against the "artificial" aspect of Kant's restrictions upon human reason, i.e., the rigidity of the mental structure which he envisages—a rigidity which, as Lewis has shown, is not required by the Kantian view generally.

Yet, among all the despised "rationalists," Kant fares by far the best at Reichenbach's hands. "Kant's system," he declares, "though proved untenable by later developments, was the attempt of a great mind to establish rationalism on a scientific basis." [32] Indeed, the scientific element in Kant's philosophy is more fundamental than the antiscientific; for his basic doctrine, that of the synthetic a priori, is "proved by reference to scientific procedure" in terms of the science of his day.[33] Reichenbach has sufficient confidence in the genuineness of Kant's scientific foundations to believe that "Had Kant lived to see the physics and mathematics of our day he might very well have abandoned the philosophy of the synthetic a priori." [34]

Thus Reichenbach recognizes clearly that much that is obsolete in Kant is attributable to the science and mathematics at his disposal. The fact "that there is no synthetic a priori" has become known "only now, after the physics of Newton and the geometry of Euclid have been superseded" [35] and after "the establishment of the formalistic conception of logic." [36] Indeed, Reichenbach sees that Kant's "question concerning the existence of a synthetic a priori," not his acceptance of it, is remarkable, entitling him to "a high rank" in the history of philosophy.[37] In regard to mathematics, for instance, as long as no alternative geometries were known, the Euclidean was naturally assumed to be necessarily that of the physical world; so that

It was Kant's merit to emphasize . . . that the coincidence of mathematical and physical geometry calls for an explanation, and his theory of the synthetic a priori must be regarded as the great attempt of a philosopher to account for this coincidence.[38]

Reichenbach, then, recognizes clearly the purpose for which Kant's concept of the synthetic a priori was developed, that of accounting for the applicability of the a priori to the synthetic. He believes nevertheless that it is an erroneous solution of the problem; and it is against this doctrine that his attack upon Kant is primarily aimed.

Reichenbach's summary of Kant's position and of the reasoning behind it is both accurate and extraordinarily clear and enlightening.[39] He then argues that, if the alleged synthetic a priori principles cannot be disproved by any experience, no matter what its character, they must be analytic. If they are a priori, in other words, they are not synthetic. This, however, is not the case, he asserts; the principles are synthetic, because we can imagine experience of a kind that would contradict them. And if we can imagine such experience, it might possibly occur; therefore the Kantian principles are not a priori. Kant's answer would be, according to Reichenbach, that experience would be impossible if the principles in question should fail to apply; but this answer is inadequate, because "experience in the Kantian sense" *may* become impossible. Indeed, the Kantian categories have already broken down in physics; "The axioms of Euclidean geometry, the principles of causality and substance are no longer recognized by the physics of our day." [40] And if such principles are indeed so "questionable," they certainly cannot be valid a priori; they must be recognized as "empirical hypotheses" and nothing more.[41]

It is remarkable that, although much of this is true, an important element is left out of Reichenbach's account—an element which brings Kant back into the picture. We must observe, first of all, that Reichenbach, when he notes that "experience in the Kantian sense" may become impossible, does not really contradict Kant, who definitely recognizes that there may even now be other types of minds than we in fact have. Kant asserts, rather, the analytic truth that, the human mind being as it is, no sense perceptions unamenable to organization in terms of the categories which such a mind employs would be understandable by us. With this Reichenbach agrees, when he argues that a man born with blue glasses (his analogy for the Kantian notion of human beings as born with a particular mental structure) cannot therefore count on the "necessary" existence of a blue world; he would merely see nothing if there were no objects with the wave-length of blue.[42] That we understand only what is understandable *to the human mind* is just what Kant tells us; if no understandable material were presented to us by our senses, we should most assuredly understand nothing. Actually, since Reichenbach believes (with Lewis) that the human mind is alterable and can eventually develop new categories to make new types of subject matter understandable, the possibility of being subjected to incomprehensible data, with nothing conceptually organizable, should be at least as remote for him as for Kant, with better reason. In any event, neither the possibility of other types of mind than we actually have nor the possibility of existential occurrences incomprehensible to the human mind is contrary to the Kantian doctrine, in spite of Kant's apparent uncertainty as to the extent to which we can be at all conscious of the latter.

What Kant does deny is the possibility of objective "experience" —or, equivalently, of a physical world—incomprehensible to the human mind as that mind is in fact constituted; because Kant *defines* "experience" and the physical world in terms of our *understanding* of our sense perceptions, and because we can understand only by using the minds that we in fact have. Reichenbach implicitly recognizes the definitive status of the Kantian categories when he speaks of "experience in the Kantian sense." In terms of experience *in the Kantian sense*, however, i.e., in terms of experience as defined by Kant, the categorial principles are analytic, and hence apply a priori to any occurrences to which the term "experience" correctly applies. It is nevertheless true, as Reichenbach points out, that some day there may be no such occurrences; but this means, as we have seen, that the empirical *applicability* of the principles is synthetic, not that the principles themselves (as part of the conceptual structure definitive of experience) are synthetic.

In regard to the principles of geometry, Reichenbach's argument is essentially the same as in regard to the categorial principles, although complicated by the fact that both pure and applied mathematics are involved. Reichenbach argues that *physical* geometry, as distinguished from *mathematical* geometry, is synthetic, and therefore empirical and *not* a priori.[43] He recognizes, very acutely, that the discovery of alternative geometries may be interpreted as supporting rather than breaking down the Kantian notion of the geometry of space as a contribution of the mind; for it has been shown that all geometries can be applied to the same physical world, by means of different definitions co-ordinating geometrical terms with physical data.[44] The philosophy of conventionalism associated with Poincaré, therefore, is rightly seen by Reichenbach as an extension, on the basis of multiple geometries, of the Kantian view that space is conceptual.

Reichenbach himself, however, opposes the conventionalist view along with Kant's, arguing that the geometry of space is empirical. Alternative geometries are applicable, he points out, only in combination with alternative physical laws; and all the applicable geometrical-physical *combinations* are empirically equivalent, while other combinations would not be equivalent and would not apply to the same empirical data. Thus geometry, if it is to be applied to the physical world at all, must be stated in combination with physical laws; and the resulting statement is empirical.[45] Physical geometry, then, is not a priori.

This argument draws our attention to an important point which conventionalism tends to obscure, if not actually to deny, but which Kant emphasizes. It reminds us that *there are facts* to be taken into account; that there are empirical data, which are of some determinate character and not otherwise, and which must be incorporated in any conceptual structure that is to be called "knowledge." It reminds us also of another very Kantian point—that all of knowledge is implicitly a single system, in which all parts must be adjusted to each other; thus, just as no one physical law can be applied except on the basis of a network of other physical assumptions, so not even the entire body of physics can be applied empirically unless a geometry is assumed, and vice versa. Reichenbach establishes also that there are nonequivalent descriptions, both of which cannot apply to one set of empirical facts; but he does not establish that an inapplicable description cannot be made applicable (and equivalent to the other applicable ones) by some change in conceptual assumptions not contained in the description itself.

Suppose we consider, for example, the reasoning by which Reichenbach attempts to prove that the "natural" geometry of our world is *in fact* non-Euclidean for astronomical distances. Einstein shows us, he says, that Euclidean geometry is applicable for such distances only if we assume the distortion of light rays by "universal forces." Reichenbach then adopts as "the normal system" the one in which there are no "universal forces," and its geometry (i.e, the non-Euclidean) as the "natural geometry." We may note, however, that the decision to rule out "universal forces" and to regard the geometry applicable without them as "normal" or "natural" is itself a conventional decision. Moreover, even the nonequivalent description, combining Euclidean geometry with the absence of universal forces, could be adopted if some new physical theory other than that of "universal forces" were invented to account for the distortions of light rays. That we do not have such a physical explanation available is no indication that none is possible. That we do not feel the need of one, as long as the substitution of non-Euclidean geometry can take care of the situation, is an indication that the Kantian ideal of systematic unity is operative.

A further argument in support of the empirical character of the geometry of space is to be found, Reichenbach supposes, in Einstein's linking of geometry and gravitation. Space, in this interpretation, is a system of relations between transported solid bodies and light rays —"a very general feature of the physical world." [46] Yet surely the theory of gravitation, although intended to apply to and explain empirical data, is itself a highly abstract conceptual system. Its relation to the data is indeed no different from that of a geometrical system, although the concepts in which it deals are physical rather than geometrical. The linking of geometry and gravitation may well be interpreted as evidence of the abstractness of physics, rather than as evidence of the empirical character of geometry. And if, by this linkage, "space" is shown to be a "feature of the physical world," we must remember that "the physical world" is itself a highly abstract conceptual system into which empirical data are incorporated; and it is on the most abstract levels of this system—certainly not among its incorporated perceptual data—that so "very general" a feature as spatial relations, or even gravitation, must belong.

There is, of course, a sense in which the distinction "between mathematical and physical geometry" is valid. If, however, we mean by "physical geometry" the interpretation of geometry in terms of physics, we are still dealing with abstractions and with an analytic system of concepts, even though they are physically relevant concepts; and "space" in this sense is that mathematical space which Lewis so helpfully distinguishes from perceptual space. If, on the other hand, by "physical geometry" we mean *applied* geometry," calculations about actual, observable empirical facts, the question of how and why mathematical geometry is employable as physical geometry, how and why systematic concepts are applicable to empirical data (i.e., the question of the apparent synthetic a priori), still remains.

The empirical *applicability* of the geometrical and physical concepts alike is, of course, *hypothetical;* in this sense, Reichenbach quite correctly refers to both types of principles as "empirical hypotheses." [47] This means that we adopt them provisionally, trying them out to see how far they can be applied to the empirically given; in other words, we adopt as "regulative" (in the Kantian sense) a synthetic assumption as to the empirical applicability of the analytic conceptual system. When Reichenbach seeks to indicate, by calling geometric and categorial principles "empirical hypotheses," that these principles are themselves synthetic, he neglects to take note of a fact of which he is fully aware in other contexts—the conceptual nature of hypotheses, the role of deductive, analytic reasoning in the development of the hypothetical structure itself, quite aside from the empirical evidence as to whether or not the hypothesis is applicable. Thus, while it is quite true that the Kantian categorial structure *may* cease to be applicable, that—as a definition of experience—it may become empty, empirically irrelevant, yet this fact in itself does not invalidate the *regulative* function of that structure, the attempt to understand whatever we can, in terms of the means of understanding at our disposal.

Have the developments of post-Kantian science shown that the Kantian concepts are *now* empirically irrelevant, that a definition of the physical world in terms of them is empty, or at least woefully inadequate? And if so, have these developments shown that *any possible* categorial structure is empirically irrelevant, that we live in a world which is not understandable even to an evolving human mind?

On the macrocosmic scale, Reichenbach points out that Einstein's "closed universe" is incompatible with Euclidean geometry if we adhere to the principles of "normal causality"; whereas Kant regarded *both* Euclidean geometry and "normal causality" as valid a priori.[48] We must observe, however, that both *are* valid a priori (i.e., analytically, as abstract systems); and that, as to empirical applicability, Einstein assumes—just as surely as Kant—that *some* geometry must be applicable if we are to understand the physical world. In fact, it is to preserve the applicability of *both* geometry and causality that Einstein invokes a non-Euclidean geometry when application of the Euclidean system results in inconsistencies.

A more difficult problem and more fundamental challenge is presented by the peculiarities of quantum mechanics. The difficulty, as Reichenbach sees it, lies in the fact that subatomic particles "do not lend themselves to a unique determination of unobservables"; [49] in other words, the Kantian concept of necessity does not apply to them. This situation makes it impossible to deal with them in terms of a "normal system" (which means, as we have seen, the Kantian concept of "substance") or in terms of homogeneous causality. But how, then, can Reichenbach's own interpretation of the physical world in terms of coherent, continuous objects and "physically necessary" laws be maintained? Only on the assumption that a categorial structure which includes substance and causality and necessity is still required for the macrocosmic world of physical objects, since it *defines* those objects. Surely this is Reichenbach's own assumption. When he says that, in reference to the subatomic world, because of the difficulties just mentioned, we cannot "speak of unobservables in the same sense as is implied for the world of everyday life," he must mean that we cannot there apply the concept of physical *objects*, which are to be defined (quite in the Kantian manner) in terms of the relation of "observables" to "unobservables" in a "normal system." [50] We are thus left with an area in which the standard categories do not apply—an area of something other than physical objects; but we still "construct homogeneous laws, as far as it is possible." [51] In other words, the categories involved are "regulative."

Reichenbach objects, however, to the Kantian doctrine that a "regulative" assumption is required. In order to look for a cause in any specific case, he argues, and to find that cause if there is one, we need not assume that there is a cause in every case. No causal law presupposes that there is always a cause for everything, but only that there is a cause in cases of this particular kind; and we find out that there is one when we find out what it is.[52] Kant, however, surely does not mean to indicate that universality is *proved* by the existence of any individual instance of causality. Rather, as we have seen, he contends that wherever and whenever we recognize *an objective physical thing*, an instance of causality is presupposed; that whenever and wherever we *understand* our experience, a causal law is presupposed; that therefore we could not experience physical things, or develop a meaningful science by which to explain them, without the concept of causality as part of our equipment.

The anomalies of quantum mechanics must, of course, complicate this view; for even if subatomic phenomena are not objective physical things, they are still part of science—a part which we must understand if physical things themselves are to be understood. We need, then, a concept of explanation which will not make explanation synonymous with discovery of causal laws of continuous objects, and which will be applicable outside that field of physical objects which is defined in terms of such laws; the possibility of explanation of some sort, then, could still be assumed as a "regulative" principle. That the development of such a new concept is possible, some assurance is given by the adaptability of the human mind, in terms of the evolutionary development of new categories to deal with new types of data—a development in which Reichenbach, like Lewis, explicitly believes. The concept of "corporeal substance," for instance, he regards as "the product of a conditioning through environment" —our environment of physical things perceived by the senses. Thus the new type of "experiences offered by atomic phenomena" require a new type of "description"—which, presumably, these experiences will condition us to produce.[53] Even now, where we cannot speak of continuous physical objects, we can speak of "waves" and "particles"; [54] so that *some* conceptual organization is still indicated.

Moreover, we may recall that, in many areas where "homogeneous causal laws" are not possible, laws of another type, the statistical, are nevertheless conceivable; and through Reichenbach's analysis of probability we shall be able to see to what extent they fufil the same explanatory role. We shall then see, also, whether we can still regard explanation, identified with systematic unification of *some* sort, as the regulative goal of knowledge; for this Kantian doctrine, too, is one that Reichenbach apparently accepts in some sense but finds challenged by the new physics.

Reichenbach's criticism of Kant, however, rests upon the new developments not only in physics but in logic. Unlike many more superficial critics, he does not merely criticize the obviously *synthetic* a priori, the a priori in the synthetic fields of physics and physical geometry, but launches an attack upon "apriorism" in logic itself.

Since logic is ordinarily regarded as the legitimate field of the a priori, however, some explanation is here in order.

Reichenbach identifies "the *aprioristic interpretation*" of logic, that of Kant and the other rationalists, as the view that "logic is a science with its own authority, founded in the a priori nature of reason, or in the psychological nature of thought, or in intellectual intuition or evidence." [55] The "*formalistic interpretation*," on the other hand, rejects this concept of "an authority in logic" and sees logic merely as "a system of rules which by no means determine the content of science, and which do nothing but furnish a transformation of one proposition into another without any addition to its intension." Thus logic is a "domain of tautological formulas"; and since a tautology, by Wittgenstein's definition, is "a formula the truth of which is independent of the truth-values of the elementary propositions contained in it," logic is characterized by "material emptiness" (i.e., it asserts a relation between propositions, but nothing about their empirical truth or falsehood and therefore nothing about any facts to which the propositions may refer). He accounts for the element of "necessity" in logic, with Carnap, as "a relation between symbols due to the rules of language." [56]

This distinction, as Reichenbach states it, seems quite simple. We may recall, however, that Kant, at least, among Reichenbach's "rationalists" and "apriorists," entirely agrees with the "formalists" as to the tautological character of logic; thus he speaks of "general logic" as "analytic," "formal," asserting no "material (objective) truth . . ." [57] We may be startled, on the other hand, to find Reichenbach's own textbook on logic introducing its subject as in some sense, at least, an "*analysis of thought*." [58] We may wonder, too, how Reichenbach's "formalistic" view can simultaneously deny *both* that logic is a "material science" and that it has "an a priori character," [59] although we may well understand his objection to the simultaneous *acceptance* of both (i.e., to the concept of logic as synthetic a priori). Finally, we may wonder why we must resort to the concept of "language" to explain logical necessity, when it has already been explained in terms of tautology.

The basis for at least some clarification of these confusions is provided elsewhere by Reichenbach in his distinction between the contents of logic itself and the facts *about* logic which explain why its contents are valid; i.e., between the "object language" of logic and its "metalanguage." In formal logic itself, he says, a formula is merely symbols manipulated according to rules. These rules, however, must be stated in words, so that we will know what they mean; and they must have meaning, so that they can tell us what we may do with the symbols. That is, they must be stated in a meta-language.[60] Of course, since some of the rules themselves are tauto-logical, we might try, Reichenbach suggests, to formalize the meta-language in turn, as another tautological system. (This seems to be what Lewis does in his logic of "strict implication," which, we may recall, is intended to formulate a "canon . . . of deductive in-ference.") Then, however, as Reichenbach points out, we need a "meta-metalanguage" to state the rules of this new system so as to tell us how to operate it. Such explanation is an infinite regress, and we may as well not embark upon it; for we must stop somewhere with our rules unformalized after all.[61]

How shall we explain, then, the validity of our rules, i.e., of our statements in the metalanguage? This is what Kant explains by the concept of a standard human mind, and what Lewis explains by the concept of "meaning," and what Reichenbach wishes to explain by the concept of linguistic structure. Any disagreements between Reich-enbach and the Kantian type of "apriorist" are disagreements not as to the nature of the statements and deductions contained in logic, which both regard as analytic, empirically empty, and in that sense a priori, but rather as to the nature of the rules which determine those statements and deductions—the reason *why* the statements are analytic, or tautological, and the deductions valid. It is the *rules* of logic that Reichenbach wants us to recognize as neither possessing a priori "authority" nor existentially "inherent in things" [62] (whether physical things or mental things).

Nevertheless, like Lewis, who criticizes Kant for admitting into logic a psychological element which he himself cannot quite exclude, Reichenbach himself runs into difficulties in trying to maintain and elaborate the "formalistic" view as here defined. Starting out with the notion of logic as *"analysis of thought,"* he tries to differentiate it from the psychological analysis of *actual* thought processes by calling it a *"rational reconstruction"* of these processes (analyzing the "justi-fication" of their conclusions rather than the manner in which these conclusions are actually obtained). This implies a criterion of logic outside of actual thought itself; but what, then, is the nature of the criterion? Reichenbach apparently intends to find it in language; yet he points out that "Not all rules of language are arbitrary; for instance, the rules of deduction are not, but are determined by the postulate that they must lead from true sentences to true sentences." [63] As soon as we recognize such an extra-linguistic determination, however, the interpretation of logic as "analysis of language" becomes futile for the explanation of logical validity. It does not tell us how these rules of deduction are obtained, or *why* they "lead from true sentences to true sentences"; or, moreover, why they do so *necessarily* (since invalid reasoning, too, may sometimes happen to do so, but only coincidentally). And here we are dealing with facts of some sort; for, as Reichenbach recognizes, while inferences in logic are necessarily valid because they are tautological, "*The statement that a given formula is a tautology, is not a tautology but an empirical statement.*" [64] Thus Reichenbach, scorning the "rationalistic" and "aprioristic" view of logic as a "material science," acknowledges nevertheless that "*formal manipulations with formulas of the object language are made possible through material thinking in the metalanguage.*" [65]

What kind of "fact," then, does the "statement that a given formula is a tautology" express? Reichenbach flounders from one suggestion to another. A "syntactical fact" rather than a "logical fact"? [66] This is the linguistic interpretation again; and we have seen how little this helps. A "posit," on which we rely "as long as we have no evidence to the contrary"? This sounds empirical; but actually, any "evidence to the contrary" must be *logical* evidence, the discovery that we have reasoned mistakenly—a discovery which can be made only by further reasoning (i.e., further "posits" of the same kind). Perhaps aware of this difficulty, Reichenbach now resorts to an ultimate "rule of logical evidence," which would have to appeal to "a psychological criterion, since evidence is a psychological phenomenon." Yet it is the despised rationalists, we may recall, who found logic upon "the a priori nature of reason" or "the psychological nature of thought" or "intellectual intuition or evidence"!

Finally, Reichenbach declares that the entire question as to the validity of logic is meaningless in any event. We can justify any logical system in terms of a metalanguage, which we can then formalize and justify in terms of another metalanguage, and so on;

but to justify *all* such metalanguages, since we cannot use a language outside all of them, we must "include the language we are speaking in our considerations"; and such "self-referent language" always results in "antinomies." To question the validity of logic is to assert "that the validity of evidence is not evident." Such a question, therefore, is "contradictory" and "cannot be meaningfully asserted."

Here Reichenbach has landed us in a very Kantian "antinomy." He himself points out an analogy with "the question 'why,' " which "can reasonably be asked with respect to every physical phenomenon," but not "with respect to all phenomena simultaneously." [67] Surely this is just what Kant says: "The concepts of reality, substance, causality, even that of necessity in existence, . . . can be employed . . . to explain the possibility of things in the world of sense, but not to explain the possibility of the *universe itself*." Such concepts "lose all meaning," Kant adds, when we try so to extend them.[68] And surely the search for final validation described by Reichenbach fits Kant's description of a pursuit of "such a completeness in the series of premisses as will dispense with the need of presupposing other premisses." [69] It is indeed the Kantian dialectical process which Reichenbach sees in that "mechanism of thought" which, "turning to more and more general questions, is carried on by a certain inertia to run idling when there is nothing left to be asked." Quite characteristically, he adds a remark obviously intended to dispel any impression of Kantian resemblances. "What is asked is nothing; and it is no breakdown of human capacities if to such a question no answer can be given." [70] It is doubtful, however, whether Kant envisages a "breakdown of human capacities" in this respect, in any sense in which Reichenbach does not; any difference on this score reduces to one of emotional tone, and that more in intention than in fact. Much more important is an illuminating by-product of the discussion of "evidence," a revelation of the very direct amenability of the Kantian antinomies, now so often regarded as trivial or as no antinomies at all, to interpretation in terms of the currently admired concept of the antinomies of "self-referent language."

It is important, too, to note what we accept when we stop short of antinomy, retaining as an indispensable assumption the belief that *some* logic is valid and will lead from true premises to true conclusions. It is that validity of "logical evidence" which involves, as Reichenbach points out, a "psychological criterion." Like Lewis, he is unable to ban the psychological element entirely. His more explicit distinction between the "object language" and "metalanguage" of logic, enabling him to keep the psychological element clearly outside the *formal* sytem, may be regarded as a source of clarification which Lewis lacks in any explicit form, partly because Lewis's formal system itself is designed to fulfil the metasystematic function of a "canon."

On the other hand, Lewis's explicit identification of the psychological element in logic in terms of "meaning" may be regarded as a source of clarification which Reichenbach lacks. Indeed, the concept of logic as "analysis of language" is most fruitful when we think of "language" in this connection as *meaningful* language. When Reichenbach does so, he can identify both the value of logic and the point of distinction between logic and the analysis of all "actual thought." "It is the value of such an analysis of language" (i.e., logical analysis) "that it . . . distinguishes meanings and the relations between meanings from the blurred background of psychological motives and intentions." [71] For meaning, as we have learned from Lewis, is that which language communicates, the basis of language in that *common* conceptual equipment by which the subjective experience of each individual is organized into the objective world consciously shared by all.

Reichenbach's objection, then, turns out to be not an objection to the conception of logic as a priori (in an analytic sense), nor even as mental (to an extent which any view of logic as conceptual must admit in the end), but rather, like Lewis's, an objection to the conception of the mental structure as fixed and unalterable, and the logical structure therefore as determined a priori to be of a particular kind, based on particular rules, which can be known once and for all. The objection to "apriorism" is an objection to *synthetic* "apriorism," in logic as elsewhere. The question may be raised, of course, whether Reichenbach's belief in "logical evidence" is not a synthetic a priori of sorts; for it is obviously a priori, and affirms those statements "that a given formula is a tautology" which he definitely regards as "empirical" statements. Moreover, it is introduced precisely in the Kantian manner—as a "presupposition of knowledge." In any event, we have here one more bit of evidence—as if more were needed— that the question of the nature of logical validity is a difficult and perplexing one, to which no one has provided a thoroughly satisfactory answer. Reichenbach is unsurpassed in the persistence and genuineness of his attempt to carry explanation of it as far as possible, even though it means the exposure of unanswered questions and unexpected resemblances to the theories which he opposes.

We may conclude, then, that Reichenbach, like Lewis, and in spite of a far more hostile and perhaps shrewder attack upon Kant and the synthetic a priori in all fields, retains a large residue of Kantian doctrine, although in a more flexible form than the original, a form influenced by and adapted to the flexibility of modern science and logic. It will be wise to take the precaution, here, of guarding against any exaggeration of resemblances. Reichenbach is certainly not a Kantian, in any sense in which a philosopher dealing in theories of knowledge and of science today can consistently fail to be a Kantian. Indeed, the persistent Kantian elements in Reichenbach, for whom Kant represents the climax of the philosophy to be opposed, are an excellent indication of the ubiquitousness of Kantian influence at the present time. Observation of these elements should prepare us for the role of Reichenbach's theory of probability as an expansion of the fundamental Kantian approach, the analysis of knowledge in terms of the applicability of the a priori to the synthetic, into the field of probable knowledge.

7

Reichenbach & the Applicability of the A Priori in Probable Knowledge

For purposes of further discussion, we must first see just what Reichenbach's doctrine of probability is. Once we have done so, we shall be in a position to see how much of it can be restated in terms of the Kantian structure.

This doctrine takes as its starting point the mathematical calculus of probability, because that calculus is a standard procedure, used in science.[1] In it, probability is always evaluated numerically "by the ratio of two frequencies—the frequency of the events of the narrower class considered and the frequency of the events of the wider class to which the probability is referred."[2] This ratio represents the probability that events of the second class will belong to the first class. Reichenbach argues that this concept may be accepted as standard, applying also to those vaguer instances of probability, outside the field of exact science, in which actual numerical determination is not practically feasible. When we say that a particular event will probably occur, for instance, or that a given proposition is probably true, the alleged single case must be included in some class if the attribution of probability to it is to have any meaning; the evidence for it must be tacitly included in classes of similar evidence, the frequency of whose reliability is estimated (however vaguely), if we are to regard the occurrence of the event or truth of the proposition as "probable."[3] Thus we need not, like Lewis, explain probability of this vaguer sort in terms of "degree of credibility," a concept which shifts ambiguously between the logical and psychological and which cannot be satisfactorily analyzed. We are justified, rather, in interpreting *all* probability in terms of relative frequencies and applying the mathematical rules for dealing with such frequencies.

There is also a more fundamental reason why the frequency ratio, or relative frequency, does not appear to exhaust the meaning of "probability." Even in science, the probability to which we ordinarily refer when we say that something is "probable" is the probability of *future* events, while the relative frequencies which form the basis of our calculations and determine the numerical value of that probability are the frequencies of *past* events. To conform his definition to this situation, Reichenbach invokes the mathematical concept of a *limit,* defining probability not as the observed relative frequency itself but as "the limit of the relative frequency in an infinite (or finite) series." [4] Each successive observation, added to all previous ones, changes the frequency ratio slightly; and, listing all such successive ratios in a series, we find a probability only if the series *"converges toward a limit,"* i.e., if there is some point in the series beyond which the successive relative frequencies fluctuate above and below a fixed ratio by not more than a particular very small quantity.[5] That fixed ratio, or limit, is what we call the *probability* (that events of the one series will be events of the other).

From this definition of probability, Reichenbach deduces the rules of the mathematical calculus of probability, without invoking any additional axioms. This achievement establishes the calculus as "tautological" (in terms of the definition).[6] It also establishes the desirability of the definition, for Reichenbach, by demonstrating its relevance to the actual procedure of science. From the mathematical calculus, in turn, Reichenbach deduces a complete formal "system of probability logic," in which the two truth-values (truth and falsehood) of ordinary logic are replaced by a continuous scale of degrees of probability ranging from truth to falsehood.[7] Thus both the mathematical and the logical system become analytically valid in terms of a scientifically relevant definition of probability, i.e., "justified . . . within the formalistic interpretation . . ." [8]

From this deductive system, too, Reichenbach further deduces the method and conditions required for *prediction* of probabilities in physical science. (He believes that prediction of certainties would be a special case of the same procedure, in which the predicted probability is equal to 1, but that in any event the assertion of such a prediction would itself be merely probable; so that all possible kinds of prediction are included.) The definition of a limit implies that, in order to find a limit, we must be able to set up the kind of series which will converge toward it after a certain point. This, obviously, is what we do in the use of induction. *"The aim of induction is to find series of events whose frequency of occurrence converges toward a limit,"* i.e., to foresee the future with some degree of probability. Inductive procedure sets up a series of observed events to find out whether they converge toward a limit, and, if so, what that limit is. Thus, from the definition of a limit (and of probability as a limit of a particular kind), we may infer tautologically that induction is a valid method of finding probabilities; it will reveal the limit if there is one, and thus "the applicability of this procedure, as a whole, is a necessary condition of the existence of a limit . . ."

There may be other methods, Reichenbach admits, such as clairvoyance; but if clairvoyance is accurate, the relative frequency of its successes will form a series with a limit, and induction will apply. Indeed, only by induction can we tell whether an alleged clairvoyant is reliable or an impostor.[9] Moreover, since prediction is equivalent to discovery of probabilities (prediction of certainties, if any, being a special case), it can take place only if there *is* a limit of relative frequency; and therefore "the applicability of the inductive procedure," which we have seen as "a necessary condition of the existence of a limit," is also "a necessary condition of predictability" because *"it is a logical consequence of the definition of predictability."* [10] In other words, in the deductive system which Reichenbach constructs on the basis of his definition of probability, a tautological equivalence is established between probability, predictability, and accessibility to induction.

Does this mean that Reichenbach has established deductively that induction can predict (approximately, at least) the course of actual events? He is quite clear that it means nothing of the sort. Mathematical calculations, such as those used in the determination of probabilities, can determine the future (i.e., presently uncalculated) direction of a mathematical series, because the known "initial segment" can give us the "prescription" for the series and can therefore determine its limit. There is no guarantee, however, that events will follow any such prescription; the series may, in the future, take a course different from that of its initial section, and cease to converge toward a limit.[11] Nevertheless, in induction as in the mathematical determination of probability, "the relative frequency observed statistically is assumed to hold approximately for any future prolongation of the series"; i.e., we *assume* that the series of events will continue to converge toward a limit.[12] Such an assumption is justified, even though events may later prove it to be mistaken; for unless the future follows the same course as the past in some respect, at least approximately, we have no means of predicting anything about it at all. Induction will provide "the best assumption concerning the future . . . relative to what we know"; and how can we select any assumption except on the basis of what we know? The world *may* be too "disorderly" for the construction of any "series with a limit," but in that case prediction will turn out to be impossible.[13]

Thus the "principle of induction," stating the *assumption* that the relative frequency observed in the past will hold approximately for the same series of events in the future, and will converge to a limit which is close to the frequency already observed, is a nontautological assumption; that is why it "can teach us something new . . ."[14] (I.e., it is synthetic.) We do, however, make this "posit," or "wager," because we can prove deductively that it is our *best* posit;[15] it may be mistaken and will then lead to failure, but "it must lead to success if success is attainable at all."[16] As Hume saw, we cannot prove by logic that induction will apply to events, nor can we infer this from the past successes of induction without circularity.[17] We can prove by logic, however, that induction will predict whatever is predictable.

The concept of a "posit"—or, more precisely, of a "best posit" —has various important functions in Reichenbach's theory. For one thing, it enables him to explain what we mean by the "probability" of a single case. Strictly speaking, we should not use this expression, because the probability ratio is a frequency and can apply only to a class. However, the frequency with which members of a class have a certain property gives a corresponding "weight" to the expectation that any particular member will have that property. We may, therefore, *posit* that such will be the case, with a *weight* in our favor derived from experience with similar instances.[18] Thus the best posit, even though it may often be disappointed, is still the one supported by induction; for if it is disappointed so frequently that there is no longer any point in counting on it at all, this means that the series will by that time have lost its convergence toward a limit. Reichenbach, then, accounts for the occurrence of the "improbable" without destroying (as Lewis appears to do in this connection) the empirical relevance of probability determinations.

By a further use of the concept of "weight" attaching to a "posit," Reichenbach meets also another fundamental problem which Lewis raises, that of the "initial credibility" which must exist prior to an induction if we are to have any idea where to begin. Since this initial credibility is sometimes so strong that relatively few favorable cases —sometimes only one crucial experiment—may be regarded as sufficient to establish an induction, it appears to embody a type of probability not involving frequency. Reichenbach, however, accounts for these circumstances by differentiating between a "blind posit," a mere stab in the dark without any grounds for expecting it to lead to success, and an "appraised posit," which has a "weight" assignable to it on the basis of some prior induction.[19] In Reichenbach's example, the melting point of each known metal except carbon has been found inductively, and located at a constant temperature with a frequency approaching certainty. In a "cross-induction," or "concatenated induction," on the next level, the very high frequency with which metals have been found to have fixed melting points leads us to posit that carbon also has one, although a higher one than we have been able to produce. If a scientist should some day succeed in exposing carbon to a temperature high enough to melt it, we should be almost certain, even without further trials, that any carbon would melt if it should be exposed to the same temperature. The confirmation of our posit that all metals have fixed melting points will greatly increase the weight of our posit that the melting point of one sample of carbon will be the melting point of all samples. In general, this means that a probable prediction is itself *probably valid* in terms of the frequency with which other predictions of a similar type have been valid; and Reichenbach works out mathematical procedures for the construction of a "probability lattice" to determine the enhancement of weight involved. The process may continue indefinitely from one level to the next; so that "every case is incorporated in the whole concatenation of knowledge."

Thus knowledge, even in terms of probability, is a system. This does not mean, however, that it is a final system or certainly valid; for the positing of a probability on a new level is always "blind" until it can be assigned a weight by means of a cross-induction on the next level. Thus we must always stop somewhere with a blind posit, and every instance of knowledge involves some uncertainty.[20] "The system of knowledge is written in the language of probability logic . . ."[21]

It is sometimes said, in criticism of such a view, that a system of knowledge based on a "blind posit" becomes not merely uncertain, but certainly invalid; that all probabilities within it are reduced to zero. This criticism is unjustified, because the blind posit is treated as *true* in all probability determinations; and legitimately so because the very attempt to know involves the assumption that some knowledge is valid. Nevertheless, the possibility that any particular attempt at induction may fail is a result not only of the possible unpredictability of the future events which that induction aims to predict (i.e., the possible failure of the series to converge), but also of the possible invalidity of past inductions on which the present one depends for its data and initial weight. Thus the blind posit, the foundation of ignorance on which all knowledge is based, injects an element of radical ignorance into every instance of knowledge.

This, in outline, is Reichenbach's theory of probability and induction. His extensive mathematical and logical expositions fall within the limits of that outline; they are designed to construct the deductive system which it involves, thereby validating its assumption that such a system is possible. We are now in a position, therefore, to consider the theory as a whole, in relation to the present discussion. And our first impression may well be that any such relation is rather remote—that a "system of knowledge . . . written in the language of probability logic" is one which could hardly be less Kantian. Nevertheless, a careful examination will show us otherwise.

As we should expect, the major difference is rooted in the difference between the science of Kant's day and that of our own. The science with which Reichenbach deals includes laws which state frequent and probable relations, not only laws which state universal and necessary relations; indeed, the view that there are *any* laws of the latter type is sometimes challenged. Yet this radical difference is, in terms of Reichenbach's theory of probability, an expansion, or generalization, with the new type of logical structure including rather than replacing the old; for "causal" (universal) laws are merely "a special case" of "inductive" (probable) laws, the case in which the limit of relative frequency is "equal to 1, or at least approximately equal to 1." [22] Reichenbach applies this analysis even to laws ordinarily regarded as clearly "explicative," pre-eminent examples of the deductive element in science. The law of gravitation, for example, embodies a concept which Newton invented in order to provide a "causal explication" of the facts, and his mathematical structure has "no resemblance" to probability calculations. Yet Reichenbach analyzes Newton's law as the result of a "cross-induction" (or "concatenated induction") based on prior inductions by Galileo and Kepler, with a resulting increase of certainty for the validity of both prior theories (because the evidence for both now combines to validate the entire structure). [23]

We may recall, at this point, Reichenbach's acceptance of the conceptual element in knowledge, the concept of "physical necessity" (i.e., logical necessity as applied to physical events through laws), the postulate of a "normal system" (or "homogeneous causality") as required for inference from the observed to the unobserved; and we must wonder whether all of this fits in without inconsistency. With a little further reflection, we find that it can be made to do so, although we may well wish that Reichenbach had done it for us more explicitly than he has. He does explain, at least, that "the hypothetico-deductive method," or "method of constructing explanatory hypotheses," may be expressed "in terms of deductive methods, with the sole addition of induction by enumeration." Reichenbach accords due importance to both elements.

These structures are superior to a simple induction by enumeration because they contain so much deductive logic—but their inductive content is exhaustively described as a network of inductions of the enumerative type. [24]

The manner in which the two elements are interrelated is not explicitly made clear. It seems, however, that Reichenbach would recognize the inductive element as establishing the applicability, or empirical relevance, of the law and of any deductive implications derivable from it, while the laws or systems of laws validated by means of induction and cross-induction may themselves be the basis of extensive deductive systems. The inductive series of relative frequencies which Reichenbach points out in connection with Galileo's and Kepler's laws are series of cases in which these apply; but the laws themselves are constructs, from which deductive (i.e., tautological and therefore necessary) mathematical inferences show us how to identify these cases—what *must* happen under given circumstances if the laws are to apply. Similarly, in Reichenbach's "cross-induction on the next level," other laws are a series of special cases in which Newton's theory applies, and thus validate it inductively (and probably) through their own inductive validity—but only because they *are* special cases of Newton's theory, as deductive (and necessary) inferences from it. Newton's theory both explains them deductively and increases the inductive probability that they are applicable, just as they in turn explain observations of particular planetary motions and increase the probability that those observations are correct. And the affirmative observations render increasingly probable the empirical applicability of the entire deductive structure in terms of which they are necessary.

There are, of course, many laws which explicitly *state* probabilities short of certainty; and it is the status of these that must now concern us. On the basis of such laws, too, we can see that deduction is possible, with the degree of probability expressed in any law being transmitted to the deductive implications of that law. As Reichenbach points out, the necessity attributed to an "if-then" relation in an individual case, e.g., "If I turn on this faucet, the water will run," derives from the generality of the implication; we believe in it because we believe that "all faucets in the world" behave in this way. Similarly, the probability (or "weight") attributed to a prediction in an individual case, e.g., that the patient has a seventy-five percent chance of recovery, derives from the belief that, in a great number of similar cases, that percentage has recovered.[25] Thus, whether the general law is universal or not, the inference from it to the individual case is deductive. Moreover, Reichenbach's concept of a "normal system," too, may easily be expanded to include homogeneous statistical laws (i.e., probable laws) as well as "homogeneous causality" in the narrower sense; for indeed, inference from the observed to the unobserved is precisely the purpose of probability calculations.

Still more important, perhaps, at least in terms of the present discussion, is the fact that *induction itself is shown by Reichenbach to consist in the application of a deductive system*—a system particularly designed to be applicable to frequencies short of the universal. Thus Reichenbach, like Kant, is concerned primarily with the *applicability of logic to experience*, although the logic involved is of a different type, suited to a science of a different type. This is the fundamental resemblance between them, and is the source of many others. If we now re-examine Reichenbach's theory of probability and induction in this light, its function in the adaptation and expansion of the Kantian structure will be readily apparent.

First, we have observed that Reichenbach takes the actual structure of science as his starting point, setting out to account for the validity which he assumes it to possess. Like Kant, he does so because he regards science as the pre-eminent example of knowledge ("knowledge in its most successful form"); [26] so that by this approach he hopes to achieve the most adequate possible analysis of knowledge in general.

Next, we have seen that Reichenbach discovers in science the use of a set of mathematical rules (those of the "calculus of probability"), and incorporates them in an entirely formal logic of probability within which they are then seen to be tautological. This gives us what Kant calls a "general logic," although not the Aristotelian system which he believed to be the only conceivable one. Still more interesting is Reichenbach's next step—the derivation, from the definition of probability (as a limit of relative frequency) assumed by the mathematical calculus, of the nature of induction as a procedure for finding the probability of *events*, i.e., for prediction. For this means that induction receives its justification in terms of a formal logic (or, as Kant would say, a priori), and at the same time provides an existential interpretation for that logic—or, rather, a schema for such interpretation, to be assigned specific content whenever actual series of events are considered. Thus the conceptual structure involved in induction is related to probability logic just as Kant's categorial structure is related to Aristotelian logic; it is probability logic interpreted in terms of the conditions under which it would be applicable to events. For only if a series of relative frequencies does have a limit can induction be successfully applied to it. Moreover, only under such conditions do we know objective events at all; for "the relations between impressions and physical facts are probability relations." [27] The logic of induction, therefore, is in a very precisely Kantian sense identifiable as a "transcendental logic," although we may be sure that Reichenbach would have disapproved of the term. Only the connotation of involvement with the structure of the mind is lacking, at this point; and we shall soon see Reichenbach supply this element also, just as we have already seen him resort to it in the case of deductive logic.

Up to the present point in the argument, however, Reichenbach is speaking of induction as a method, without regard to whether or not there are events such that the method can actually be used. Induction, or inductive logic, in the sense in which it is deductively justified, is prediction of events in intension (to use the distinction which we noted in connection with Lewis) but not necessarily in extension. It *means* prediction of events, but cannot tell us a priori that there are events which are predictable. The "inductive principle," on the other hand, stating the *assumption* that induction and (through it) the logic of probability do have extension, that they are in fact applicable to events (i.e., stating just what Kant's "principles of pure understanding" state in regard to the applicability of his categories), is seen by Reichenbach as *synthetic*—"the only synthetic principle on which the application of the calculus of probability is based." [28] In a sense which he makes very clear, it is also an a priori principle; for "logic can prove . . . that the use of the principle is advisable" if we want to predict, and "This proof, the justification of induction, is constructed in terms of analytic considerations." [29]

Is the inductive principle, then, synthetic a priori? It not only states the same assumption that Kant's synthetic a priori principles state, but performs the same function; for we must note that it is the *application* of the calculus of probability, not the calculus itself, that Reichenbach sees as requiring this "synthetic principle." It is offered, indeed, precisely with the intention of solving that problem of the applicability of a logical system which Kant, too, confronts at the same stage of the analysis of knowledge and sees as the focal point of that analysis—the problem presented by the fact that no type of logical structure or logical operation can guarantee the occurrence of any event. Kant sees this problem in terms of the need to explain the conformity of the physical world to universal laws, and Reichenbach in terms of the need to explain the use of mathematical calculations (in which the initial segment of a series determines the remainder of the series) for the prediction of a series of events (in which there is no such determination); but it is the problem of applicability in both cases.

This agreement as to the central problem is further attested by the fact that Reichenbach, like Kant, identifies it with the problem raised by Hume, although Reichenbach thinks of the Humean dilemma primarily as a threat to the concept of induction, while Kant thinks of it primarily as a threat to the concept of causal necessity and thus to the validity of "human reason" [30] (including science). Reichenbach is concerned rather with induction as establishing something short of causal necessity but nevertheless scientifically valid; yet he sees that even a probable inference from past to future is in need of justification as a synthetic assumption about events, and finds "the logic of science . . . a failure so long as we have no theory of induction which is not exposed to Hume's criticism." [31] In that case, "science might as well not be continued"; for "if there is no justification for the inductive inference, the working procedure of science . . . can no longer be justified by the applicability of its results for the purpose of actions." (I.e., we cannot infer future applicability in action from past applicability in action.) Reichenbach recognizes, moreover, that "It was the intention of Kant's synthetic a priori to secure this working procedure against Hume's doubts"; and, since he is sure that "Kant's attempt at rescue failed," because "the formalistic conception of logic" has shown the impossibility of a synthetic a priori, he sets out to find a substitute form of rescue "within the frame of logistic formalism." [32]

What, then, are we to substitute for the synthetic a priori? How is Reichenbach's "inductive principle," analytically derived but stating something synthetic nevertheless, to be differentiated from the synthetic a priori? *"Although the inductive inference,"* says Reichenbach,

is not a tautology, the proof that it leads to the best posit is based on tautologies only. The . . . "something new" furnished by the inference is not maintained as a true statement but as our best posit . . .

In other words—more specifically, in Kantian words—it is maintained not as a constitutive principle but as a regulative principle. The principle that would be synthetic a priori if it were a "statement" is permissible under a "formal conception of logic" if the synthetic element is only a "posit." The nature of the posit, moreover, is determined by "the logical relation of the procedure to the aim of knowledge." [33] For Reichenbach, as for Kant, the synthetic a priori element in knowledge reduces to the "posit," or "regulative" assumption, that knowledge is possible.

Thus, in a manner so Kantian that Reichenbach himself is compelled to take note of the unwelcome resemblance, the occurrence of events amenable to systematic treatment (of the kind required for induction) is "a necessary condition of knowledge." [34] Such events *may* not occur; but if they do not, there can be no prediction and hence no knowledge. This is why we must apply a principle of whose success we have no advance assurance, based on an assumption of whose truth we have no assurance. We can have no knowledge except where the assumption is true and the application successful, and we cannot find out where this is the case except by trying out our "posit" that it is. If the posit proves to be unwarranted, the venture fails; but then it could not have been successful by any other means either. "It is the concept of necessary condition on which our reasoning is based." [35]

Reichenbach attempts to differentiate his concept of "a necessary condition of knowledge" from Kant's, by pointing out that in his own view "this quality of the inductive principle does not spring from any a priori qualities of human reason but has its origin in other sources" —the definition of predictability and the "usual practice of language" to which we want our definition to have some degree of relevance. Thus no "restriction or . . . renunciation of predictability in another form" is signified.[36] We may well question, however, the extent of these differences. Surely the derivation of the inductive principle from a definition (that of predictability, which for Reichenbach is an element in all knowledge) is a derivation a priori; and surely the "usual practice of language" determining that definition is itself determined, at least in part, by the mental processes of the beings who communicate in terms of it and who have developed it for that purpose. The "qualities of human reason," of course, are not as they are because of any "a priori" determination; indeed, as we have seen, it is questionable whether Kant so regards them. They are, however, a priori in relation to our knowledge, to the extent that we must use them in knowing anything at all. Surely the fact that we must use our own minds, just the kind of minds that we have, in order to know anything, is no "renunciation" of knowledge "in another form," any more than Reichenbach's definition of predictability is a renunciation of anything. Indeed, the former is implied by the latter; for, if the definition of predictability is to be restricted by the claims of relevance, as Reichenbach admits, the relevance in question is surely relevance to the nature of *human* experience.

Because the nature of human experience can be accounted for genetically, in empirical terms, the a priori (tautological) principles determining the "best posit" can be seen all the more readily to be inherent in it; for successful prediction is clearly essential to human life and development. This idea, which we have seen thoroughly worked out by Lewis, Reichenbach develops with an interesting twist of his own. Most people, he observes, believe in induction through habit, as Hume supposed, and not through logical analysis. Consequently, they believe that induction *will* succeed, although logical analysis justifies only the belief that it will succeed *if* success is possible at all. Both beliefs, however, determine the same course of action, so that the difference does not matter practically.

This happy coincidence is certainly to be explained by Darwin's idea of selection; those animals were to survive whose habits of belief corresponded to the most useful instrument for foreseeing the future.[37]

This is why a nontautological (synthetic) inductive inference can be proved tautologically (a priori) to be the "best posit"—i.e., why a method for discovering empirical truth can be validated by a logical proof—with some chance of success, some assurance that true conclusions will sometimes actually result.

By "the aim of knowledge," here, Reichenbach clearly means accurate empirical prediction. Is this, then, the point at which we may find his ultimate divergence from Kant, for whom the final goal of knowledge is conceptual, a systematic unification enabling us to understand (and therefore also to predict) empirical events? There is, indeed, a difference in emphasis; but closer consideration will show us that, for Reichenbach as for Kant, the two aims are interrelated; that, in the very process of observing and predicting, we build up the conceptual system in terms of which our experience is progressively unified and understood, making further prediction possible.

When, in order either to explain or to predict a particular event, we demonstrate its "necessity" relative to initial conditions in terms of a physical law, those initial conditions, according to Reichenbach, must include all the knowledge that we already possess.[38] This is equally true, of course, when the law states a probability and the weight which we necessarily assign to the event is therefore short of certainty. In both cases, all the given conditions have "initial weight" determined by "the whole system of knowledge"; [39] the induction from them to predicted events has a weight determined by a "concatenated induction" involving other similar inductions and so again "the whole concatenation of knowledge"; [40] and the choice among scientific theories, when several can explain the data, is made on the basis of "the general body of knowledge, in the face of which some explanations appear more probable than others." [41] Clearly, when "The system of knowledge is written in the language of probability logic," [42] it is still a *system* of knowledge—just what Reichenbach calls it.

To this system, moreover, laws which are merely statistical present no threat. Nor need observations which disappoint our expectations, even on the basis of such laws, be excluded; for the improbable may happen. Only where a series of relative frequencies fails to conform to *any* limit, however low, does the system fail; and then it still applies regulatively, for we can still seek other series in which the same events may be included more successfully. And since subatomic occurrences do follow statistical and probable laws, even though they do not follow universal and causal ones, the fundamental Kantian concept of a physical system as a progressive conceptual unification of empirical data can be expanded to include such occurrences and need not be negated by them. Reichenbach, indeed, seems rather carelessly to claim more than this, in speaking of "every case" as "incorporated in the whole concatenation of knowledge"; [43] for no one has, at any given time, systematized all human knowledge—or even all of his own knowledge—into a complete "concatenation," nor is there any assurance that every case can be included. It is sufficient, however, if Reichenbach's more moderate claim is true—that we cannot know in advance, in respect to any particular case, that success is impossible.[44]

Unfortunately, there is one area in which, according to Reichenbach's analysis, we may indeed be said to know in advance that success is impossible. When we proceed from the statistical laws of quantum mechanics to the theoretical explanation of them, we find two interpretations, one in terms of waves and one in terms of particles. Each is required to explain a different set of phenomena, the two are mutually contradictory, and no empirical test is possible.[45] In other words, not even a probable determination is available, and we cannot even set out to find one. Here, then, we have a breakdown of *all* system, Reichenbach's as well as Kant's. As Reichenbach aptly points out, "That atomic occurrences are controlled by probability laws, and not by causal laws, appears as a relatively harmless result if compared with the . . . anomalies" involved here.[46]

Surely we have here, when we reach the level of comprehensiveness at which both theories must be taken into account simultaneously, no explanation and no conceptual understanding at all. We may overcome the idea that continuous objects and causal laws are required for all physical explanation, but hardly the idea that logical consistency is required for all explanation; for explanation seems to require logical consistency *by definition*. Does this mean that we must admit a specific limit of explanation, a limit beyond which systematically organized concepts are known to be inapplicable to empirical data and therefore have not even a "regulative" validity?

In the midst of a lengthy justification of the dual interpretation in quantum mechanics, Reichenbach reverts to the belief that this situation cannot, after all, be final. The success of physics on this basis, he declares, does not prove

that contradiction is irrelevant for physical theories and that only the observational success matters . . . I rather think it proves that the discovery of new ideas follows other laws than laws of logical order; . . . that contradictory theories can be helpful only because there exists, though unknown at that time, a better theory which comprehends all observational data and is free from contradictions.[47]

Here, again, it is Reichenbach who claims too much. Surely this synthetic a priori assumption that *there exists* such a coherent and comprehensive theory, waiting to be discovered, is far more rationalistic than Kant's unifying "ideal of pure reason" conceived as "regulative" only. Even the different assumption that it is possible to construct such a theory for "all observational data," which is probably what Reichenbach means, is neither required nor warranted. What we need is only Kant's assumption that, although such a complete conceptual ordering of all data is *not* possible, *progress in the direction* of such unification is just what we mean by knowledge. The assumption that such progress is possible is merely the assumption that knowledge is possible.

And of course we cannot really know that a logically consistent theory resolving the contradictions is *not* possible. Reichenbach himself suggests that a new logic may be devised, giving us a new conception of what is required for logical consistency.[48] Thus he recognizes that, where a contradiction exists, there is a situation which we do not understand; and that the direction which knowledge must take (in order to be knowledge) is that of the elimination of contradictions, the increase of understanding, over a more comprehensive area of empirical application and on a higher level of abstraction.

Not the least interesting feature of the parallels between Reichenbach and Kant is the fact that the former is so un-Kantian a philosopher when his work is viewed as a whole and on its own terms. Unlike Lewis, he acknowledges no special debt to Kant, and does not think in terms of the Kantian concepts, such as (for instance) the establishment of a categorial structure. The Kantian features which we have seen in his work generally are those which follow from his acceptance of the general Kantian heritage of naturalistic philosophy today—the distinction between the analytic and the synthetic or existential, and the conceptual factor in all knowledge.

Yet his theory of probability turns out to be quite precisely an adaptation of the Kantian theory of knowledge to the kind of knowledge that current science provides. It takes as its point of departure the assumed validity of science and Hume's challenge to that validity. After analyzing the logical structure of scientific laws, it works out deductively an abstract logic and a theory of the application of that logic (induction) from which such laws will result. It justifies the empirical application of the deductive system by means of an assumption, itself synthetic but analytically required by the aim of knowledge (which in turn is set by the nature of our mental capacities); and that assumption is to be tried out wherever we hope for knowledge, i.e., to be applied as far as possible, or "regulatively," because its applicability is a "necessary condition" without which there can be no knowledge. Thus knowledge is a system; more specifically, the incorporation of as much empirical material as possible in a logical structure (that of probability logic). The aim of knowledge, then, which Reichenbach would say is prediction, may also be expressed as that systematization which both explains and predicts those events that are understandable and predictable; and the two characteristics are interdependent.

Thus Kant's "synthetic a priori" is clearly seen as the assumption that the analytic and a priori, i.e., logic, including probability logic, is applicable to the synthetic and empirical. It is seen as an assumption, not an assertion, although we can assert it as true wherever we do in fact have knowledge, because the application of logical structure to empirical data (deductively or inductively) is just what we mean by knowledge. This formulation is easily seen to cover the views of Kant, Lewis, and Reichenbach equally, although with differences of emphasis; and so we see that Kant's concept is clarified and extended, but not abandoned, by the later philosophers. Nor can it be abandoned, as long as we accept both the distinction between the analytic and synthetic and the role of both in knowledge.

Those who regard Kant as the great rationalistic antagonist naturally see the Kantian element in the work of others much more readily than in their own. Thus Reichenbach finds that

It is to be regretted seriously that Bertrand Russell . . . has apparently become the advocate of a synthetic a priori in the theory of probability and induction. He believes that induction presupposes "an extra-logical principle not based on experience" (p. 412). But if knowledge is interpreted as a system of posits, no such principle is needed.[49]

Yet Russell's "postulates of scientific inference," which together constitute this presupposition, are no more synthetic a priori than Reichenbach's "principle of induction," nor are "postulates" distinguishable from "posits" (even though Russell in turn inveighs against Reichenbach's use of the latter). Both postulates and posits are determined a priori by the definition of knowledge, and both would be synthetic assertions if they were asserted at all. They are, however, merely *assumed* (or "postulated" or "posited"—or, indeed, "regulative") in the procedures of knowledge, and are valid to whatever extent knowledge turns out to be valid. Thus knowledge, as Russell views it, *is* based on posits; his "postulates" are an alternative analysis, and a very enlightening one, of the implied contents of the ultimate "blind posit" (or synthetic a priori "regulative" principle) that conceptual systems are empirically applicable—that our knowledge is valid.

Is it possible, however, that our knowledge is *not* valid? Reichenbach, recognizing "that the posits of the highest level are always blind posits," and that the "appraised weights" of other posits depend on them, concludes that "the system of knowledge, as a whole, is a blind posit . . . The uncertainty of knowledge as a whole therefore penetrates to the simplest posits we can make . . ." [50] Kant, on the other hand, seems to assume without real question that we do have valid knowledge; yet even he, though so often accused of too much certainty, also recognizes a sense in which the entire system of knowledge may be regarded as "blind," i.e., in relation to "things in themselves" as distinguished from our experience of things. To the extent that the relation—or lack of relation—to "things in themselves" is relevant to knowledge at all (as we shall soon see that it is), we have here, too, a foundation of ignorance, underlying and penetrating all knowledge, one with which Reichenbach's "blind posit"—in effect, at least, if not in structure—has much in common. Both Kant's concept and Reichenbach's indicate that knowledge is a self-contained system, having only a tenuous, "blind" relation to anything outside that system.

Reichenbach, of course, might argue that his "blind posit" is about future experience to be incorporated into the system of knowledge, and not about anything outside all experience; and that therefore the concept of anything outside the system is, at the very least, irrelevant. He might even say that it is meaningless. Yet it often becomes evident that he cannot altogether believe this; nor can most of the other present-day philosophers by whom the Kantian concept of "things in themselves" is so much maligned and misunderstood. The reasons why they cannot, the extent to which the Kantian concept (or something very similar) is implicit in their own views, the difficulties and ambiguities which clear analysis and acceptance of such a concept could eliminate, are important matters for our investigation. The central problem involved, we shall see, is a direct consequence of the Kantian epistemological structure which we have been considering, and which, it is now apparent, his present-day successors essentially share. Its clarification, moreover, can shed considerable light both on Kant himself and on his successors today.

Things: As Known & in Themselves

To RECOGNIZE the problem with which we are faced, we must re-
capitulate, at this point, *the kind of world* that confronts us as
a consequence of the Kantian epistemological structure insofar as
that structure is widely accepted today; i.e., the kind of world that
confronts us as a consequence of the clear-cut distinction between
the analytic and the synthetic and of the resulting conceptualization
of experience and the objects of experience.

Such a world, clearly, is analyzable into two elements, one of which
is known analytically (or a priori) and the other synthetically (or
empirically). Since only the latter type of knowledge can indicate
the existence of anything, it follows that the entire rational element,
the element of conceptual structure to be found in even the simplest
experience of everyday objects, is an abstract construction. It is not
a thing, not an event, but is real only by virtue of its applicability
to something that exists or occurs. What exists or occurs is what
we experience by means of our senses, as distinguished from any conceptual element; and whether or not it is ever actually found apart
from any conceptual element, it is distinguishable from any such
element by inspection of any human experience.

This rather simple analysis, fairly commonplace today (though
not when Kant introduced it), has a curious consequence which is
not always noted. The bare content of sensory awareness (with which
we are left when the entire conceptual content of cognitive experience is abstracted), the sole concrete, *existential* element in our experience, is also the *subjective* element. Its nature is determined, at
least in part, by the nature of our sensory apparatus, and it could
not exist at all if there were no beings capable of sensation. Indeed,

our own sense perceptions are thus dependent upon our own *individual* sensory apparatus. The *objective* element in our experience, on the other hand, that which transforms the mere content of experience into an object of experience, is the *abstract* element. The sensations of various individuals may differ, and our own sense perceptions of the same object may never be identically repeated; but when they can be incorporated into one conceptual structure related analytically to a definition of the object, we have a continuous, identifiable object in a common world.

It is here that we are confronted by a perplexing question. What *is* there, apart from the content of consciousness? Physical objects? Existentially, these *are* the content of consciousness; for, to the extent that they are more than that, they are conceptual abstractions, and cannot be said to exist at all. The "existence" of a physical object is the applicability of an abstract concept, or definition, to actually occurring events; and if these are objective physical events, in the first instance, they in turn are defined by abstract concepts, and "exist," or actually occur, as subjective events to which these concepts are applicable. (Lewis's analysis of objective or "non-terminating" judgments in terms of "terminating judgments" makes this essentially Kantian notion quite clear, in more modern terms than Kant's.)

A world that is a combination of the subjective and the abstract is an "objective" world in terms of human experience. Kant, indeed, *defines* objectivity in terms of this combination, speaking of "the only objects in regard to which our knowledge can possess objective reality, that is, in respect of which there is an intuition corresponding to the concepts." [1] In his view, "*Understanding* and *sensibility* . . . can determine objects *only when they are employed in conjunction*." [2] This "objective" world is not, nevertheless, a world existing independently of human experience. If there were no human beings, having the kind of experience that our physiological structure and mental processes determine, not only would there be no sensory occurrences, but also—unless we resort to a Platonic rationalism which our initial premises (and Kant's) have made impossible—there would be no concepts. In short, there would be no objects; there would be *nothing* that is part of that world which is the object of our experience. This means that our world, if we accept the analytic-synthetic distinction and its consequences, is a *phenomenal* world—

which is just what Kant says it is. The only question is, then, whether there is anything non-phenomenal in any way indicated by it.

Most naturalistic philosophers today, although they accept the analytic-synthetic distinction and the consequent analysis of the physical world in terms of sensation and applicable abstraction, are quite unwilling to accept the label of phenomenalism which they sometimes attempt to attach to each other; yet they are also unwilling to take Kant's avenue of escape from it, the doctrine of non-phenomenal "things in themselves." A simple review of the premises which they share with Kant, however, may already have shown us that their attempts to find an escape from phenomenalism entirely *within* the physical world as known, i.e., within the *objects of experience* as such, are necessarily doomed to failure, and can lead only to inconsistency and confusion. We shall now see how this works out; the analysis of the Kantian concept itself will be more interesting and significant after we see more precisely how and why that concept is needed.

Here, once more, it is highly instructive to consider the point of view expressed by Einstein. Just because he was a scientist and not a philosopher, although a scientist interested in and articulate about the philosophical aspects of his scientific work, his difficulties with the concept of "reality" or a "real external world" may serve to indicate the needs of contemporary science itself in this respect.

"The belief in an external world independent of the perceiving subject," Einstein says, "is the basis of all natural science." [3] Just what he means by such a statement, however, is extremely difficult to pin down. According to his analysis of knowledge, we may recall, both physical objects and scientific theories are products, on different levels of abstraction, of one process—the "free creation" of concepts and their ultimate application to sense perceptions.[4] In this context, "every assertion of a theory lays claim to 'objective meaning' (within the framework of the theory)," [5] although the theory itself acquires "cognitive value" only through some connection with "sensible experience." [6] The theory, in other words, is a definition of reality, or objectivity; and applicability to sense perceptions renders the definition valid as a means of cognition, or knowledge of something existent.

Very often, nevertheless, Einstein quite clearly thinks of the "external world," or "reality," as something *known by means of* conceptual constructs, not as constituted by them. The "axiomatic basis of physics" is identified with "our concept of the structure of reality," [7] not with that structure itself; and a "distinction" is drawn "between the objective reality, which is independent of any theory, and the physical concepts with which the theory operates." [8] Scientific theory is characterized as a "representation of real things," [9] a "model of reality . . . which represents things themselves and not merely the probability of their occurrence." [10]

What, then, is this "reality" which science "represents," and what represents it—the conceptual structure, the sense data, or both? One might suppose that the sense data must be "reality," or at least its "representatives," since they have been said to provide the sole "cognitive value" of any theory; yet sense data are also classified as "psychic experiences of a special kind," [11] and are said to provide "information of this external world or of 'physical reality'" only "indirectly." [12] Are there, then, *relations* between sense data, existing somehow independently of knowledge, which the conceptual structure attempts to represent? Einstein does say that "the empirical contents and their mutual relations must find their representation in the conclusions of the theory"; [13] but he also contradicts this view, asserting that scientific theories set up logical connections between phenomena which have *no* connection in experience.[14]

Moreover, the notion that the conceptual structure of science "represents" anything at all, or—a vaguer alternative often asserted by Einstein—that it is a means by which we "grasp" reality,[15] or even that it is itself a predetermined "right way" of interpreting nature which has a reality of its own and which "we are capable of finding," [16] all seem obviously to contradict Einstein's frequent characterization of that structure as "fictitious," a "free creation," a "free invention of the mind." Einstein tries to reconcile the contradiction by explaining, at one point, that the scientist's "liberty of choice" is not that of a "writer of fiction" but that of a man solving a word puzzle. "He may, it is true, propose any word as the solution; but, there is only *one* word which really solves the puzzle in all its parts." [17] This does not seem, however, to be quite what we ordinarily mean by "invention"—or, indeed, what Einstein himself often appears to mean. There seems to be no way of reconciling all of Einstein's statements about "reality."

What is the difficulty behind all this confusion? In Einstein's very Kantian analysis of *knowledge* which we considered earlier, there is no confusion at all. There, however, we find a world which is in large part "invented" by the human mind and whose reality is analytically determined by the criteria of the invented system itself; and Einstein is not quite satisfied that this kind of "reality" is all there is. It is the reality that distinguishes physical objects of knowledge from illusions; but what about *independent existence*—a reality existing whether or not there is human knowledge or human beings? Einstein distorts his otherwise coherent and lucid analysis of knowledge in the attempt to locate this element within it; but actually it cannot be so located, but must be added outside it, as Kant saw.

There are involved, then, two very different meanings of the term "reality," both of which accord with common linguistic uses; and the term may readily be used in both senses interchangeably, with confusing results, unless the distinction is noted. That distinction, however, is none other than Kant's very unpopular one between the "phenomenal world," or things as known, and "things in themselves," both of which may be regarded as "real" in different senses of the term.

This conclusion may suggest that perhaps a scientist is not, after all, the one most expert in analyzing a philosophical concept of this sort, with which science need not concern itself at all. We may suppose that philosophers, aware of the structure of science which Einstein points out but looking at it from the outside, may provide a more satisfactory answer—perhaps one more satisfactory to science itself. And so, temporarily refraining from attaching too much weight to Einstein's opinion, we shall return to the consideration of those philosophers today who, like Einstein, accept the Kantian epistemological premises and see by what means and with what degree of success they avoid the Kantian conclusion as to "things in themselves." We shall continue to consider Lewis and Reichenbach primarily, since they are representative contemporary philosophers whose direct relation to Kant we now have clearly in mind; but the results will be more enlightening if we refer briefly to some other alternatives also, to see whether there is any way out of the difficulty which both Lewis and Reichenbach overlook.

We may readily begin, then, with the positivist view, which Reichenbach sets forth very clearly for us before he proceeds to attack it. Here we find perhaps the simplest analysis of the physical object, and one whose essential agreement with the views of both Kant and Einstein should be easily apparent. This analysis, Reichenbach tells us, proceeds from the concept of "impressions as basic facts of knowledge." Since only impressions can be directly observed, only sentences about impressions can be directly verified; and only through verification do we have knowledge.[18] To this starting point, the positivist analysis applies the *"truth theory of meaning,"* which states that *"two sentences have the same meaning if they obtain the same determination as true or false by every possible observation."* [19] Thus propositions about physical objects, which are indirectly verified by sense impressions, have the same meaning as the corresponding propositions about the impressions. When we say "There is a table," we are making an inference from various sensations; therefore "The table exists" and "I have impressions of such and such kinds" are equivalent in meaning. The "indirect sentence" (i.e., one not mentioning impressions directly) is "reducible" to "direct sentences" (i.e., "impression sentences").[20] Since all meaning is to be found in verifiability by impressions, the meaning of any "indirect sentence" must be found "by constructing the observation propositions from which the indirect proposition is inferred"; this is called the *"principle of retrogression."* [21]

Once more, then, we find sense impressions identified as cognitions of a physical object through incorporation in a deductive conceptual system; for it is the deducibility of the existence of the object and the existence of the impressions from each other that constitutes their "equivalence." Existentially, the object is the impressions; in the sense in which it is also a conceptual *system* of impressions, identifiable by a definition denoting some impressions and not others, it is an abstraction. "The existence of concreta is to be reduced to the existence of impressions in the same way as the existence of abstracta is reduced to the existence of concreta." [22] Objects, in other words, in the sense in which we distinguish them from impressions, are abstractions; what we usually call "abstractions," as distinguished from objects, are merely abstractions on a higher logical level.

Thus we have, as we anticipated, a world of impressions and abstractions only. This result, moreover, has followed directly from the development of the Kantian doctrines that all existential knowledge is synthetic and that a physical object is to be identified by the conformity of sense perceptions to a conceptual structure. The phenomenalism implicit in this view is clearly pointed out by Reichenbach. Our impressions obviously do not persist after our death; therefore, neither do physical objects whose existence *is* the existence of our impressions.[23] Nor does inclusion of other people's impressions help much; for the inference from our own impressions to those of other people seems even less "permissible" than the inference to the "independent existence" of physical things; and in any event, the difficulty would still remain as to the existence of anything before or after the existence of mankind.[24] All of Reichenbach's departures from the positivist view are based on this recognition of and objection to its implicit phenomenalism. Whether his own alternative overcomes this difficulty, however, remains to be seen.

Reichenbach rejects in positivism both the "impression basis" and the means of proceeding from that basis—the truth theory of meaning and the resulting principle of retrogression. As contrasted with the "impression basis," we may recall his view that the subject matter of our immediate awareness is not sense impressions, but "concreta" —"immediately existing things . . . entering into our knowledge without any intellectual operations being performed by us." [25] From these the existence of impressions is "inferred" as part of the same process by which we construct physical objects.[26] It is the mistaken attempt to explain knowledge as built on subjective impressions, Reichenbach believes, that creates the insoluble "existence problem" in regard to the objective "external world"; for any inference from "events . . . of my private world" to "things of an independent existence" is uncertain, and we become uncertain as to whether there are such things at all.[27]

There are many difficulties in this view, but we need not consider them; for, however we may identify or describe the data of immediate awareness, it is their status *as such data* that makes of them a "private world." Awareness is always someone's awareness; the immediate is always immediate to someone and inaccessible to others. *Recognition* that such data are private as given, whatever status we may subsequently or simultaneously attribute to them, of course requires "intellectual operations"; but that is not the point at issue. If they are indeed "things, or states of things" [28] as well as data, surely that fact cannot be known immediately either.

Can it, then, be inferred? As we have already seen, it is by a process of conceptual construction of physical laws and inference from them that Reichenbach explains the sorting out of our data into objective and subjective, real and unreal, in accordance with the concept of a physical object.[29] This is quite different, however, from any inference as to "things of an independent existence," if we mean independent of both the perceptions and the intellectual operations of any observer. Reichenbach, recognizing this lack, is not satisfied with such an analysis, which up to this point he shares with the positivists. Consequently, he superimposes upon it an essentially different view, in which our conceptual construction is such that "the world is doubled," and "impressions within me" *correspond,* some more accurately than others and some not at all, with the independently existing physical world.[30] Those "immediate things" classified as subjective are now subdivided into those which have a "coupled objective thing" (e.g., perceptual errors, as when we mistake a bush for a man) and those which have none (e.g., dreams); while objective things, unlike subjective ones, may be either "immediate" also (i.e., perceived) or not.[31]

There is, of course, a serious discrepancy involved here. We are told, on one hand, that objective things, when observed, *are* immediate things; this, indeed, is Reichenbach's purpose in identifying the initial data as "immediate things" rather than as "impressions." On the other hand, we are told that our sensory "impressions"— which must surely be regarded as our means of knowing objects— are subjective things "within me," providing correct knowledge when they are correctly "coupled" with objective things. This would have the strange consequence that the immediate things (or data) which are not subjective are not impressions. Moreover, either the objective things with which our veridical impressions are coupled must be the same ones that we know as immediate things (in which case the impressions are superfluous), or they must be different ones (in which case we have two physical worlds rather than one).

Such a position is, of course, totally untenable. Therefore, in spite of Reichenbach's insistence on the concept of "concreta," or "immediate things," as a means of avoiding an "existence problem" as to the objective world, we find that the *objective* immediate things soon drop out completely; "even the concreta are only subjective things, of the type to which an objective thing of different form is co-ordinated." Their "correspondence is closer" than in the case of illusions, but "there always remains a deviation . . . it is a substitute world in which we live." [32] But how can we tell when the correspondence is closer, since we cannot get outside the "substitute world" to make the comparison? For Kant, this "substitute world" *is* the real physical world, both objective and knowable because constructed by standard human cognitive equipment. For Reichenbach, who sees the need for "things of an independent existence" but insists that physical objects must be those things, the physical world itself becomes inaccessible to knowledge—just the consequence that Kant regards as inevitable if we take "phenomena" to be "things in themselves."

Reichenbach has, however, another device for establishing an independently existing world, a device that he regards as valid and effective whatever may be the nature of the primitive data. This device, which involves his second major disagreement with positivism, is a method of inferring the objective world from the data (whether these are "impressions" or "concreta"), in such a way that its existence independent of the data is automatically inferred also. The method is called by Reichenbach "projective construction," or simply "projection"; and it is intended to provide his conclusive alternative to phenomenalism.

Reichenbach argues that the existence of a physical object is not equivalent in meaning to the occurrence of the observations from which it is inferred, because it also means other observations which may (or may not) occur in the future. Indeed, it has a infinite number of such implications, and thus its meaning cannot be exhausted by any finite set of observations; it has a "surplus meaning" not equivalent to them and therefore not deducible from them. The type of inference by which we proceed from observations to the prediction of other observations not included among the premises and not certain to occur, is the *probability* inference; and indeed, we are well aware that the inference from our observations to the existence of a physical object, although highly probable, is sometimes mistaken. It is also possible, though very improbable, that the physical object may exist without the occurrence of the observations which we should expect. For "physical truth meaning," therefore, Reichenbach substitutes "physical probability meaning" as a formulation of what we mean when we say that a physical object exists. [33]

This method of constructing a physical object from empirical observations is what Reichenbach calls "projection." The physical object is not a "reducible complex" of the observations; it is not equivalent, or *reducible*, to them; but it is a "projective complex" of the observations, co-ordinated with them by a probability connection. Thus the object does "mean" the set of observations, and vice versa, in the sense of "physical probability meaning"; but this is not an equivalence, since one *may* exist without the other. Each, therefore, must have "an independent existence." [34] Just *what* has this independent existence remains to be seen.

By means of this same concept, Reichenbach claims (in opposition to the positivists) a difference in meaning for theories all of whose empirical consequences are identical. Since theories are not equivalent, or reducible, to the observations on which they are based, but merely probable inferences from the observations, they may be distinguished from each other by the different *weights* of the inferences. Here, again, the independent existence of objects is maintained. When two sets of observations are co-ordinated in experience, we may assume either the theory that one set causes the other or the theory that there is an outside cause of both. The same series of impressions, therefore, may be interpreted either in terms of the earlier causing the later, or in terms of a persisting physical object causing all of them; but these two interpretations do not mean the same thing, because the latter is more probable (i.e., has more weight).[35] The persistence of physical objects after my death does not mean the same thing as their existence only during my life, even though my impressions of them would be the same in both cases, because the former alternative is more probable (since objects have persisted after the death of many other people).[36]

To find out what is wrong here, we may begin with the concept of "probability meaning." Just what is the "surplus meaning" involved, beyond the meaning in terms of the observational premises? There are, of course, future observations which are predicted by the assertion of the existence of a physical object on the basis of past observations; probable (or inductive) inferences do, while deductive inferences do not, lead to such predictions about the occurrence of events not included in the premises. Then, however, we have still not left the observational field.

On the other hand, Reichenbach's analysis also implies that it is the uncertainty of the predictions that is important, that "probability meaning" differs from "truth meaning" by including the predicted

observations that do *not* occur, as well as those that do, since both
sets have been legitimately regarded as "probable." But what *are*
events that do not occur? Surely nonexistent events cannot add to
the *existential* content of any conceptual structure; on the contrary,
it is only in terms of a conceptual structure that we can significantly
speak of probable or possible observations which do not occur. When
we turn to Lewis's view, we shall find a far-reaching clarification of
this point and revelation of its extreme importance.

Meaning in terms of conceptual structure enters the picture, though
rather obscurely, through Reichenbach's argument that meaning is
"a function of propositions," not a "something" to which a proposition refers; that, indeed, it would be better to say that a proposition
"is significant," rather than that it has meaning. All we need to know
is the conditions under which a proposition has meaning and those
under which two propositions have the same meaning; "we need
not know what the meaning is." If Reichenbach is saying here, as
he appears to be saying, that a proposition does not *refer to* any actual events, his "functional theory of meaning" directly contradicts
the "verifiability theory of meaning" in which he intends to incorporate it. His attempt to reconcile the two views by admitting the
reference to impressions as an "intuitive representation" of meaning, though not as constituting meaning, seems only to confuse the
issue further.[37]

Neither concept, moreover, justifies the odd notion of difference
in weight without difference in consequences, by which Reichenbach
claims to give both meaning and validity to his assertion of the independent existence of objects. In assigning to this assertion more
"weight" (or probability) than to the contrary assertion that objects
consist only of impressions, he argues from his own observation of
the persistence of objects after the death of others; [38] but all that
he can infer in this manner is their continued observation by others
after his own death, not their existence at a time when there may be
no observers. We still have an *empirical* inference, with consequences
in terms of observation. Indeed, if "weight" is equated with "predic-
tional value," [39] it seems self-contradictory to assert that propositions
which do not differ in any possible empirical consequences can differ
in weight, or that we can give meaning, on this basis, to any distinction between objects and their verifications.

The same difficulty is revealed in a different manner when Reichenbach uses his analogy of two synchronized sets of shadow pictures, explainable in terms either of one set's causing the other or of an external cause of both. Reichenbach assigns more "weight" to the theory of an external cause, even though its predictions are identical with those of the other theory and thus not more probable, merely because external causes have been found in similar situations in the past.[40] Yet we may remember that the assignment of "weight" to a theory on the basis of similarity to established explanations of similar situations is carefully analyzed by Reichenbach as a "cross-induction"; from the success of similar theories in the past, we predict that the theory in question will probably be successful also. If the theory in question, then, cannot be either more or less successful than its competitor, if it has no distinctive empirical consequences to predict, there seems to be nothing that a cross-induction can predict about it. (We cannot predict that the external cause will be found, because Reichenbach has ruled out that possibility, to preserve the analogy with the theory of an independent object as the cause of our impressions.)

If we cannot avoid the belief that, nevertheless, the theory analogous to other theories would still be the one chosen, that choice must be justifiable on some grounds other than its superior weight or probability; and of course there are such grounds. It would be chosen because it would fit more manageably into the conceptual structure of a world about which similar theories are already asserted. This is true also of the assertion of the existence of permanent physical objects; such an assertion is *not* "probable" (or improbable), but gives a standardized, communicable conceptual structure to our experience which the series of impressions alone, without such conceptualization, would lack. (The assertion that a particular kind of physical object exists at a particular time and place would, of course, assert the empirical applicability of the concept under actual circumstances. It would, therefore, have empirical consequences, and therefore also a "weight," or degree of probability.)

It is in this sense—i.e., in terms of conceptual construction—that meaning may perhaps be regarded as "a function of propositions." Then, however, the physical object meant is also "a function of propositions." The object exists, therefore, only in the sense that "objective existence is a determinate logical function of subjective existence." [41] It is impressions, in other words, that exist; and the "objectivity" of the object consists of an abstract system, which "exists" only through its applicability to impressions.

This is hardly the "independent existence," the escape from "phenomenalism," that Reichenbach was to establish through his concept of "probability meaning"; rather, it is the Kantian phenomenal object once more. Nor need this surprise us; for Reichenbach himself has taught us that the system of probability logic is an abstract, analytic system, though applicable in inductive operations. Naturally, then, the object conceived in terms of probability logic turns out to be an abstract construction just as inevitably as the object conceived in terms of deductive logic, though perhaps a somewhat more flexible one. Moreover, in misplacing the existential element so as to attribute "independent existence" to this abstraction, Reichenbach has misplaced the element of probability as well. It is not meaning that is probable; for meaning, even when it states a probability, is established by definition; only the occurrence of the empirical referents, the relevance of the definition to experience, is probable.

It is evident, then, that Reichenbach's discussion of physical objects involves a great deal of confusion. This confusion arises, we can now see, because, attempting to avoid the "phenomenalism" of the positivist view, he seeks within the physical object some feature to which existence independently of any observer can be attributed; and this is impossible if the object is conceived as empirical data organized in a conceptual system. In Reichenbach's attempt to regard the data themselves as in some sense "things," knowledge becomes subjective and the physical world unknowable. In his attempt to regard the conceptual system as in some sense involving independent existence, that system is cut off from its empirical moorings; knowledge becomes abstract and the empirical world a mere "intuitive representation" of it. In either case, the physical world loses even its phenomenal objectivity, and Reichenbach, like Einstein, throws his own clear and impressive analysis of *knowledge* into confusion in his attempted analysis of *reality*.

Consideration of Lewis's view, if it does not solve all the difficulties, will at least clarify them. For him, we may recall, an assertion about a real physical object is a "non-terminating judgment," equivalent to an infinite ("non-terminating") series of "terminating judgments," or predictions as to the content of experience that will follow if certain conditions are fulfilled; [42] and we know this equivalence analytically, "in knowing what we mean by our affirmation of objective fact." [43] Thus Lewis, like the positivists whom Reichenbach criticizes on this score, interprets "objective statements as meaning what would verify them"; the non-terminating judgment is equivalent to the set of terminating judgments which expresses its possible verifications because "each is deducible from the other." [44] After considering Reichenbach's criticisms of such a view, unsatisfactory as they may be, we must nevertheless wonder whether Lewis has not overlooked thereby the element of probability in empirical knowledge.

We find, however, that Lewis has not overlooked the role of probability, but, on the contrary, has set in order Reichenbach's confused allocation of it. He agrees with Reichenbach that no *actual* set of verifications obtainable by any human knower can ever be equivalent to the objective fact verified. The *possible* empirical verifications implied by any objective statement are inexhaustible; [45] moreover, we cannot go back in time to experience those empirical consequences of the event that could have been experienced in the past, nor can we experience the alternative empirical consequences which would follow if we took alternative actions at a given time. [46] Lewis also agrees with Reichenbach that empirical verifications of an objective statement are never more than probable, not only because of their unavoidable incompleteness, but also because one empirical disconfirmation is not regarded as a conclusive disproof, as it would be if the predicted experience were a deductive consequence of the statement. The objective statement means that, if certain test routines are followed under certain conditions, certain empirical observations will probably follow; and each of the statements as to tests and conditions, being itself an objective statement, must in turn be interpreted in this same manner to reveal its observational meaning. [47] These probability relations, moreover, are learned inductively; and it is because they occur in our experience that we construct and understand concepts which are applicable to them, and whose applicability we assert in our assertions of objective beliefs.

Nevertheless, when we do make these assertions, "such connections are contained" (i.e., analytically, or deductively) "in the objective belief itself: it is *these meanings themselves* which we learn to entertain and to understand from past experience." [48] The objective statement is *equivalent* to a set of "terminating judgments," which are probability statements in terms of sense impressions. Thus the predictions, the factual inferences, are probable and not certain, but meaning is nevertheless definitive and analytic, and the confusions of Reichenbach's conceptions both of "probability *meaning*" and of "physical necessity" are avoided. Indeed, Lewis applies to the interpretation of physical objects the doctrine of probability which is pre-eminently Reichenbach's achievement; and he does so much more clearly and consistently than its own author. Physical objects are analyzed, in the Kantian manner, as logical constructs, ordering and explaining sense data in terms of physical laws. These laws are analytically "necessary" in terms of theories constructed to explain them, and also in terms of their consequences for classes of relevant events; yet they are probable laws (i.e., laws which state probabilities), and their relevance to any particular event is also probable. Obviously, however, this analysis does not break through the circularity of concepts that have existential meaning only in terms of sense data, and sense data that are objective only in terms of appropriate concepts. We must still ask what, if anything, does break through this circularity to establish an independent world.

Lewis, like Reichenbach, often seems to take the position that the data themselves provide the way out of this circularity. In his view, however, they are clearly identified as sense impressions; it is their status as the fundamental and certain subject matter of knowledge that qualifies them for their special role. Objective statements, Lewis says, being only probable, must find their ultimate evidence in data which are given and therefore certain (i.e., which *are* their own evidence); otherwise, we are involved either in an infinite regress of probabilities or in a circularity of mutual coherence. "If anything is to be probable, then something must be certain"; for "objective judgments *none* of which could acquire probability by direct confirmations in experience, would gain no support by leaning up against one another in the fashion of the 'coherence theory of truth.' " [49]

Lewis thus stresses, in this connection, two features of sense impressions, their certainty and their givenness. The former seems to be the less important; for Reichenbach has shown us that a "posit" as to the reliability of initial premises may take the place of actual certainty, and Lewis himself gives up the requirement of certainty in dealing with the data of memory.[50] It is quite true, however, that, if anything is to be probable, something must be *real;* that there must be something for knowledge to be about; that, if our objective knowledge is self-justifying and circular as a standard of objectivity, it is nevertheless an unacceptable standard unless there is an existing subject matter independent of it, to which the standard may relevantly be applied. The fact that our concepts cannot create or change data, however much they may juggle them around, distinguishes knowledge from fiction; and Lewis realizes this when he speaks of "the *givenness* of what is given" as part, at least, of what we mean by "the independence of reality." [51]

This "givenness," this feature of sense data as forcing themselves upon us, is what Kant recognizes as a *"necessary unity* of apperception in the synthesis of intuitions," which "is intended by the copula 'is' . . . even if the judgment is itself empirical, and therefore contingent"—a necessity that is absent from "relation according to laws of the reproductive imagination, which has only subjective validity." [52] It is to be distinguished from that "necessity" which means *"conformity with a rule"* and determines *"relation to an object,"* [53] and which (when the rule is one applying to sequence of perceptions) is identifiable as causality. It is a confusion of the two concepts— the unavoidable character of sensation and the logical necessity of conceptual relations—and a corresponding confusion of givenness and objectivity, that makes Kant's "proof" of causality so difficult to follow. For Kant sometimes seems to be arguing that *all* succession of given sensory material is causal succession, or that every event is the cause of every event immediately following it, while at other times he seems to be arguing, with more consistency and validity, that conformity of a sequence of sense perceptions to some conceptual structure of logically necessary relations distinguishes it as objective, in contrast with nonconforming sequences which are subjective.

This confusion arises very readily because the compulsory character of sense data does seem to constitute objectivity of a sort, as Lewis sees; not objectivity in the sense of belonging to a physical object (since many illusory perceptions are equally inescapable), but objectivity in the sense of originating in some sense independently of us. Yet there is a serious ambiguity in Lewis's statement that "the given is a condition of reality independent of the mind." [54] After all, there could be nothing given if there were no mind to which it could be given; nor could the character of the given be just as it is, if our senses were not as they are. It is through independence of our *volition* alone that sense data arouse in us a rather vague *feeling* of their objectivity. Does this feeling justify us in the assumption that something *existing* independently is "given" through our sense perceptions, or is the sensory content itself, dependent as it is on the nature of our sensory equipment, *all* that is "given"?

In *Mind and the World-Order* Lewis argues at considerable length that the obvious relativity of perception to our senses does not prevent it from revealing veridically the character of the independently real object. The "independent nature" of the object can be known through its relation to the knower, he says, because, although what we know about it is relative, yet the statement of that relation is absolutely true. Moreover, if the object had no character of its own apart from our minds, there would be nothing for our experience to relate to the mind.[55] And we *know* that character; for if we know the mind and the relation, we may infer the object; and we *do* know the mind, just as we know the object, by the nature of our experience. Indeed, the nature of our perceptual experience is "a function of two variables," the subject (or mind) and the object;[56] what we observe depends both on us and on the thing observed.[57] If it depended solely on us, the content of experience would be deducible from the nature of our minds.[58]

Upon closer examination, however, some of this alleged knowledge of independent reality turns out to be merely that conceptual organization of sense data with which our discussion of objects began. We are said to know the independent nature of the object by knowing its relation to mind and also by knowing the nature of mind; but this is a fallacious argument if mind is known (as Lewis makes quite clear) just as we know the object and not prior to our knowledge of the object. For then what we know of both is only their interrelation in experience; they must remain only "variables," neither of which ever has a determinate value because the other has not. Only their relation (i.e., experience) is known. We may, of course, *assign* such values to them as will provide maximum continuity between one experience and the next; in this way the concept of our experience as "a function of two variables" is (as Lewis at one point recognizes) a conceptual means by which we "introduce order into the procession of given presentation,"[59] but not a means of penetrating beyond the given presentation to something existing independently of it. Thus the two variables, like Kant's "transcendental object" (to be discussed later) and "transcendental unity of apperception," are constructs for the ordering of experience in terms of object and subject, not prior existents which experience brings together.

Similarly, the fact that "the content of presentation is an authentic part or aspect or perspective which is ingredient in the objective reality known" (e.g., that "an elliptical appearance may be genuine ingredient of a real round penny") [60] is certainly a fact about that categorial "reality" whose very purpose is the coherent organization of this content into a "physical world" by means of such concepts as "perspective"; for this *is* "the objective reality known." Nothing whatever is indicated here as to any reality independent of knowledge. That the electron which "nobody can perceive" is nevertheless "partially given" in our "experiencing those laboratory phenomena which oblige us . . . to believe in the existence of electrons" is no closer to the point; for it is precisely as a logical construction to explain the "laboratory phenomena" that we "believe in" electrons, and Lewis's analogy with the existence of "the fountain pen in my hand" serves only to impress upon us the conceptual factor in the latter.[61] And Lewis himself asserts that "the validity of understanding does not concern the relation between experience and what is usually meant by 'the independent object'; it concerns the relation between this experience and *other experiences* . . ." [62]

If, however, we assume in addition (as Lewis does) that there *is* an independent world, something besides our sense data and our abstract logical constructions, something existing whether it is known or not, it appears that Lewis's view of the sense in which we may be said to know that world is much closer than he intends to Kant's view in regard to "things in themselves." He asserts the reality of the physical world on the grounds

(1) that "appearances" themselves must constitute one kind of reality . . . (2) that reality of any sort is definable and meaningful only in terms of *some* experience, actual or hypothetical, and (3) that regardless of the relativity of perception, appearances inevitably are, for a rational understanding, a ground of *true* knowledge of the reality which appears even though that knowledge should be incomplete.[63] (Numerals added.)

With the first of Lewis's points Kant would obviously agree; the "one kind of reality" mentioned here is just what he calls "phenomenal" reality. The third point is taken by Lewis to constitute a denial "that the real object is a *ding an sich*," although there may be things unknowable to us because of "our human limitations." He admits that if we conjecture that reality has aspects forever beyond the reach of human beings, we must do so by the metaphor of some mind differently organized than our own. But when we know that other humans have greater auditory range than ourselves, and can reasonably suppose that insects possess senses which directly register stimuli which we do not, what prevents us from conceiving that there are ranges of the real beyond the direct apprehension of any human, or even of any animal that happens to exist?

Nevertheless, while our "human limitations" do mean a certain amount of inevitable "ignorance," they do not mean any inevitable "error" or "untruth of our knowledge to reality." [64] Lewis apparently believes that Kant's view is otherwise; but we shall soon see, when we consider that view, that it is not.

There remains Lewis's assertion "that reality of any sort is definable and meaningful only in terms of *some* experience, actual or hypothetical." Here, of course, is a characterization of physical, objective reality as "possible experience" with which Kant would agree completely; but in the inclusion of reality *of any sort* in the specifications, there is a prima facie difference from Kant's view of "things in themselves." It is also a difference from Lewis's own view in the passage just quoted. To credit him with as much consistency as we can, we may suppose that he has in mind a distinction between "any human or even any animal that happens to exist" and some being that *might conceivably* exist; it would then be in the latter sense only that "reality of any sort" must be definable as possible experience of some observer. This, however, is the very concept of "some mind differently organized than our own" to which we have just seen Lewis allude as merely a "metaphor"; so that it is obvious that he does not know, here, quite how far he wishes to go in the matter.

In *An Analysis of Knowledge and Valuation*, however, Lewis has reached a clear distinction between belief in "reality which is unknown" and belief in a "thing or fact whch is intrinsically unknowable—which could not be empirically evidenced to any actual or even any supposititious observer." [65] Vigorously disclaiming the latter belief but accepting the former, Lewis carefully builds on that acceptance his proposed escape from phenomenalism and subjectivism. We may wonder whether the distinction can be consistently maintained, and, if so, whether the concept advanced by Lewis is adequate to fulfil the role which he claims for it. If a "supposititious observer" means an observer of a *kind* that does not actually exist, the distinction between the unknown and the unknowable appears pointless; for surely it is as difficult to attribute meaning to the concept of a hypothetical experience of a hypothetical *kind* of observer, the kind being completely unspecified, as it is to attribute meaning to the concept of an unobservable existent in the first place—if indeed the two are not synonymous. On the other hand, if a "supposititious observer" means a possible *human* observer, the distinction makes sense, but appears unjustified; for if there can be existents outside the range of experience of any existing human being, as Lewis's earlier argument demonstrates, why not existents outside the range of experience of any being of the human *kind?* Moreover, although the concept of a possible human observer (which is probably intended) does provide a more determinate "meaning" for the concept of an unobserved but not unobservable existent, does it not, in so doing, turn the "unobserved existent" into an abstract conceptual construction, constitutive of *phenomenal* reality?

In spite of such difficulties, it is through his interpretation of the unknown but knowable (or, more precisely, "the verifiability of what remains unverified") [66] that Lewis makes a genuine and fruitful contribution to our understanding of the physical object, in terms of both the phenomenal and the independently real. It is a contribution which points the way toward a new understanding of the relation between them—an understanding which, although still somewhat obscure, may perhaps be clearer than Kant's own. To this analysis we must now turn.

Lewis here approaches the problem in terms of what we *mean* by objective statements, or statements implying the existence of a physical object. Like the positivists, he accepts the doctrine of "objective statements as meaning what would verify them," which derives, as we have seen, from the Kantian view of physical objects as conceptual (categorial) structures into which sense perceptions can be incorporated in accordance with physical laws. Like Reichenbach, Lewis objects to any implication of an existential *reduction* of objects to sense data; but he has an altogether different method for its elimination, based on his distinction between holophrastic and analytic meaning. His analysis does not, therefore, depend (like Reichenbach's) on the application of a new kind of logic, that of probability, to the relation between data and objects, but rather uses that new understanding which he has given us of the manner in which any logic is empirically applied.

The equivalence between statements about physical objects or events and statements about sense perceptions is an equivalence of "meaning in the sense of intension, for which two empirical statements have the same meaning if each is deducible from the other." Consequently, "what either of them requires to be the case in order to be true is . . . the same as what the other requires to be the case . . ." Nevertheless, two statements equivalent in intension may differ in "analytic meaning"; the *constituent terms* of one may not have the same meaning as the constituent terms of the other, and through these terms the two statements may *refer to* different things or events. The *occurrence* of the objective event (or existence of the physical object) is one fact, or "space-time slab," and the *occurrence* of any observational verification of it (simultaneously or not) is another; thus "phenomenalism" on this score is avoided. Yet a *statement* that the objective event has occurred and a *statement* (or rather an infinite series of statements) that various observations have occurred under certain conditions or would occur under certain other conditions are logically equivalent in meaning (i.e., imply each other) although they do not refer to the same facts.[67] The relation between the statements is deductive, a relation of equivalence; the prediction that the observations will occur, or, equivalently, the inference that the object actually exists, is probable.

We are left, at this point, with an important question still unanswered. What is the "fact" to which the objective statement refers? For that matter, what are the *actual* facts to which the series of observational statements refer? Many of those statements, we have already learned, are hypothetical; they are statements that *if* certain actions were taken under certain conditions, specified observations would follow. Where, then, is the factual reference? It is this latter phase of the problem which Lewis now confronts in illuminating detail.

It is obvious that "the givenness of what is given" cannot, in this connection, constitute what we mean by independent reality, because when the hypothetical action is not in fact taken, nothing is given. Givenness as such is an indispensable *part* of what we mean by the reality of a physical object; but, since that object is to be regarded as existing also when no one is observing it, we must mean, in addition, "the truth of those 'If-then' propositions in which the process of possible experience, starting from the given, could be expressed," and therefore, further, "the transcendence by reality of our present knowledge of it . . ." [68] But what is possible experience, or unknown experience, empirically? In *Mind and the World-Order,* Lewis considers Broad's solution in terms of "unsensed sensa," dismissing it as "verbal nonsense," with the acute observation that it introduces "a new kind of *ding an sich* . . . inappropriately named so as to suggest its phenomenological character." (We shall see, however, whether Lewis himself can avoid introducing a *Ding an sich* of his own—not one like Broad's, but perhaps one more like Kant's.) The existence of an unobserved object, the fact that *"if* any observer *were* there he *would* observe it," Lewis says, means not that "unsensed sensa" exist in the meantime, but "that . . . whenever an observer *is* there he *does* see this." This is the only possible empirical meaning, because no empirical test is possible when no observer is there.[69]

This interpretation, however, is precisely the one which Lewis later rejects, taking great pains, in *An Analysis of Knowledge and Valuation,* to demonstrate its inadequacy. The statement that *if* an observer were there he *would* observe the object means something quite different from the statement that *when* an observer is there he *does* observe the object. It is just because the former statement asserts something that is true *now,* even though no observer is now there, that it can express (along with other similar statements) the meaning of the assertion that an object exists. As Lewis puts it, the relation "If *A* then *E,*" in such cases, is not the relation of "material implication" (which means merely that the consequent cannot be false if the antecedent is true), because it "intends an assertion whose truth or falsity is not affected by the truth or falsity of the hypothesis '*A.*'" This distinction is identifiable with the distinction between "objective reality" and "subjective experience"; for "I believe the terminating judgment 'If *A* then *E*' to be true when I do not act in manner *A,* just as I believe a real thing is still there when I do not look to see." A material implication asserts nothing additional, either as true or as false, when the antecedent is asserted to be *false;* but the statement that an object exists, or its equivalent series of statements that *if* an observer performed certain actions he *would* experience certain observations, means that "although certain hypotheses are now false, they have certain consequences . . . *and not others.*" Such relations, in other words, are "facts which obtain independently of being experienced." [70]

If the relation is not one of material implication, what kind of implication is it? It is not a relation of logical entailment, or deducibility, Lewis points out; i.e., the consequent is not logically implied by the antecedent, because "The situation which would prove it false is logically thinkable . . ." [71] Nor is it explainable as a formal implication (i.e., one holding "For all values of x"); for this is a form of logical entailment if we mean "Every *thinkable* thing," and a form of material implication if we mean "Every *existent* . . ." (The "existent" to which Lewis here refers, of course, is the antecedent of the implication, not the "object" with whose existence the truth of the implication has been equated.) Like the formal implication, however, the implication with which we are dealing is "implicitly general." [72]

The "If-then" relation with which we are concerned, then, is one whose "consequent . . . is not logically deducible from the antecedent," but whose truth nevertheless "is independent of the truth or falsity of the antecedent" because the antecedent "has the same consequences whether it is true or false"; and "Hence this hypothetical statement may be significantly asserted when the hypothesis of it is contrary to fact and is known to be so." [73] The "If-then" relation in question, which "has no name" in standard logic, Lewis says, is a relation of "matter-of-fact connections" or "natural connections" or "real connections," because it is a relation "connoted in any assertion of causal relationship or of connection according to natural law." It obtains "because of 'the way reality is' or because the facts of nature are thus and so." The connections so expressed are those which determine what experience is "possible." They are just "what Hume meant by 'necessary connection of matters of fact,'" although the notion may and should be expanded to include "real" *probable* connections; and Hume was quite right in pointing out that the only alternative to their acceptance is complete scepticism—an alternative, however, which Lewis rejects because of the exigencies of action. And it is the acceptance of such *real* connections, he believes, that finally saves "pragmatism" or "a 'verification-theory' of meaning" from phenomenalism by accounting for unverified though not unverifiable facts.[74]

It is instructive to compare, at this point, Reichenbach's theory regarding this same type of statement, which he, too, regards as implied by physical laws. Laws about "all *x*," he says, are regarded as true even when no *x* now exists; therefore they must be regarded as true of "all possible *x*." When a law co-ordinates two kinds of objects, *x* and *y*, it means that "If *there were* an *x*, *there would* be a *y*" in a specified relation to the *x*, which must mean in turn that "in the domain of possible things there is a *y* coördinated to every *x* such that for these two possible things" the specified relation holds.[75] Thus Reichenbach introduces, in this connection, the very kind of existential interpretation of logic that he usually condemns as "aprioristic," turning a hypothetical assertion of existence into an assertion of hypothetical existence. What we need here is some feature of the *existing* world that may be indicated to us by the counterfactual statement. It is this, probably, that Reichenbach has in mind when he insists, as we have seen, on maintaining a concept of "physical necessity" which he himself sees a way of avoiding on a logical basis.

Lewis's treatment of the problem clearly recognizes that x and y do *not* exist when we say that "If there were an x, there would be a y," and are not asserted as existing in any sense whatever; data of experience do not exist when not experienced. It is the *connection* between them that is asserted as existing, in his view. Lewis recognizes also that the truth of the statement must depend somehow on "the facts of nature." Yet, although he avoids Reichenbach's "domain of possible things" in this way, his own concept is in some respects still more ambiguous. Indeed, it may ultimately amount to the same thing; for what sort of "reality" can be attributed to a "real connection," existing with nothing to connect, except a metaphysical existence of the same kind as the "existence of possible things"? On the other hand, how can we include a "necessary connection" among the "facts of nature" unless we mean that it is a synthetic a priori connection?

It is strange that Lewis does not appear to recognize that a statement of "necessary connections of matters of fact" is *by definition* "synthetic a priori"—that matters of fact, in terms of his own clear initial distinction between the analytic or a priori and the synthetic or empirical, *cannot* be connected necessarily. This oversight is all the more strange in that he is aware of the relation of his concept not only to Hume, who refutes it, but also to Kant, whom Lewis himself has blamed for employing just such a "synthetic a priori" principle. In a very revealing footnote, he tells us that

Kant also uses the word "necessary" (*notwendig*) in this sense, particularly in his discussion of the Analogies of Experience. And he indicates the correlative sense of "possible" in his discussion of the categories of modality. He also uses the phrase "according to a rule" (*nach einer Regel*) as equivalent to "necessary" in this sense. According to his conception the particular rule of connection is not necessary in the sense of a priori, but he believes it assured that there must *be* such rules if the objective order of fact is to be distinguished from the subjective connection of mere association of ideas, and from the merely temporal order of experience as given.[76]

I.e., conformity to physical laws distinguishes the objective from the subjective, by definition; it is what we mean by the existence of a physical object. Any *particular* "connection" of this sort, however, must be learned empirically; it is not "necessary in the sense of a priori." In what sense, then, *is* it necessary? If it is necessary only that there be *some* connection, what is the kind of connection required to explain the "If-then" relation under discussion? and how is the particular connection expressed in any one such statement "necessary" at all? Surely Kant recognizes *no* necessity that is not a priori. As we have seen, his most consistent doctrine is that the particular physical law is "necessary" in the very sense in which the existence of *some* physical law is "necessary," i.e., definitively and regulatively, although it is not so deeply rooted in the structure of our minds nor in our definition of the objective world and may more easily become irrelevant. It defines a particular kind of object as the applicability of *some* law defines a physical object in general. Yet it is never "necessary" that any particular data belong to such an object; indeed, there may or may not be any such object. This, moreover, is Lewis's own analysis, which he seems here to have forgotten but which we may readily recall.

As to the sense in which the particular "If-then" relation between an action and an observation is a necessary relation, Lewis himself gives us a hint, not only in Kant's terms ("according to a rule") but in his own terms as well. Arguing that the consequent in this relation is not deducible from the antecedent, he points out in passing that nevertheless "the terminating judgment itself" (i.e., the "If-then" statement as a whole) "*is* deducible from the objective judgment in which it is a constituent," because "it is contained in the meaning of the objective statement." [77] Lewis fails to note, however, that this makes the consequent deducible from the antecedent *plus the objective statement*, though not from the antecedent alone. Thus the necessity involved is *logical* necessity, a priori necessity, after all; and Lewis, in neglecting to call attention to this point, has made precisely the same mistake as Reichenbach, who, as we have observed, sees an available means of translating his "physical necessity" into logical necessity but somehow regards it as undesirable to do so. The prediction that events will coincide with the conceptual structure is, of course, strictly empirical and probable.

The real difficulty in regard to the "If-then" statement concerns not its necessity, which is logical, but its existential truth, which we should expect to be empirical. The existential premise from which it is logically derived can give us no help, for it is that very statement of objective fact that we are trying to explain. What, we must ask, is the present *fact* by virtue of which the hypothetical statement is *now true, in an existential sense*, although the hypothesis is now false and there are no relevant empirical facts presently given? A "connection" is conceptual, and cannot be a fact, although its applicability to something actual can be a fact. What we need is *real existents* for the connections to connect—or, more precisely, real existents by virtue of which the connections connect those empirical data which do actually occur, and which exist also at those times when no relevant empirical data actually occur. Lewis expresses the situation most correctly when he says that the "If-then" relation is one that obtains "because of 'the way reality is' " [78]—not, however, *physical* reality, or *objective* reality, which is *constituted* by the relation in question and the actual data thus related, but a reality which exists even when we entertain no relevant data or concepts and which would continue to exist even if there were no observers at all. What we need to complete our conception of objective (i.e., phenomenal) reality is not the concept of synthetic a priori connections; that concept, or rather the concept that Kant calls by that name, is abstract and phenomenal, the very opposite of what we need. What we do need is a concept of *things*, given as sense perceptions and understood by conceptual organization of these, but *existing independently* (i.e., existing "in themselves").

Philosophers tend to dislike this concept. Nevertheless, the concrete, existential element which it supplies is one whose lack must ultimately be felt; and if this element is not placed where it belongs, it is likely to be misplaced elsewhere. Lewis properly shows us that the concept of the verifiable but unverified, i.e., the concept of the truth of counterfactual statements, is the point at which this need becomes especially clear; but he then attributes the required independent existence to "connections" which can only be conceptual. Reichenbach attributes it instead to "possible things," which can only be conceptual also, or—in another context—to things having a probability connection with our sense perceptions, things which must be either more constructs (in terms of probability logic) or actual sense perceptions in the future. When we observe, however, that the "necessity" of the counterfactual "If-then" statement is really logical necessity, based on the deducibility—which Lewis points out—of the entire statement from a more general premise (e.g., from the concept, or definition, of a physical object), the problem is seen to be that of the existential reference and validity of the statement at any time when no relevant observations are being made.

What is there, we now ask again, outside our consciousness? Not what do we see when we go to the next room, nor even what should we see if we were there now, but what *is there now*, factually and not counterfactually? Empirically, in terms of observations, or sense data, there is nothing; and logically, in terms of concepts and deductions from them, there is never anything. In what sense, then, does the presence of a table in the next room mean that there is now something? Only one answer suggests itself. It means that *reality is such that* if we went into the next room we should have visual sensations of a particular kind, and that if we took certain other actions we should have sensations of certain other kinds. It means that *reality is such that* the objective statement "There is a table in the next room" will be applicable to any relevant observations that may occur. And the term "reality," as used here, means *whatever* there is independently of being observed. The only possible description of the table is in terms of the observations themselves, actual or hypothetical, and the statement in terms of "reality" adds nothing to the description; but it anchors the description, assuring us that there is something to describe besides the description itself. And this, when misunderstandings are cleared aside, is what Kant means by "things in themselves."

The objection may perhaps be raised here that the whole concept of "independent reality" is an irrelevant and misguided one; that, while it does indeed lead inevitably to the notion of things existing "in themselves" in a manner different from their manner of existence as physical objects, we need not and should not become involved with any such concept in the first place. This, of course, is the position which Dewey purports to adopt; and, unless we take it into account, at least briefly, we cannot presume that we have reached any conclusion.

First of all, we must take note of the fact that the physical world, for Dewey, is a constructed world, just as it is for Kant, Lewis, Reichenbach, and all others who both recognize a rational element in that world and regard any rational element as conceptual and nonexistential. There is, of course, something that is "given" (or, as Dewey prefers to say, "had"),[79] an existential subject matter of knowledge; and this, Dewey vigorously asserts, is not at all a collection of "sensations" or "mental" states,[80] but rather "experience," a "total field or situation" from which immediate qualities are "taken" (actively selected) as data for inquiry. This concept, however, of an initial "experience" from which qualities are "taken" solves the problem as little as does Reichenbach's concept of "immediate things" from which impressions are "inferred." For surely qualities cannot be "taken" unless they are first *there* (i.e., "given"); when we make a selection, we must have at least a rudimentary prior consciousness of that which we select. Indeed, what else there is in "experience" Dewey never specifies. Certainly physical objects are not; they are results of "inquiry," described in terms of "what is *not* then and there observed,"[81] on the basis of qualities which "hang together as dependable signs that certain consequences will follow when certain interactions take place."[82]

The initial experience, then, is not experience of objective things, which are a product of knowledge. What, then, is it? The total content of consciousness? Dewey does not regard it as within consciousness. If it is prior to sense data, objects, and consciousness, must we regard it as transcendental in the Kantian sense—indeed, in the most obscure Kantian sense, that of the preconscious synthesis which Kant regards as necessarily prior to analysis? This would require further consideration; but in any event, though "experience" may not be subjective as differentiated from the objective, since it precedes differentiation, we must have difficulty in conceiving an "experience" that exists when no one is experiencing it. Whatever it is, it is not an independent existent.

As for the physical object, we may note that Dewey's conception of it, unlike Lewis's, is expressed in terms of *future* actions and consequences rather than hypothetical, counterfactual ones. (We may recall that Lewis's earlier concept, later discarded, is comparable.) Does Dewey thereby avoid the problem of the *present* truth of objective statements, the *present* existence of physical objects, which leads Lewis on into the search for something that is *now* independently real? Dewey obviously sees no such problem, because for him "consequences not antecedents supply meaning and verity." [83] Lewis, while attempting in an extremely confused chapter to maintain this view also,[84] bases his entire discussion of counterfactuals (as well as other features of his analysis) on the contrary assumption. For Dewey, on the other hand, the question of what is true *now* does not arise; indeed it would appear to him self-contradictory. The statement about a physical object is true not by virtue of some fact of existence, obtaining now, but by virtue of future verifications. In that case, however, to take only the most obvious difficulty, there would be no conceivable distinction between the truth and falsity of the statement if tests were never carried out. I.e., if I now say that "There is a table in the next room," and if the house should be completely burned to ashes an hour from now, so that no one would ever again see the table, my statement would turn out to have been neither true nor false *when uttered*. And as soon as verifiability is substituted for actual future verification as constituting truth, we are confronted by Lewis's problem as to the truth of counterfactual statements, and not helped by Dewey's evasion of it.

In any event, Dewey himself is not quite ready to assert that there *are* no "antecedent facts," although he often creates that impression; what he asserts is merely that such facts are not objects of knowledge. There are no "antecedent *truths*," either of reason or of sensation,[85] but merely because nothing antecedent can be a basis of truth as Dewey defines it. There is "existence antecedent to search and discovery," but this is not what we know; knowledge is a "re-construction" of it.[86] The situation becomes quite vague, however, if we stop to think what this antecedent existence is. If it is to be identified as the existence of "experience," i.e., of the given content of consciousness (with which knowledge does not need to be concerned because

"Direct experiencing itself takes care of that matter"),[87] then it is difficult to understand why we should need to reconstruct what we already have, or, indeed, how a construction involving such "logical" concepts as substance and causality [88] can be a reconstruction of purely existential subject matter. If the physical world purports to be a reconstruction of anything, does it not thereby refer us to a world logically and genetically prior to "experience" of any kind, which experience merely conveys to us according to our capacity?

Moreover, what are those "things as they really are" with which knowledge, according to Dewey, need not concern itself, because we "experience" them by noncognitive value experiences? [89] Surely any experience by which we "experience things as they really are" is cognitive *by definition*, whether or not it follows Dewey's pattern for knowledge; and if he has in mind here the direct, immediate experience of value qualities, there appears to be no more reason for interpreting this as a grasp of "things as they really are" than there is for interpreting the experience of sensory qualities in this manner. Indeed, Dewey seems to drop the point in later books.

Aside from these and other confusions along the way, it is clear that, if knowledge is not "a disclosure and definition of the properties of fixed and antecedent reality," [90] or even "related to an antecedent reality," [91] we have only two alternatives: *1*] there *is* no antecedent reality, or *2*] there is an antecedent reality which is not an object of knowledge, i.e., which we do not know. It is Dewey's attempt to reject both alternatives that lands him in confusion.

Dewey cannot, however, avail himself of Kant's solution, i.e., the second alternative, because he so thoroughly misunderstands it. True to the dominant conception of Kant as an exponent of "rationalistic idealism," Dewey argues that Kant's doctrine requires a world that is "rational through and through"; and that it cannot account for the "blind and unordered situations" which experience often presents to us, except by distinguishing between the "phenomenal" world in which these situations occur and "the world in its reality." [92] Actually, in Kant's view, it is not things in themselves but the phenomenal world that is rational (not "through and through," since its existential material is extrarational sense perceptions, but "regulatively," insofar as it is objective). Kant argues, rather, that our rational concepts do not apply to things in themselves at all, but only to the sensory subject matter that constitutes, as organized by those concepts, the phenomenal world. Dewey, however, is by no means alone in such a misconception. It is essential, therefore, to see what Kant's doctrine of things in themselves really is, in order to understand how it may supply the missing existential factor—the element of concrete objectivity to supplement the abstract objectivity of the physical world—in all the philosophies which are based on Kant's widely accepted premises today.

Kant's Doctrine of Things

KANT'S INTERPRETATION of the physical object, with which we are already familiar,[1] is expressed largely by the three "Analogies of Experience" and the subsequent "Postulates of Empirical Thought in General." These principles assume as empirically relevant and apply as definitions of objective experience those categories which we have in mind particularly when we think in terms of *objects*, or *things*, as definite, identifiable entities distinguishable from subjective impressions; those categories which Kant sometimes calls "regulative." The "analogies," comprising the principles of substance, causality, and reciprocity, tell us what aspects of experience may be so interpreted and assign them their place in the categorial structure. The "postulates," defining the possible, the actual, and the necessary in experience, tell us how the concept of objective things may, or indeed must, by means of the categorial structure, be extended beyond the immediate content of actual experience to include "possible experience" as well. It is extremely interesting to note that Kant finds it necessary to insert in his second edition, precisely at the completion of this discussion, a "Refutation of Idealism," intended to establish anew, in answer to his critics, the *reality* of the real objective world so conceived; to prove that experience of an objective world, so analyzed, is indeed *"experience,* and not merely imagination of outer things . . ."[2] Is this a mere recapitulation, or is it an effort to remedy a lack of which Kant is aware in his doctrine of things as it stands in the preceding discussion? In the light of what we now know of the struggle of his successors with the same problem, it will not surprise us to find that the latter alternative is indeed the case; that the difficulty consists of the exclusively *phenomenal* character of the real world as here conceived; and that Kant's genuine refutation of idealism is to be found not in the involved assertion of "empirical realism" which he presents under that title, but rather in his doctrine of *independent* reality, of things as existing not only as objects of experience, or phenomena, but also *in themselves.*

A revealing analysis of the problem of physical objects is to be found in Kant's discussion of causality, although it may readily be seen that precisely the same problem can be formulated in terms of any one of the "analogies of experience" by which physical objectivity is defined. The analysis is particularly revealing because it contains the essential elements of Lewis's confrontation of the same problem, although without the benefit of those devices of modern logic by which Lewis is able to convey his meaning more clearly.

Kant's discussion is an outgrowth of that distinction between the order of our sensations and the order of objective events which is a chief foundation of his concept of causality. "The apprehension of the manifold of appearance," he begins, "is always successive"; but this fact does not necessarily indicate that the same "representations . . . also follow one another in the object . . ." The distinction drawn here is a distinction between two senses of the word "object." In the first sense, "Everything, every representation even, in so far as we are conscious of it, may be entitled object." This is the sense in which we use the term "object of consciousness" to denote the *content* of consciousness. As Kant puts it, "The appearances, in so far as they are objects of consciousness simply in virtue of being representations, are not in any way distinct from their apprehension"; or, as Lewis would say, *actual* experience, the mere stream of consciousness, is exactly whatever it seems to be. In the second sense, however, we use the term "object," as Kant usually does, to mean the *objective thing*, "what the word 'object' ought to signify in respect of appearances when these are viewed not in so far as they are (as representations) objects, but only in so far as they stand for an object." [3] It is this second sense that presents a serious problem; for we know by immediate awareness what our "representations" are, but we do not know in this manner what some other entity may be for which they "stand."

We have already observed Kant's recognition that sense perceptions cannot qualitatively "represent" an abstract concept. Kant now recognizes that they cannot thus "represent" a nonsensory, nonqualitative object either. Our perceptions cannot and need not tell us "How things may be in themselves, apart from the representations through which they affect us"; it is only *as perceived* (i.e., as "appearances") that things are objects of knowledge. Nevertheless, the objects of knowledge are not *reducible* to our actual sensory perceptions of them. (This, we may recall, is pointed out by Reichenbach in criticism of the positivists, and by Lewis in distinguishng "real connections" from material implications; and both find it difficult to explain. Kant's own explanation is complicated by a shift in his use of the term "appearance," which we have just seen him apply to sense perceptions and which we shall now see him apply to the phenomenal object as distinguished from our perceptions of it. Such shifting use of this term is habitual with Kant, as pointed out by Kemp Smith, although we need not therefore accept the peculiar significance which Kemp Smith finds in the various shifts.[4])

We know that objects are not reducible to perceptions, Kant asserts, because a different "connection in time belongs to the manifold in the appearances themselves" (i.e., in the physical objects) than in "their representation in apprehension"; we regard the object as permanent and its parts as simultaneous, while our perceptions of it are "successive." That the parts of a house, for instance, exist only successively, "is what no one will grant." Thus, although what we mean by a "house" is the house *as perceived* and not as it exists unperceived, though in this sense "the appearance . . . is nothing but the sum of these representations," nevertheless the "appearance" (i.e., the house) is not identified with the "representations" but is "viewed as their object."

This solves, for Kant, the problem of "representation." Sense perceptions can "represent" an object because the object *consists* of these (and other actual and possible) sense perceptions, but differently related to each other than in our immediate awareness. In this way, "my concept" of the object is, quite properly, one "which I derive from the representations of apprehension." We have not yet seen, however, what the object is "as an object distinct from them," with which my concept of the object must "agree" (i.e., what constitutes the different "connection in time" which we attribute to the sensory qualities when we regard them as properties of an object). Kant sees the problem as that of explaining "how the manifold may be connected in the appearance itself, which yet is nothing in itself."

In other words, since the only existential feature of knowledge is sensory, the *object of knowledge* can have no actual *existence* apart from being perceived; and the "connection" which is its distinguishing feature, establishing its continuity as a physical object, must therefore be abstract and conceptual (i.e., the connection must constitute "only . . . the formal conditions of empirical truth"). Such a formal (or defining) condition of a physical object is the requirement that "it stands under a rule which distinguishes it from every other apprehension and necessitates some one particular mode of connection of the manifold." [5]

Kant, then, like Lewis, sees objective perceptions as distinguished from subjective ones on the basis of a particular kind of connection obtaining between them. As to the logical structure of that connection, he is of course less precise and less enlightening than Lewis, whose analysis in terms of factual and counterfactual "terminating judgments" is undoubtedly a major addition to our understanding of physical objects. Yet Kant's recognition of the abstract (or "formal") character of the connection is, at this point, "synthetic a priori" notwithstanding, clearer than Lewis's. He confronts, like Lewis, the problem of the continuous reality of an empirical object which is not always—and never completely—under observation, the continuous objectivity of a concept which at a given time may apply to nothing empirically occurring. "To call an appearance a real thing," he declares, "prior to our perceiving it, either means that in the advance of experience we must meet with such a perception, or it means nothing at all"; for appearance "consists merely of representations, which, if not given in us—that is to say, in perception—are nowhere to be met with." [6] The reality of a physical object as such, then, is that of an "appearance itself, which yet is nothing in itself."

Kant, however, need not, like Lewis, try to turn the abstract connection which is the basis of objectivity in this appearance into an independently existing connection, because he assumes that the physical object is the appearance *of something*—the appearance of an independently *real existent*, a real "thing" existing independently of being known (i.e., existing "in itself"). The conceptual connection is still needed to supply the definition in terms of which the object is identified and takes its place in the physical world, and in terms of which the relevant perceptual data become "necessary" and thus objective; but this function is one that a "formal" connection can fulfil.[7] Kant's emphasis, in this passage, is on the role of this formal connection; and quite rightly so, since he is here concerned not with independent reality but with physical objectivity, that property of the object of knowledge which distinguishes our knowledge of it from the subjective consciousness occurring in illusion or dreams. Yet his passing reference to the question of "How things may be in themselves" shows that he has in mind the fact that things (unlike their appearances) are *something* in themselves, quite aside from the question of phenomenal objectivity with which he is here primarily concerned; and thus he need not confuse the analysis of phenomenal objectivity by trying to attribute to its abstract structure an existential character that it cannot possess.

Thus, when Kant goes on to speak of "real connection in an experience in general," he does not mean a connection of the kind envisaged by Lewis, one that somehow exists independently of knowledge. Rather, he means "the connection of the object with some actual perception, in accordance with the analogies of experience . . ." It is the *perception* that is "actual," and that determines the reality of the object connected with it, and in that sense the "reality" of the connection also. The connection itself is "formal" —belonging to "the formal conditions under which in experience anything whatsoever is determined as object" (i.e., to the *definition* of a physical object in experiential terms); and it determines a real "possibility of things . . . only in relation to experience" (i.e., in a hypothetical sense only—for any such experience that we may have, if and when we have it. The *actual* "existence of the thing" is to be interpreted in terms of "a possible experience, . . . the series of possible perceptions," but only by adding to the formal connection an *actual perception* to be connected by it with possible ones. We need a relevant actual perception because we need an empirical premise if *any* "connection" is to yield an empirical conclusion. Having that, however, we need no new and different kind of connection, but only the "formal" categorial connection, in order "to make the transition from our actual perception to the thing in question" (i.e., to the possible experience which, together with the rule and the actual experience by which jointly its possibility is indicated, constitutes the objective reality of the object).[8]

"Reality" in this sense, then, is synonymous with physical objectivity, and consists of the coincidence of conceptual structures—

ultimately, of the conceptual structure which defines the physical world—and sense perceptions. Lewis has shown, we may remember, how this notion may be expanded and clarified (in a manner at which Kant also hints) to include such occurrences as illusions and dreams, and perhaps all the content of sensory awareness, since it is conceivable that all may be incorporated in *some* conceptual structure and may therefore be regarded as "real" in some capacity, e.g., as a real dream, if not as a real physical object. In any event, we have here the data of sense perception as existential subject matter and the abstract conceptual structure as determining the objectivity (or, in an equivalent sense, the "reality") of that subject matter, but nothing that is an independent existent. For the existence of sensory qualities is obviously *not* independent of being known; there is—in an immediate, qualitative sense—no color without eyes to see it and no sound without ears to hear it. Shall we say that there are light waves and sound waves, independently of being known? Kant is the first to show us clearly that these are abstractions; that, along with the still more abstract and general "substance," or even "nature," they are our own explanatory concepts, by which we construct a coherent physical world, incorporating the actually seen colors and heard sounds in a system and so making them understandable. Such concepts are our ways of knowing, of organizing existential subject matter, determined by our mental equipment as our perceptions are determined by our sensory equipment. Thus they are neither independent of knowledge nor indicative of the existence of anything. Existence is sensory, and objectivity is abstract; when the object is unperceived, when it does not *appear* to anyone, the concept is not applicable to any existent but is a mere abstract definition—retained, however, as part of the conceptual structure of knowledge. The reality of the object, then, is indeed a phenomenal reality, determined by knowledge (sensory and conceptual) and dependent, therefore, on being known, directly or by implication—the reality of an "appearance itself, which yet is nothing in itself."

Kant's awareness of the further problem as also demanding solution, his sense of the inadequacy of this kind of objectivity in terms of what we mean by "reality," his recognition that we do in fact all believe that there must be *something* "in itself" (i.e., independently of being known) and not merely an object which is "nothing in itself," are evidenced by his selection of this point in the discussion to insert his so-called "Refutation of Idealism." What he intends to refute is the criticism of him as a subjective idealist which followed the publication of his first edition.[9] Unfortunately, when Kant makes a special effort to clarify an idea to the reader, he often succeeds only in confusing himself. Thus, although the difficulties in which Kant involves himself in the "Refutation" are themselves illuminating, as we shall see, we shall still have to turn to other, much better refutations of idealism—or, more precisely, of phenomenalism—by Kant, in order to get out of these difficulties.

Somewhat surprisingly, the would-be "Refutation of Idealism" is no such thing, because Kant here makes the very mistake which we have seen his successors make, and tries to locate the element of independent reality within the object of knowledge, within the world as known. This error is already involved in his statement of the problem here. Kant defines *"material* idealism," the theory which he wishes to refute, as "the theory which declares the existence of objects in space outside us either to be merely doubtful and indemonstrable or to be false and impossible." Actually, the real issue concerns the existence of objects *independently* of us, not "in space outside us"; for no one denies the existence of spatial objects, however that existence may be interpreted; and spatial objects are "outside us" by definition, because "outside" is itself a spatial term. Kant, apparently aware of this to some extent, does try to shift his emphasis from the spatial externality of the objects to their reality; but, since he has limited his problem to the reality of objects "in space outside us," it is their physical objectivity that he now emphasizes—the proof "that we have *experience,* and not merely imagination of outer things." In other words, he sets out to prove just what he has already made clear enough—the phenomenal reality of objects, their objectivity as distinguished from the subjective content of consciousness, not their existence independently of all consciousness.

Assuming that idealism is based chiefly on the argument "that the only immediate experience is inner experience, and that from it we can only *infer* outer things . . . in an untrustworthy manner," Kant argues that, on the contrary, inner experience is dependent upon outer experience, and that therefore the latter (and not the former) must be "immediate." Inner experience includes consciousness of time, and thus "presupposes something *permanent*"; but nothing is perceived "in me" except my impermanent "representations," and the permanent must therefore be "a *thing* outside me." [10] It is obvious, however, in terms of Kant's entire analysis, that the presuppositions of experience are conceptual, that we need here a *concept* of a permanent "thing outside me" rather than the independent existence of such a thing, and that the "thing" which Kant here distinguishes from its "representations" is precisely the phenomenal thing, the physical object, knowable "immediately" because the so-called "representations" do not really *represent* it but rather *constitute* it (together with possible representations inferred from them by the application of conceptual laws). There is no indication here that we know—immediately or otherwise—anything that *exists* also when unknown, although spatial and other *concepts are valid* (i.e., in terms of "possible experience") when the object is unknown.

The "proof" that consciousness of the permanent object is logically prior to consciousness of the continuous self, moreover, is unconvincing; for if my consciousness of my own existence is temporal, so is my consciousness of objects. More convincing, at least on this score, is the otherwise rather similar refutation of idealism in connection with the "paralogisms," in which consciousness of the continuous self and of the continuous object are given equal cognitive status; "the existence of matter" is seen as "proved in the same manner as the existence of myself as a thinking being is proved." [11] We may recall that Lewis, too, uses this argument at one point, and is unsuccessful in establishing thereby the independent reality of anything.[12] Kant is similarly unsuccessful, and for the same reason; *both* the "thinking subject" and the "outer objects" validated "upon the immediate witness of my self-consciousness" can be so validated only because, existentially, "in both cases alike the objects are nothing but representations, the immediate perception (consciousness) of which is at the same time a sufficient proof of their reality." Because "the objects of outer sense" are *not* "something distinct from the senses themselves," Kant's theory "allows to matter, as appearance, a reality which . . . is immediately perceived . . ."

Thus the "realism" that Kant establishes in these passages is indeed an "empirical realism," a belief in the "reality" (i.e., the actual occurrence) of sense data, in the "reality" (i.e., the conceptual coherence and empirical content) of the physical objects in terms of which we organize such data, and in the distinction between reality and illusion within experience—a "realism" which few people, if any, would question, and which is quite consistent with outright phenomenalism. The spatial character of these objects, and their consequent spatially "outer" character, is hardly relevant to the question of their independent existence, if "the space itself is in us." [13] It makes no difference, moreover, if we emphasize (like Lewis, and more explicitly than Kant was able to do) the distinction between perceptual space as a characteristic of all our sense data and mathematical space as a conceptual structure. Since the conceptual structure is applicable to the data, both are "objective" in the Kantian sense; but both are nevertheless "in me" in the sense that "if I remove the thinking subject the whole corporeal world must at once vanish." [14] Only by rejection of a "transcendental realism" which would regard space and time—and also, we may add to Kant's exposition, scientific laws—as "given in themselves" (i.e., only by rejection of an existential interpretation of them in favor of their interpretation as definitions of reality) is Kant able to identify the perceived objects determined by them as "real." If the reality of the objects of knowledge is to mean *independent* reality, he cannot establish it at all. It is on this basis that Kant calls himself an "empirical realist" and "transcendental idealist." [15] The "transcendental" conditions determining the physical world (i.e., those conditions which make coherent knowledge of it possible) are "ideal" (i.e., conceptual); and the empirical world, the world as known, is "real" (as distinguished from subjective or illusory sensation) because its reality is then a matter of definition, not because we know it "in itself."

This distinction, then, does not establish an independently existing reality in any sense, although it does establish a world having that kind of existence which consists of being perceived, that kind of independence of being perceived which belongs to an abstraction, and that independence of any one individual mind which belongs to its status as a common world of all human beings. Kant does, however, believe in an independent (not merely "empirical") reality, existing in itself as well as in knowledge, although it is in knowledge, as a system, that the physical world is constituted. The corporeal world that must "vanish" with the knowing subject is the world *as known,* and *all* that we know about the world is included; but that which exists whether known or unknown is unaffected by the existence or nonexistence of the knowing subject.

It is not as an "empirical realist," then, that Kant refutes the phenomenalistic view which he calls "material idealism" or "empirical idealism," but rather as an *ontological realist;* for his "transcendental idealism" is an *epistemological idealism* only. It is knowledge and the objects of knowledge that are part conceptual and part sensory, dependent upon the categorial equipment of our minds and the nature of our senses; our cognitive apparatus determines what we can know, and its method of operation enters into the construction of its object. Recognition of this fact may be called epistemological (or "transcendental") idealism, if we choose, although it extends today—in some form or other—far beyond the ranks of those who regard themselves as idealists of any sort. On the other hand, whatever becomes an object of knowledge is also *something* when we do not know it, as is much else (we may well suppose) that we never know at all; and what exists or what occurs (other than the occurrence of mental or sensory processes themselves) is not determined either by our minds or by our senses. Recognition of this fact may be called ontological realism; and although Kant does not so designate it, this is clearly the view that he expresses. He declares explicitly that "we cannot treat the special conditions of sensibility as conditions of the possibility of things, but only of their appearances"; [16] and there is no reason to suppose that he ever contradicts or changes this view, if we realize that "appearance," for Kant, means the physical object, and is thoroughly "real" in the phenomenal sense determined by the categorial structure, while "things" as contrasted with "appearance" are things *in themselves.*

The concept of things in themselves is a relatively simple and straightforward one, so long as it is not entangled with other more complex and often more dubious concepts which Kant frequently presents in association with it. It is an outgrowth of Kant's view that our knowledge of independently existing things is not direct and immediate; that things are not somehow seized bodily, just as they are when unobserved, in our cognitive grasp, but rather appear in consciousness as sensations and are transformed into objects of experience by our organization of these sensations in terms of a conceptual structure; "that our representation of things, as they are given to us, does not conform to these things as they are in themselves, but that these objects, as appearances, conform to our mode of representation . . ." Thus the main point to be understood is the distinction between "things, so far as we know them, that is, so far as they are given to us," and things "so far as we do not know them, that is, so far as they are things in themselves . . ." [17]

This analysis, of course, may suggest that of Locke, to which Kant indeed refers in support of his own. At least since Locke, he argues, many predicates of things have been seen "to belong, not to the things in themselves, but to their appearances"; and he proposes to extend this treatment to "the remaining qualities of bodies also." [18] There are, however, important differences. Kant, unlike Locke, identifies the physical object with the "appearances," to which the predicates *do* belong, and not with that entity to which they are shown not to belong. He can do this because the nonsensory features of the physical object, such as substance and causality, are shown to be conceptual, and as such to belong (as *applicable* concepts) to the appearances also. On this point, Kant is quite clear. Matter is "a particular way of representing an unknown object," and "motion is not the effect of this unknown cause, but only the appearance of its influence on our senses"; and both are "representations in us," [19] although they determine the objectivity of representations. Thus our "representations" may be said to "represent" a real, objective, physical world of which it is an actual part, as well as an independently existing something to which no identifiable qualities can be attributed; and the former is immeasurably strengthened, while the latter appears, from this point of view, to have even less function for Kant than for Locke.

That there *is* something more than the actual content of experience, something existing independently of conscious experience, then, it is possible to question; indeed, this is the path which Berkeley and Hume follow with Locke's position as the starting point. Kant, however, argues that "The existence of the thing that appears is . . . not destroyed" by Locke's analysis, nor even by his own transfer of everything else that we know about it to the phenomenal world also; "it is only shown that we cannot possibly know it by the senses as it is in itself." [20] The implication is that we *do* know it by the senses, and that thus we do not know it "as it is in itself," but that it nevertheless *is* in itself; for Kant regards as "absurd" the "conclusion that there can be appearance without anything that appears." Thus the concept of "things in themselves" is the concept of a reality existing independently of being known. It is not, however, a reality that is numerically distinct from the world of experience (the world as known), but merely one that does not, when and as it exists unknown to any conscious being, contain either the sensory qualities or conceptual structure that constitute our experience of it; for sensory qualities could not exist without our senses, nor concepts without our minds.

The distinction between the "appearance" and the thing whose appearance it is, in other words, is not a distinction between a physical and a nonphysical set of objects, but rather a "distinction . . . between things as objects of experience and those same things as things in themselves . . ." [21] Thus "things in themselves" *are* "the objects of our senses"—but they are "the objects of our senses as they are in themselves, that is, out of all relation to the senses." [22] Conversely, "the things which we intuit" are the same things that exist in themselves, but they "are not in themselves what we intuit them as being." [23] We experience only "representations, which, in the manner in which they are represented, as extended beings, or as series of alterations, have no independent existence outside our thoughts"; [24] but we need not therefore deny the existence of the things represented, as a reality independent of our "thoughts," in a manner *different* from that in which they are "represented." "What the objects may be in themselves would never become known to us even through the most enlightened knowledge of . . . their appearance"; [25] but we can, nevertheless, legitimately and meaningfully refer to "things in themselves," to the extent of asserting their existence; for we are referring not to an unknown set of things, but to an unknown aspect of those things that we do in some sense know. What Kant is asserting is not that entities of a nonsensory, nonphysical, unknown kind, designated as "things in themselves," exist, but rather that the things which we transform into objects of knowledge by our cognitive processes, sensory and conceptual, are things which also exist in themselves (i.e., exist whether or not they are known).

Naturally, there are difficulties involved in speaking of anything unknown, even of a completely unknown aspect of things; and Kant is not always sufficiently on his guard to maintain thorough consistency. He says of things in themselves, for instance, that "their relations" are not "so constituted in themselves as they appear to us." [26] Actually, he should not speak at all of the "relations" of things in themselves, since relations are conceptual, in his view, and empty unless applied to sensory subject matter. That is why we are not only unable to perceive by our senses but equally unable to "conceive by pure understanding what the things which appear to us may be in themselves." [27]

This objection applies also to Kant's occasional treatment of things in themselves as the *cause* of our sensations, speaking of "representations" as "appearances of an unknown cause," [28] or "the way in which our senses are affected by this unknown something"; [29] for causality, as a category, applies to "things *as objects of experience only*" [30] and not as they are in themselves. Yet such passages are the exception, and by no means the rule. In most passages where Kant is often thought to be committing this error, he does not have the thing in itself in mind at all, although it may suggest itself to the reader. Sometimes, as we shall see later, he means the transcendental object, which is something else entirely. More often, he means the empirical, physical object, and the reader is thrown off the track by the resemblance of Kant's mode of expressing the situation to that of Locke. For example, when Kant defines "sensation" as the "effect of an object upon the faculty of representation, as we are affected by it," we readily think of Locke's independently existing "substance" affecting our senses and causing our sensations. Kant, however, is not here speaking of the thing in itself at all, but of the physical object, part of that physical world within which causality obtains and within which our sensory equipment, being physical also, performs its functions; and this object is indeed the cause of our sensations, according to causal laws applicable in the physical world. That Kant does mean precisely this in the definition under discussion, becomes quite clear when we observe that the "object" has just previously been mentioned as "*given* to us by means of sensibility, and . . . *thought* through the understanding"; [31] for it is the physical, phenomenal object, the object of experience, and never the thing in itself, that Kant analyzes in these terms.

Another typical example is the statement that

sensuous perception represents things not at all as they are, but only the mode in which they affect our senses; and consequently by sensuous perception appearances only, and not things themselves, are given to the understanding for reflection.[32]

If "the mode in which" things "affect our senses" is identified as the physical object, the thing as an appearance, the statement makes sense in Kant's framework. For those very things which we do not know "as they are" appear to us in experience; and *in that mode*, as objects of experience, they do affect our senses and are represented by our senses, and we do know them.

The same objection that applies to references to the thing in itself as cause, has sometimes been raised in regard to references to the thing in itself as existing. It is said that, since existence, too, is a category, and therefore applies only to experience, Kant contradicts himself whenever he says that there *are* things in themselves. We must note, however, Kant's recognition (made explicit in another connection, but highly relevant here) of a sense in which

existence . . . is not a category. The category as such does not apply to an indeterminately given object but only to one of which we have a concept and about which we seek to know whether it does or does not exist outside the concept.[33]

In other words, the *category* of existence refers to phenomenal existence, actuality as an object of experience, as indeed becomes clear when we see that the "principle" applying it is the postulate defining the "actual." To "have a concept" of such an object means to have a definition of it, interpretable in sensory terms; and the object exists "outside the concept" if we have sense perceptions which either fit the definition or provide a basis for the inference that other sense perceptions fitting the definition would occur under other conditions. But the thing in itself is "indeterminately given"; we can, in the nature of the case, have no definition of it in sensory terms, but recognize it as *something* existing, of such character that beings with human sensory equipment will experience it in a certain way, as a certain kind of object, but existing independently of such beings.

What is involved here is a more general and fundamental meaning of "existence," one that is very difficult to define, but one that we may recognize by thinking of a physical object as existing in the categorial sense just analyzed, and then thinking of the annihilation of all beings capable of perception. We cannot properly say that the existing thing would still be a "physical object," nor can we describe that which remains (except in terms of a hypothetical observer); but there is no reason to suppose that the thing would have ceased to *exist*. There would still be something. A parallel analysis, of course, may be made of the term "reality" as applied to the phenomenally real and the independently real. When Kant speaks of things as existing "in themselves," he means that there is *something*, regardless of whether or not anyone knows it, about which we know only how it appears to beings with the cognitive equipment that human beings in fact have.

This is Kant's doctrine of the thing in itself, taken in isolation. Unfortunately, Kant does not always take it in isolation, but attempts to merge it with the very different concept of the "noumenon," and, in so doing, entangles it also with the still different concept of the "transcendental object." If we start with a reasonably clear idea of these other concepts, we can see both the reasons for this entanglement and the means of escape from it.

The transcendental object, like everything that Kant calls "transcendental," is part of the conceptual equipment by which we organize our sense perceptions into coherent and understandable experience. It is, as we have already seen, "a correlate of the unity of apperception." In every occurrence of consciousness, even the most rudimentary sensation, there is not only the continuity with other such occurrences that marks it as an occurrence of *my* consciousness, but also the contrasting recognition that *something* is happening of which I am conscious. What happens is simply the sensation; but because it is an event of consciousness, it carries with it a conceptual classification in terms of both subject and object. It is not only a particular sense quality, but *something* happening to *someone;* if it were not, no one's concepts could be applied to it, and there would be no objective experience or physical world as we know it.

Thus the transcendental object is the abstract concept of an object—not of any particular object, nor of any particular kind of object (not even of a physical object), but rather "the concept of an object in general," the concept of *something* ("a something $= X$," Kant says) which we have in mind whenever we regard anything as an object—even as merely an object of consciousness; i.e., whenever we have coherent experience of anything. Yet it is not a formal uninterpreted concept of logic, but a "transcendental" concept; not *merely* "the concept of an object in general," but "the representation of appearances under the concept of an object in general"; and "not in itself an object of knowledge" (because an object must have sensory content and there is no sense perception of "something" as distinguished from a particular thing), but applied through the categories whenever they are applied (i.e., in all knowledge).[34]

Thus the transcendental object seems to have a definite place in Kant's system of knowledge, and it is difficult to see why he eliminates it in his second edition—except, perhaps, as part of one of his sporadic attempts at clarification which too often miscarry. Indeed, he still speaks of a "form of thought" which both determines physical objects and enables us to "think objects in general, without regard to the special mode . . . in which they may be given." [35] Surely this is still the transcendental object after all.

In some cases where Kant is accused of applying the category of causality to the thing in itself, it is the transcendental object that is involved. The causal role of the latter is most apparent in connection with knowledge of the past. Past events are "possible experience" only theoretically (since we cannot go back to them in time); but the *concept* of an object (i.e., the transcendental object) *means* something with a past, and we are therefore justified in reasoning backward from present experience "by the light of history or by the guiding-clues of causes and effects," even though empirical verification can itself be referred to the past only by conceptual means. "Thus . . . the real things of past time are given in the transcendental object of experience," though not in experience itself, which is always present.[36] The transcendental object may be regarded as the conceptual ("non-sensible" or "intelligible") cause of our experience of an object as continuous with its past, just as the transcendental subject, or unity of apperception, may be regarded as a conceptual cause of our experience (of an object) as continuous with our own individual past.

The transcendental object, then, resembles the thing in itself in several respects. It is not an "object of knowledge," no determinate character can be attributed to it, and it is nevertheless present in all experience. Moreover, as "the completely indeterminate thought of *something* in general," [37] it may be regarded as the *concept* of a thing in itself; for the thing can be conceived "in itself" (apart from the description of our actual and possible experience of it, i.e., the description of its "appearance") only as an "indeterminate . . . *something*." Nevertheless, it is not the *thing* in itself, but rather, in a sense, the very opposite; for the transcendental object is entirely conceptual and abstract, while the thing in itself is entirely existential. The transcendental object is not an object of knowledge because *it does not exist;* but it is implicitly thought whenever we know any object. The thing in itself, on the other hand, is not an object of knowledge because, by definition, it is the thing not as known but as it exists when unknown. The transcendental object is so abstract and general that it is "one and the same for all appearances"; [38] the thing in itself, too, must be regarded in the same way for all appearances, but merely because its character is not known to us except as to its ways of appearing.

The relations and distinctions among the various means by which Kant provides continuity to physical objects can become clearer to the modern reader in Lewis's language than in Kant's. By means of the concepts of substance and causality, we infer from present experience the fact that other experiences are *possible,* i.e., that they *would* occur if certain actions were taken under certain conditions; for instance, that we should see the table if we went into the next room. The table is a continuous object because we could, if we so desired and if other physical conditions permitted, perform this action; when we believe that this condition no longer obtains, we say that there is no longer a table there. When we say that the table was there yesterday, however, we mean that certain observations would have occurred if we had gone into the room yesterday; and we can say this even if we did not in fact do so and if no one did so. We are speaking of something, however, that is not now a possible experience. Indeed, when we speak of the history of the earth prior to the existence of any conscious observer, we are speaking of something that *never was* a possible experience. We can say that it would have been possible if there had been observers; but this is a purely abstract possibility, as the conditions of which we speak are such that there could not have been living observers of any known kind on the earth.

How, then, are we justified in referring our categories backward to a time which no one can ever again experience—and even to a time when there never was any real possibility of experience? Only because a continuous object *means* an object with a past; so that when we verify our concept of it in terms of present experience, or affirm that we *could* do so, the verification is regarded as extending also to its implied past. This extension, however, is "transcendental" (to revert to Kantian language once more); it is conceptual, in terms of the "transcendental object," or "concept of an object in general"; it is not empirical, in terms of conceptual but empirically significant categories, like a reference to the present or future existence of an object. The extension is abstract, expressible only in counterfactual terms; and we still believe that there is more to the situation, though not to our knowledge or possible knowledge of it, than counterfactual or hypothetical statements can directly express. There must be some *fact* which they express—a factual and not merely a counterfactual past—if they are to be true in any but an abstract, analytic sense; *something must exist* (and while the present tense is used here because there is no tenseless verb, no temporal specification is intended) *such that* the hypothetical observations would have occurred under the hypothetical circumstances. Phenomenalism makes literally nothing of the unobserved past, as Reichenbach has pointed out; and logical construction can add nothing existent, but only abstract concepts of existents. If we regard the unobserved past as existentially something, and, indeed, if we so regard the unobserved present, which will become past before we can in fact verify it, we thereby assert not only the transcendental object (the *concept* of a thing which may be observed or unobserved, by which the categories defining physical objects may be referred back to a forever unobserved past), but the *existence* of a thing independently of being observed (the thing in itself).

Now that the situation may have become reasonably clear, another concept unfortunately appears on the scene to complicate matters all over again. This is the concept of "noumena," defined by Kant as "mere objects of understanding," or "intelligible entities." They are not perceptible by the senses but are cognizable, in a direct, intuitive manner analogous to perception, "by a special mode of intuition, namely, the intellectual, which is not that which we possess . . ." In other words, they are conceptual existents, objects whose existence is identical with the concept of it. This is just what Kant proves to be impossible in his analysis of the ontological argument for the existence of God; but, in dealing with noumena, he appears to regard it as impossible only for an object of the kind of cognition that we in fact have, in which the recognition of existential subject matter is exclusively sensory and separate from the abstract understanding of concepts. That is why, with the kind of cognitive equipment available to us, we cannot *know* noumena in a "positive sense," although we can *think* them in a "negative sense" (i.e., by contrast with the "sensible" objects that we do know).[39]

As objects of understanding but not of sense perception, noumena resemble the transcendental object; but as a concept of something that *exists* without being perceived (i.e., a "something in itself"), the concept of noumena resembles that of things in themselves. Thus this concept may be understood as an attempt by Kant to attribute an existential character to the transcendental object, or (conversely) to make the thing in itself somehow "intelligible" in conceptual terms. It is an attempt by Kant, in other words, to combine the transcendental object with the thing in itself, in violation of all the principles of his analysis of knowledge, while accounting for the violation on the grounds that noumena are not objects of our kind of cognition but may be objects of some other kind. Kant rightly says, at first, that "the transcendental object . . . cannot be entitled the *noumenon*" because it is "the object of a sensible intuition in general"; [40] yet elsewhere he uses the expression "thing in itself (transcendental object)" [41] as if these two were identical, and also the expression "things in themselves (*noumena*)" [42] in the same manner. Kant's alleged argument for the existence of noumena—that it is established by the existence of phenomena, because "if the senses represent to us something merely *as it appears,* this something must also in itself be a thing"—is actually an argument for things in themselves, and not for noumena at all; and Kant's addition of the phrase "and an object of a non-sensible intuition, that is, of the understanding," [43] is a complete nonsequitur.

Apparently aware of something wrong here, but nevertheless rephrasing and repeating the very same argument in his second edition, Kant there tries to justify it by qualifying his conclusion so as to assert the existence of the noumenon "in the *negative* sense" only; it is to be regarded merely as "*not an object of our sensible intuition,*" not as "an *object* of a *non-sensible* intuition." Regarded in this way (i.e., merely as "non-sensible," not as "intelligible"), the noumenon is properly identifiable with the thing in itself; but the retention of the term "noumenon" involves an ambiguous retention, in association—however "problematic"—with the thing in itself, of the concept of "intelligible entities." This, indeed, is the manner in which Kant wishes us to retain the "concept of a *noumenon*—that is, of a thing which is not to be thought as object of the senses but as a thing in itself, solely through a pure understanding . . ." [44] Actually, there is no reason why something that is merely "*not an object of our sensible intuition*" should be called a "noumenon" (i.e., "object . . . of the understanding") at all, in however "negative" a sense. Indeed, if we did have "intellectual intuition," and if there were things which we perceived as noumena by means of it, the noumena would then be "appearances" of the things (though not sensory appearances), and their character "in themselves" would still be unknown; for, no matter what kind of knowledge might be available, it is a tautology that we can know things only as known. Even the concept, then, of anything as a noumenon *in itself* is self-contradictory, as we do not—and logically cannot—know *what* anything is in itself.

Kant does, however, sometimes conceive things in themselves as noumena, and therefore as known to be determinately different in character from the phenomena which we perceive through the senses. Thus they cannot be the same sets of things after all, and we now have a "division . . . of the world into a world of the senses and a world of the understanding . . . generically distinct from one another." [45] Not as a definite statement of fact, but at least "in a merely problematic sense . . . as setting limits to sensibility" (i.e., as a statement of something that phenomena are *not* and that things in themselves might be), Kant suggests "applying the term noumena to things in themselves." [46] Thus he contradicts his explicit statement that "appearance" is not "illusion," [47] as well as all his clear indications that the things of experience *are* the things which also exist in themselves (even though we do not experience them as they are in themselves).

Unfortunately, many of Kant's successors today, appalled at such a distinction between phenomena and noumena, with its implied relegation of the former to an inferior ontological status, carry over their dismay to the distinction between phenomena and things in themselves. They apparently do not realize that the latter distinction is separable from the former and quite different in character and function. To this confusion many commentators on Kant have contributed, even though they do not ordinarily go so far as Heinrich Cassirer, who flatly declares that not only the term "noumenon" but also the term "transcendental object" must be "understood as an exact equivalent of the term 'thing-in-itself.' " [48] And once such an identification is assumed, legitimate objections to noumena are illegitimately directed against things in themselves.

Thus Reichenbach's horror at Kant's doctrine of "things of appearance and things-in-themselves" [49] is based on the belief that it "leads," at least, to the view "that ultimate reality is reserved to ideas, whereas physical objects are but poor copies of the ideal ones." Yet, although noumena may perhaps be approximately identified with Platonic "ideas," things in themselves certainly many not. Reichenbach's association of the Kantian doctrine which he has in mind with "God, freedom, and immortality" makes it very evident that it is noumena, and not things in themselves, that are at issue. [50]

Lewis, on the other hand, recognizes that Kant's doctrine of things in themselves would invalidate neither science nor common sense knowledge, both of which are based on "connection according to a rule" rather than on any ontological "ground." [51] Even Lewis, however, in trying to eliminate the doctrine of things in themselves, shifts to the other interpretation of them, denying a *"ding an sich"* on the grounds that "we must not confuse limitation of knowledge with misrepresentation or mistake" [52]—a confusion of which Kant is never guilty when dealing with things in themselves in the context of epistemology rather than in the context of noumena. And we can now see that Dewey, too, when he interprets Kant as distinguishing between "the world of phenomenal appearances and the world in its reality," the latter being "rational through and through" [53] and the former consisting of "perceptual material" which "gets completely in the way of knowledge of things as they 'really' are," [54] must have noumena and not things in themselves in mind. If things in themselves *are* noumena, and not otherwise, they must be a separate set of things, not appearing to us *as* phenomena but poorly duplicated by them.

Such an interpretation is both reflected and enhanced by the custom, adopted by many writers in English, of spelling "thing-in-itself" with hyphens. This device, for which surely there is no linguistic reason, obscures the fact that Kant, in dealing with this concept on its own terms, has in mind one set of things—as known and in themselves. And the division into two sets, a phenomenal and a noumenal, combined with the exaggeration of Kant's echoings of Locke's theory of perception, establishes the very mistaken impression—against which

Kant himself already found it necessary to defend himself—that knowledge and its objects, as presented by his analysis, are illusory, and that an underlying "rational" world is designated by that analysis as the only "reality."

Naturally, the varied interpretations would not arise without some foundation. It seems evident that Kant means by the transcendental object, at least, something entirely different from the thing in itself, in spite of his one lapse (noted above); [55] but there is little doubt that he often thinks of things in themselves as noumena, although he believes that there may be other noumena also. It is noteworthy, however, that when Kant advances in support of noumena the line of reasoning that actually leads to the establishment of the doctrine of things in themselves (i.e., the line of reasoning from "appearances" to that which appears), he does not treat them as separate things; rather, he distinguishes merely between "the mode in which we intuit them" and "the nature that belongs to them in themselves." [56] When, on the other hand, the concept of noumena is advanced, not in order to indicate a foundation of concrete, independent reality for phenomena, but rather to indicate that "a place remains open" for the application of theological concepts, the situation is quite different; it is not the objects of sense perception as they are independently of being perceived, but "other and different objects" entirely, that are to occupy the open place. Indeed, it is clearly for theological purposes that Kant attempts to turn the thing in itself into a noumenon, recognizing that the noumena of his theology can fulfil their role there with validity only if they can be established as in some sense noumena *in themselves*. It is the concept of noumena, however, not that of things in themselves, that is the theological concept for Kant.

Thus, while we cannot deny that Kant himself often identifies the thing in itself and the noumenon, it is clear that the two concepts are logically separable; the concept of something that exists independently of being known in any way and the concept of something whose existence can be known by a "pure understanding" which involves "intellectual intuition" are by no means logically equivalent. For the latter concept, Kant's analysis as a whole provides no grounds —not even a "place," if the noumenon is to be regarded as something whose nature "in itself" is specified in any way. The other concept, however, is required for the completion of his analysis of knowledge, and also for the completion of those more recent analyses of knowledge which derive from the Kantian premises.

In respect to things in themselves, when he is *not* thinking of them as noumena, Kant is quite clear in his view that they are entirely "unknown to us as to what they are in themselves." [57] They must, when unknown, have some character that is incommunicable to us, since the sense data by which we perceive cannot exist when our senses are not functioning, and since our concepts are not cognitive except in application to these data. Moreover, we do not actually *know* that things exist "in themselves," independently of our knowledge of them. Kant never proves it; indeed, it is in the nature of the case unprovable. If things in themselves were logically required, they would be conceptual constructs; and if they were inductively indicated, they would be "possible experience." Kant's implicit argument is merely that *either* there are things independent of knowledge which "appear" in our knowledge only in a manner made possible by the nature of our cognitive equipment, sensory and conceptual (i.e., "transcendental idealism"), *or* there is nothing but the object of knowledge precisely as known, consisting of sense data and abstract concepts (i.e., "empirical idealism" or phenomenalism). Either the world *as object of knowledge* is our phenomenal view of a reality independent of knowledge, or this phenomenal world is all there is and nothing exists independently ("in itself"). For surely "being known" means something other than "being," except for bare events of consciousness; and either there is *something* prior to and different from our knowledge of it, or there is nothing but events of consciousness. Kant himself adopts the former view, and if his successors reject the other alternative (which they clearly intend to do), they must accept it also. This is no proof, but should be sufficient to break down the common prejudice against the Kantian doctrine.

Nevertheless, acceptance of the "thing in itself" must be regarded as "blind" in a more final and total sense than acceptance of Reichenbach's "blind posit" that future experience will conform to laws applicable in past experience. For future experience will become present, and the "blind posit," validated for at least some of it, is pushed continually forward in time; but the status of knowledge as either exhausting reality or constituting an appearance of something independently real, is "problematic" at every step, and cannot be demonstrated or verified for any experience whatever.

Is it preferable to adopt the phenomenalist alternative? Would our knowledge be validated? Kant would answer that our knowledge *is* validated, in any event; because the objective validity of knowledge *means* its phenomenal validity, the coincidence of concepts and sense perceptions in a coherent structure. The thing in itself has no bearing on the validity of our knowledge; for "in experience no question is ever asked in regard to it"; [58] it is not what our knowledge is about. Kant rejects—and here his very language suggests Dewey—the notion that the object of knowledge is "given antecedently to your knowledge, and not by means of it"; [59] but Kant places equal emphasis on the fact that there is *something* existing "antecedently" nevertheless.

We may ask, however, why Kant should place such emphasis on something outside of knowledge and irrelevant to its validity. Is it not possible to reject *both* phenomenalism and the thing in itself as meaningless, since the contents and validity of knowledge and experience are unaffected? First of all, we must recognize that this view itself amounts to acceptance of one of the alternatives, that of phenomenalism, because it rejects any reference to anything beyond the contents of knowledge. Second, there is Russell's argument that phenomenalism reduces to solipsism, and that there is an emotional difference—if not a cognitive one—between the view that *other people* exist independently of us and the view that they are our experience of them.[60] The strongest justification of the Kantian concept, however, is the fact that most people, including most philosophers, actually do believe that the things that we know are things which exist independently of us; that the earth (to use Reichenbach's example) existed when there were no observers; that there is something besides the sensation and abstraction by which our experience and knowledge are constituted. Kant shows us, taking the nature of our experience and knowledge into consideration, what this belief means and in what sense it can conceivably be true.

Thus a careful consideration of the doctrine of things in themselves reinforces the view that this concept alone provides Kant's effective "refutation of idealism," and that here the chief importance of the concept lies. (In this context, "idealism" is equated with phenomenalism; the rationalistic or Platonic type of idealism is refuted by the recognition of the analytic character of logic and the synthetic character of existence propositions.) "I grant by all means," Kant asserts,

that there are bodies without us, that is, things which, though quite unknown to us as to what they are in themselves, we yet know by the representations which their influence on our sensibility procures us. These representations we call "bodies," a term signifying merely the appearance of the thing which is unknown to us, but not therefore less actual. Can this be termed idealism? It is the very contrary.

And so it is; not, however, because the "representations" are those of "bodies without us" in space, not because (as Kant explains) "things as objects of our senses existing outside us are given" even though "we know nothing of what they may be in themselves," but rather because they *are something* in themselves—something which, although "unknown to us" except by its "appearance," exists whether known or unknown.[61]

Moreover—and this is the aspect of the matter that Kant habitually stresses—the affirmation of things in themselves does have certain types of relevance for knowledge. If things exist in themselves, the phenomenal character of our knowledge is emphasized by contrast; and this emphasis has both a positive and a negative significance for knowledge.

Positively, it may be said to make knowledge possible. Just because the physical object, as we experience it, is *not* identifiable with the thing in itself, just because its existential subject matter is supplied by our senses and structurally organized by our concepts, we can know that our sense data represent its own character and that our concepts are applicable to it. For "we cannot treat the special conditions of sensibility as conditions of the possibility of things, but only of their appearances";[62] it is the fact that physical objects *are* appearance that makes such treatment of them valid. And the same is true in regard to the special nature of our conceptual equipment; we understand things because their "laws" are the means by which we make them understandable to ourselves.[63] Knowledge, by its very nature, must be phenomenal knowledge.

Negatively, however, this phenomenal character of knowledge is also significant. Kant speaks of the "concept of a noumenon" as a "*limiting concept*," by which the understanding not only "limits sensibility" but also "sets limits to itself." [64] The concept of things in themselves, however, performs this function even more effectively, since we cannot describe things in themselves, even tentatively, in any terms whatever, sensory or conceptual. We assert *that* they exist —i.e., that *something* exists (although even this assertion, as we have seen, is not definitely known to be true); but the character which belongs to them when unknown is not and can never be an object of knowledge. When we acquire new knowledge, knowledge of a previously unknown thing, we apply a new concept of a particular thing (part, however, of our accustomed system of concepts) to new actual experience, inferring therefrom new possible experience; and independent, antecedently existing fact thus acquires a new aspect, that of its "appearance" in our system of experience, but is not in any part transferred into our experience as it antecedently is. Thus, however far we may extend our knowledge, we do not come any closer to knowing the antecedent reality as it exists outside of knowledge. "What the objects may be in themselves would never become known to us even through the most enlightened knowledge of that which is alone given us, namely, their appearance." [65] The extension of knowledge is the construction of new *objects of knowledge*, the acquisition and ordering of a wider body of experience and perhaps its more coherent explanation, but not a closer approach to that which already exists independently. Of the latter, we cannot even try to know anything, since our concepts do not apply to it and our sense data do not include it—and since the very attempt to know is the attempt to acquire new objects of knowledge, or new explanations of them. The thing in itself is not even an unattainable goal of knowledge; it is not even, like the "ideal of pure reason," a "regulative concept"; and the direction of knowledge is not toward it, for it determines no direction. It is simply outside the ultimate circularity of knowledge.

That we cannot know the unknown while it remains unknown, is tautological. Nevertheless, when we assert that there *is something* unknown, we make a synthetic assertion, one that is not empty; and the prior statement, understood as an assertion *about this something*, is no longer empty. The same situation obtains in regard to the statement that we cannot know that some unknown things are *not* different in kind from the things that we do know. Thus the concept of things in themselves makes us aware of a further limitation of knowledge. We have already seen that the things known to us as they "appear" are unknown to us "as they are in themselves"; we now see, in addition, that there may very well be other things, even other kinds of things, existing "in themselves" but not such as can appear to us or be known to us at all. We can think of nothing that they might be; certainly there is no reason to suppose that they are "noumena." But while "it would be absurd for us to hope that we can know more of any object than belongs to the possible experience of it," yet "it would be . . . a still greater absurdity if we . . . set up our experience as the only possible mode of knowing things . . ." [66] Kant repeatedly argues that there may be other kinds of minds than ours, capable of knowing other kinds of things; and we may recall, here, Lewis's example of insects that seem to respond to some type of stimulus unknown to us by means of some sense that we do not possess.

Indeed, it is just as plausible that there may be existents of which *no* existing mind can become aware. This concept is neither more nor less "metaphysical" than the belief that the earth existed before there were observers. We do not and cannot know that there are such existents, and the notion that there may be is one that can be of no possible use to us, practical or theoretical. No implications can be drawn from it, except that knowledge, actual or possible, need not be ontologically exhaustive in kind any more than in extent. It is not a limitation that restricts any use or development of the cognitive powers that we have; or that interferes with the validity of any knowledge, wherever it may extend; or that stops the expansion or progress of knowledge at any point. Yet it is a limitation ubiquitously present in the background of our knowledge; and Kant's system, so often charged with over-certainty, is built upon a scepticism both broader and deeper than whatever certainty it may be said to claim.

Nevertheless, it is this same concept of "things in themselves" that gives to the system of knowledge its existential anchorage.

Kant Today: *A Reappraisal*

THE TWO FUNDAMENTAL phases of Kantian influence in philosophy today, the clear-cut distinction between analytic and synthetic statements and the recognition of a conceptual factor in all knowledge, are easily discernible, as to both their Kantian source and their widespread acceptance. They were apparent to us at the outset, and surely this initial estimate has been reinforced by all subsequent considerations. It was also apparent at the outset, however, that this far-reaching influence is rendered perplexing and almost paradoxical by other, equally fundamental Kantian doctrines, particularly the concepts of the synthetic a priori and of the thing in itself, which are almost universally disapproved today; that Kant, primarily in connection with these doctrines, has acquired those labels of "rationalist" and "idealist" which make many current philosophers reluctant to admit his obvious influence, and which make his continued importance seem highly doubtful.

We may now be in a position to reassess this situation. First, we must review what we have learned about it. We have seen that it is quite possible to disentangle Kant's own philosophical premises, together with the structure founded on them, from views which he derived from scientific, mathematical, and logical equipment standard in his time but obsolete today. We have found, indeed, that his philosophical doctrines are equally well adapted—in some ways even better adapted—to the scientific, mathematical, and logical concepts prevailing today, and have in fact been developed in terms of such concepts by Lewis and by Reichenbach. Thus the "synthetic a priori" becomes understandable as signifying not an alleged basis for an existential logic but rather an assumption as to the applicability of the a priori and analytic to the synthetic and existential. This assumption can then be seen as necessary for objective experience and knowledge because it defines objective experience and knowledge, and free from arbitrariness because based on the cognitive equipment which human beings do in fact have; and it provides a basis for organization of the data of sensory awareness into conceptual systems, with complete systematization as an ideal goal.

This doctrine is greatly reinforced by Lewis, who clarifies more fully the coincidence of our concepts and our sense data, explaining the fact of its occurrence in genetic and pragmatic terms and its precise nature in terms of his theory of holophrastic and analytic meaning, and by means of the latter theory closing an ultimate gap in the Kantian structure with which its author was unable to deal. And the scope of the doctrine is greatly expanded by Reichenbach, who applies it (apparently without recognizing its full role) in the field of probable knowledge and thus insures its relevance to the science of today.

Thus we find that Kant establishes the role of the rational and conceptual *in our experience* of an objective world, i.e., in knowledge and not in existence. He can do so just because of the distinction between knowledge and existence—between the object of knowledge (as an organization of sense data in terms of abstract concepts) and the existent that is independent of being known. He is not, then, a rationalist, because he claims for logic only indispensability for knowledge and therefore applicability to the object of knowledge, but no relation to existence independent of knowledge, and no ontological status of its own. And he is not an idealist, because he regards only the nature of the object of knowledge as determined by our mental capacities and activities, but does not regard all existence as so determined; the object of knowledge is not the sole existent either numerically or in kind, nor is the existent independent of knowledge to be regarded as mental in character (in spite of some ambiguity on this point because of the additional concept of the "noumenon").

This, in outline, is the picture that confronts us when the essential Kantian structure is divested of its obsolete nonphilosophical background and restated in modern terms. We must now ask, however, what purpose such a restatement may serve. Has it been worth while to trace back to Kant, and to translate into modern language in order to trace forward again to our contemporaries, ideas which are well established and well understood in any event? I think it has been well worth while, not only in terms of an increased understanding of past and present philosophical developments, but also in terms of an increased awareness of the suggestions that may be derived for future developments.

First, as to the past, it is obvious that a matter of historical justice is involved; for only by some such reinterpretation can we fully appreciate the significance for all subsequent philosophy of a work which embodies one of the very few permanent major advances in philosophy. Even an inadequate review of Kant's doctrines, if carried out in terms more understandable and relevant today than the terms in which he wrote, and if placed in the context of the science and logic of the twentieth century rather than of the eighteenth, must make it very difficult to regard the *Critique of Pure Reason* as a dead classic of the rationalistic and idealistic past of philosophy. Unlike many philosophers of the past, Kant has not been systematically "revived" in recent years, probably because he has never been dead enough to be missed. Yet his contribution does need at least to be *renewed*, if his own work is not to fall into obsoleteness in spite of its continuing vital role in the work of others.

History, however, is the least important consideration involved here. More important is the fact that this history has specific bearing on the present; that the ideas of many current philosophers can be greatly clarified by recognition and understanding of their Kantian origin. A clarification of Kant in modern terms is at the same time a clarification of all of his direct modern successors. We have seen it in the cases of Lewis and Reichenbach. Lewis's "pragmatism," for instance, narrowed down by his own analysis to a pragmatic interpretation of the formation and selection of concepts for empirical application, is much more understandable as a development of Kant's "regulative" application of the a priori to the synthetic than as a development of the Deweyan pragmatism which interprets all consciousness, all cognition, and all truth in pragmatic terms. His theory of holophrastic and analytic meaning cannot be understood in its full significance or accorded its due importance unless it is recognized as dealing with Kant's problem, that of explaining the applicability of the a priori to the synthetic; more specifically, as treating an aspect of the problem—that of the sense in which concrete data can be "subsumed" under abstract concepts—

which Kant saw but did not properly understand; and as providing a new and altogether effective solution. Reichenbach's analysis of the problem of probability and induction, which might appear to be simply one mathematical theory among others, of interest only in mathematics, takes on new dimensions and new philosophical import when seen as incorporating this problem in the larger one of the applicability of logic.

For the interpretation of current philosophers in Kantian terms and of Kant in terms of his successors, Lewis and Reichenbach have proved to be excellent examples; but they certainly do not exhaust the field. At least one writer besides Reichenbach himself has hinted at such interpretation of the work of Bertrand Russell.[1] Similar possibilities in the work of John Dewey have been mentioned in the course of the present discussion; they involve, in addition to the type of Kantian concepts with which we have been concerned, the preconscious "transcendental synthesis" which seems so surprisingly to reappear in Dewey's concept of an "experience" prior to consciousness. An interpretation of Dewey in Kantian terms, like the similar interpretation of Lewis and Reichenbach, would serve not only to clarify its subject but to carry further the modernization and expansion of Kant's philosophy to cover later developments in science; for Dewey brings into his revised but still essentially Kantian framework the role of experiment, which Kant recognizes in passing but does not develop, and which must be put into its proper place in that framework to make it a thoroughly satisfactory one for the science of the twentieth century. And surely the very great value of the positivist contribution would be much more apparent if the widespread emphasis (by its exponents and detractors alike) on its negative aspects were supplemented by clear recognition of its role, directly in the Kantian tradition, of emphasizing and justifying once more the place of deductive logic in "empirical" science.

A further clarification would occur if, through recognition of the essential acceptability of the Kantian epistemology from the point of view of science and naturalistic philosophy today, philosophers became less embarrassed by those obvious Kantianisms, too clear and definite to overlook, that persist in turning up in their own work. They would no longer feel it necessary to introduce needless confusion by the attempt to deny such resemblances. Lewis would not have to confuse us by insisting that "reality," in spite of "human limitations" and the "relativity of perception," is *not* "a *ding an sich*."[2] Reichenbach would not have to draw complicated and insignificant distinctions in order to divest his "necessary condition of knowledge" of the "unpleasant flavor" of Kant.[3] Dewey, explaining causality as "a *logical* category," could make his concept readily understandable in terms of its Kantian background, instead of obscurely insisting that his statement is not to be taken "in an a priori or Kantian sense."[4] Surely the problems of philosophy are perplexing enough without such superfluous complication by those who attempt to solve them; and it would be worth while to remove from Kant the gratuitous "rationalist" and "idealist" labels which apparently induce such complication.

Even more important is the fact that Kant has something to offer toward the solution of problems by which philosophy is still confronted.

As we have seen, the distinction between analytic and synthetic propositions, and the consequent recognition that all conceptual knowledge is abstract and all existential knowledge synthetic, raises for Kant the problem of the relation of one to the other, i.e., the problem of the empirical applicability of logic. This problem is not only still with us, but with us in an increasingly acute form. For Kant's distinction remains firmly entrenched; general acceptance of the analytic nature of mathematics has removed the last seemingly intermediate type of concept; and the abstract, nonexistential character of logic is completely affirmed by the logicians themselves. Indeed, both logicians and mathematicians have developed their technical apparatus to a degree unimagined in Kant's day, only to insist that it means nothing at all. And on the other hand, if logic has nothing to do with the actual world, the actual world has nothing to do with logic; the converse of logical formalism is existentialism.

Nevertheless, a strange anomaly, in this context, takes on ever-increasing proportions—the steady development of mathematical physics. As logic (and mathematics along with it) on the one hand and the existent world on the other more and more insistently disclaim each other, scientific knowledge of the very foundations of the existent world is expressed more and more in mathematical symbols. This is true even of scientific knowledge about those subatomic phenomena that seem to defy rational conception; whatever fails to fit into a deductive system is nevertheless treated mathematically, in terms of probability. Thus the question of how mathematical physics is possible, and—still more fundamentally—the question of how conceptual reasoning about the physical world is possible, how logic is empirically applicable, present issues of crucial importance. We have examined Kant's reply—that such applicability is a "presupposition" of coherent, objective experience, to be assumed as a premise in any instance of such experience because it constitutes a definition of such experience. We have seen that this reply provides the foundation of any adequate solution; and that, augmented in scope and given increased flexibility by Lewis and Reichenbach, it provides as adequate an answer as crucial philosophical issues can normally be expected to have. By understanding this answer, moreover, we understand that logic is indeed analytic, but not thereby a trivial aesthetic exercise without relevance to experience; and that the facts of existence are indeed to be known by empirical means only, but that neither they nor actions in regard to them possess thereby a privileged immunity from logical analysis or from the requirements of logical consistency. "Thoughts without content are empty, intuitions without concepts are blind." [5]

Then we find before us the second urgent philosophical issue arising from Kantian sources and resolvable in Kantian terms. The conceptual element which Kant eliminates from existence, he finds in experience; not only science, but even the physical object becomes conceptualized, and to that extent abstract, and only the bare data of sense remain concrete and existential. Here again, the ever-increasing extent to which physics is understood in terms of mathematics, and mathematics in terms of logic, has served to accentuate and render still more crucial a problem which Kant produced and recognized, the problem of locating existence in a world of abstractions, independent reality in a world defined and limited by the nature of human cognitive equipment. Here again, we can see in existentialism the reaction against the conceptualized, abstract world which science and the positivist philosophy of science present to us— the revolt of the "blind" against the "empty."

In regard to this question of finding a content for the belief that something exists independently of us, that the world is in some sense neither an abstraction nor subjective nor even a combination of the two, we have found even greater confusion than in regard to the applicability of logic. Even the problem appears to be imperfectly recognized, perhaps because thorough recognition of it would itself point to that Kantian answer which is in such disrepute. Yet we have seen in an assortment of representative views a vague but continually troublesome consciousness of such a problem, and in each of these views also various hints—often retracted or diverted—at the Kantian solution. Surely we may conclude that Kant can be of genuine and vital assistance here.

In addition to the role that Kant may still have in the resolution of these two major issues confronting philosophy today, he may also—when understood in the context of that role—provide us with other ideas that may prove valuable if blanket resistance to Kantian doctrine is overcome. One such idea is the concept of the unification of knowledge as an ideal goal, establishing the direction of progress in knowledge. This concept, implicit in the search of science for more and more comprehensive theories, is challenged by the simultaneous acceptance of mutually contradictory theories in science, as Reichenbach has shown us. It is challenged also by a widespread distrust of any unified system—a distrust based on the fear of "rationalism" and enhanced by awareness of the elements of arbitrariness and occasional a priori physics in Kant's own system. When we realize, however, that Kant's limited and fixed logic and absolute physics are not necessarily involved here but are merely standard equipment of his time; that Kant's ideal of unification implies nothing whatever about the existing world but does imply something about the nature of explanation and our understanding of that world; that such an ideal is intended to be applied *so far as possible*, without any necessary assumption as to how far that may be; then the value of such a concept begins to be apparent. At least it becomes open for consideration.

Another Kantian notion that seems to deserve reconsideration is that of a fundamental relation between logic and mind, perhaps as reflected in Lewis's interpretation of logic as the analysis of meaning. We have seen that the nature and justification of logic itself, even apart from the question of its applicability, have not been explained in any adequate manner; that the reduction of logic to tautology still leaves the same question open in regard to tautology itself; that, if logic is neither self-validating nor empirical, neither itself a matter of objective fact nor derived from objective facts, it *must* be a fact about the structure of the human mind; and that *some* standard structure must in any event be attributed to the human mind, to the extent that human beings can communicate with each other in terms of a common world. Here the Kantian concept runs counter to deep-seated, widely accepted views; and indeed (as we have seen) Kant himself tries to evade it. Yet, in the continued absence of more satisfactory solutions for this extremely involved and perplexing problem, the Kantian answer, supplemented by (and reflected in) Lewis's theories of the genetic development of conceptual structure and the role of "meaning" in logic, ought at least to be considered much more carefully and sympathetically than is customary.

Finally, a reconsideration of Kant, if anything at all is gained by it, must inevitably lead to a reconsideration of the importance of epistemology and of its role in philosophy generally. Full recognition of its importance is of course implied in an approach like that of Reichenbach, for instance, who hardly changes matters by using the term "philosophy of science" instead. Yet we have seen Reichenbach, following Dewey in this respect, attempt to avoid the problem for which the epistemological approach is often held responsible, that of bridging the gap from knowledge to existence, by taking a concrete, independently existing subject matter as given and as the starting point of analysis, rather than sense data with their implied cognitive character. We have seen, too, that this approach avoids no problems whatever. Indeed, the suggestion inevitably presents itself that, if the nature of knowledge is not necessarily the first question in philosophy, it is necessarily the second; for whatever the first may be, and whatever the proposed answer to it, that answer is not established until its proponent has replied to the further question, "Why do you regard that answer as valid? *How do you know?*"

Naturally, the relevance and value of the Kantian theory of knowledge today should not be exaggerated. The body of obsolete science and logic from which it must be extricated is very considerable and very closely entangled with it. The rigidity of the Kantian categorial structure, tied up with the notions of one complete logic (the Aristotelian) on one hand and one complete physics (the Newtonian) on the other, and the consequent rigidity of structure attributed both to mind and to the physical world, have required drastic loosening—the work which has been done for us, fortunately, by Lewis and Reichenbach. And some of the subordinate Kantian doctrines that we have seen to be worthy of attention are nevertheless inconclusive.

Yet, when all possible reservations are taken into account, there remains the distinction between the analytic and the synthetic, together with the means of bridging the gap; and recognition of the conceptual element in experience and the abstract, deductive element in science, together with recognition of noncognitive, independent existents in which our concepts have no part. In other words, there remains the establishment of a major landmark in philosophy, still not left behind, together with a major contribution, still not exhausted, toward the solution of the resulting problems. The solution, moreover, is one that reinstates logic without resort to rationalism, and existence without resort to existentialism.

All of this can again be made available and effective in philosophy through adequate interpretation and reconsideration, in the language of our contemporaries and in terms of modern science, mathematics, and logic; and it is to be hoped that the present attempt may have given some indication of what is required.

NOTES

Chapter 1. Kant Today: *A Preliminary View*

1. Hans Reichenbach, *The Rise of Scientific Philosophy*, (Berkeley and Los Angeles, University of California Press, 1951), pp. 125, 140.

2. *Ibid.*, pp. 222–23.

3. Hans Reichenbach, *Experience and Prediction*, (Chicago, University of Chicago Press, 1938), pp. 334–36.

4. *Immanuel Kant's Critique of Pure Reason*, translated by Norman Kemp Smith, (London, Macmillan and Co., Limited, 1953), p. 48.

5. Reichenbach, *Experience and Prediction*, p. 335.

6. Kant, *op. cit.*, p. 530.

7. Immanuel Kant, *Prolegomena to Any Future Metaphysics*, translated by Lewis W. Beck, (New York, The Liberal Arts Press, 1951), p. 14.

8. Morton G. White, "The Analytic and the Synthetic: An Untenable Dualism," reprinted in L. Linsky, editor, *Semantics and the Philosophy of Language*, (Urbana, University of Illinois Press, 1952).

9. Kant, *Critique of Pure Reason*, p. 98.

10. *Ibid.*, pp. 287–88.

11. *Ibid.*, p. 99.

12. *Ibid.*, p. 177.

13. *Ibid.*, p. 504.

14. *Ibid.*, p. 505.

15. *Ibid.*, p. 243.

16. *Ibid.*, p. 98.

17. *Ibid.*, p. 243.

18. *Ibid.*, p. 49; cf. p. 504.

19. *Ibid.*, p. 55.

20. Kant, *Prolegomena*, p. 123.

21. *Ibid.*, p. 124n.

22. *Ibid.*, pp. 22–23.

23. Kant, *Critique of Pure Reason*, p. 93.

24. *Ibid.*, pp. 22–23.

25. *Ibid.*, p. 193.

26. *Ibid.*, p. 114.

27. *Ibid.*, p. 65.

28. *Ibid.*, p. 41.

29. *Ibid.*, p. 22.

30. *Ibid.*, p. 195.

31. *Ibid.*, pp. 22–23.

32. John Dewey, *Experience and Nature*, (New York, W. W. Norton and Company, Inc., 1925, 1929), pp. 156–57.

33. John Dewey, *Logic: the Theory of Inquiry*, (New York, Henry Holt & Co., 1938), pp. 455–56.

34. *Ibid.*, p. 123.

35. Dewey, *Experience and Nature*, p. 140.

36. Dewey, *Logic*, p. 129.

37. Henry Margenau, *The Nature of Physical Reality*, (New York, McGraw-Hill Book Company, Inc., 1950), p. 172.

38. Albert Einstein, "Physics and Reality," in *Ideas and Opinions*, (New York, Crown Publishers, Inc., 1954), pp. 291–92.

39. *Ibid.*, p. 294; cf. Margenau, *op. cit.*, p. 172.

40. Kant, *Critique of Pure Reason*, e.g., pp. 20–23.

41. *Ibid.*, p. 20n.

42. Dewey, *Logic*, pp. 454–56.

43. *Ibid.*, p. 432.

44. Kant, *Critique of Pure Reason*, p. 20.

45. Dewey, *Logic*, p. 111.

46. Carl G. Hempel, *Fundamentals of Concept Formation in Empirical Science*, (Chicago, University of Chicago Press, 1952), pp. 36–37.

47. Herbert Feigl, "Some Remarks on the Meaning of Scientific Explanation," in Herbert Feigl and Wilfrid Sellars, editors, *Readings in Philosophical Analysis*, (New York, Appleton-Century-Crofts, Inc., 1949), pp. 510–11.

48. Einstein, "On the Method of Theoretical Physics," in *Ideas and Opinions*, p. 273.

49. Einstein, "The Problem of Space, Ether, and the Field in Physics," in *ibid.*, p. 278.

50. Einstein, "Physics and Reality," in *ibid.*, p. 307.

51. Einstein, "On the Method of Theoretical Physics," in *ibid.*, p. 274.

52. *Ibid.*, p. 272.

53. *Ibid.*, p. 271.

54. Einstein, "Physics and Reality," in *ibid.*, p. 292.

55. *Ibid.*, pp. 293–94.

56. Kant, *Critique of Pure Reason*, p. 41.

57. Reichenbach, *The Rise of Scientific Philosophy*, p. 102.

58. *Ibid.*, p. 103.

59. Karl Pearson, *The Grammar of Science*, Everyman edition, (London, J. M. Dent and Sons, Ltd., 1937), p. 11.

60. *Ibid.*, pp. 60–61.

61. Hans Reichenbach, "The Philosophical Significance of the Theory of Relativity," in *Albert Einstein: Philosopher-Scientist*, edited by Paul Arthur Schilpp, (Evanston, Illinois, The Library of Living Philosophers, 1949), p. 309.

62. Kant, *Critique of Pure Reason*, p. 41.

63. *Ibid.*, pp. 121, 130.

64. *Ibid.*, pp. 243–44.

65. *Ibid.*, p. 98.

66. *Ibid.*, p. 500.

67. Kant, *Prolegomena*, p. 123.

68. Kant, *Critique of Pure Reason*, p. 97.

69. Kant, *Prolegomena*, p. 110.

70. Kant, *Critique of Pure Reason*, p. 259; cf. p. 193.

71. *Ibid.*, p. 181.

72. Kant, *Prolegomena*, p. 75.

73. Kant, *Critique of Pure Reason*, p. 614.

74. Kant, *Prolegomena*, p. 101.

75. *Ibid.*, p. 79.

76. Kant, *Critique of Pure Reason*, pp. 615–16.

77. Reichenbach, "The Philosophical Significance of the Theory of Relativity," in *Albert Einstein: Philosopher-Scientist*, p. 309.

78. T. D. Weldon, *Introduction to Kant's Critique of Pure Reason*, (Oxford, Clarendon Press, 1946), p. 203.

79. Heinrich Cassirer, *Kant's First Critique*, (New York, The Macmillan Company, 1954), pp. 225–26.

80. Quoted by Norman Kemp Smith, *A Commentary to Kant's "Critique of Pure Reason,"* (New York, The Humanities Press, 1950), pp. xxii–xxiii.

81. *Ibid.*, p. 608.

82. Kant, *Critique of Pure Reason*, p. 10.

83. *Ibid.*, e.g., p. 11.

84. *Ibid.*, e.g., pp. 32–33.

85. *Ibid.*, p. 433.

86. *Ibid.*, p. 11; cf. pp. 646–47.

87. Kant, *Prolegomena*, p. 118.

88. Kant, *Critique of Pure Reason,* pp. 431–32.

89. *Ibid.,* p. 43.

90. *Ibid.,* p. 17.

91. *Ibid.,* p. 411.

92. *Ibid.,* p. 466.

93. *Ibid.,* p. 233.

Chapter 2. The Synthetic A Priori

1. Kant, *Prolegomena,* p. 27; cf. *Critique of Pure Reason,* pp. 52–55.

2. Kant, *Critique of Pure Reason,* p. 433.

3. Kant, *Prolegomena,* p. 26; cf. *Critique of Pure Reason,* p. 433.

4. Weldon, T. D., *Introduction to Kant's Critique of Pure Reason,* (Oxford, Clarendon Press, 1946), Preface, p. v.

5. Albert Einstein, "Reply to Criticisms," in *Albert Einstein: Philosopher-Scientist,* pp. 678–79.

6. Kant, *Critique of Pure Reason,* p. 54; *Prolegomena,* p. 68.

7. Kemp Smith, *op. cit.,* p. 401.

8. Kant, *Critique of Pure Reason,* pp. 248–49.

9. *Ibid.,* p. 233.

10. Kant, *Prolegomena,* p. 22.

11. Kant, *Critique of Pure Reason,* pp. 172, 170.

12. *Ibid.,* p. 55.

13. *Ibid.,* p. 124.

14. *Ibid.,* pp. 274–75.

15. *Ibid.,* p. 162.

16. *Ibid.,* p. 180.

17. *Ibid.,* p. 97.

18. *Ibid.,* pp. 176–77.

19. *Ibid.,* p. 95.

20. *Ibid.,* p. 91.

21. Kant, *Prolegomena,* p. 29.

22. Kant, *Critique of Pure Reason,* p. 162.

23. *Ibid.,* p. 179.

24. *Ibid.,* p. 187.

25. *Ibid.,* p. 160.

26. *Ibid.,* p. 128.

27. *Ibid.,* p. 253.

28. *Ibid.,* pp. 582–83.

29. *Ibid.,* p. 432.

30. *Ibid.,* p. 41.

31. *Ibid.,* p. 128.

32. *Ibid.,* p. 263.

33. *Ibid.,* p. 220.

34. *Ibid.,* pp. 242–43.

35. *Ibid.,* p. 283.

36. *Ibid.,* p. 196.

37. *Ibid.,* p. 247.

38. *Ibid.,* pp. 214–15.

39. *Ibid.,* p. 219.

40. *Ibid.,* p. 214.

41. *Ibid.,* pp. 252–53.

42. Bertrand Russell, *A Critical Exposition of the Philosophy of Leibniz,* (London, George Allen and Unwin, 1937), pp. 40–44.

43. Kant, *Critique of Pure Reason,* p. 108.

44. *Ibid.,* p. 253.

45. *Ibid.,* pp. 224–25.

46. *Ibid.,* pp. 50–51.

47. *Ibid.,* p. 624.

48. Kant, *Prolegomena,* pp. 44–45.

49. Kant, *Critique of Pure Reason,* p. 227.

50. Reichenbach, *The Rise of Scientific Philosophy,* p. 48.

51. Kant, *Critique of Pure Reason,* p. 592.

52. *Ibid.,* p. 592.

53. *Ibid.,* pp. 124–25.

54. *Ibid.,* pp. 129–50.

55. *Ibid.,* p. 173.

56. Kant, *Critique of Pure Reason*, p. 161.

57. *Ibid.*, p. 159.

58. *Ibid.*, p. 161.

59. H. J. Paton, *Kant's Metaphysic of Experience*, (New York, The Macmillan Company, 1936), 2 vols., Vol. I, pp. 324–34.

60. Kant, *Critique of Pure Reason*, p. 124.

61. *Ibid.*, p. 160.

62. Paton, *op. cit.*, Vol. I, p. 331.

63. Kant, *Critique of Pure Reason*, p. 197.

64. *Ibid.*, p. 201.

65. *Ibid.*, p. 196.

66. *Ibid.*, p. 546.

67. Kant, *Prolegomena*, p. 38.

68. Kant, *Critique of Pure Reason*, p. 350.

69. *Ibid.*, p. 227.

70. E.g., Kemp Smith, *op. cit.*,

71. Kant, *Critique of Pure Reason*, p. 183.

72. *Ibid.*, pp. 174–75.

73. *Ibid.*, pp. 93–96.

74. *Ibid.*, p. 264.

75. Kant, *Prolegomena*, p. 46.

76. Kant, *Critique of Pure Reason*, pp. 305–306.

77. *Ibid.*, p. 324.

78. *Ibid.*, p. 175.

79. Kant, *Prolegomena*, p. 52.

80. *Ibid.*, p. 52.

81. Kant, *Critique of Pure Reason*, p. 82.

82. *Ibid.*, p. 152.

83. Kant, *Prolegomena*, p. 65.

84. Kant, *Critique of Pure Reason*, p. 147.

85. *Ibid.*, p. 580.

86. Reichenbach, *The Rise of Scientific Philosophy*, p. 123.

pp. 176–80; Cassirer, *op. cit.*, p. 58.

Chapter 3.
The Synthetic A Priori and Kant's Interpretation of Science

1. Kant, *Critique of Pure Reason*, p. 148.

2. *Ibid.*, p. 172.

3. *Ibid.*, pp. 147–48.

4. *Ibid.*, p. 247.

5. *Ibid.*, p. 655.

6. *Ibid.*, p. 214.

7. Kant, *Prolegomena*, p. 5; cf. *Critique of Pure Reason*, p. 229.

8. Kant, *Critique of Pure Reason*, pp. 230–31.

9. *Ibid.*, p. 249.

10. *Ibid.*, p. 249.

11. Kant, *Prolegomena*, p. 68.

12. *Ibid.*, pp. 53–54.

13. Kant, *Critique of Pure Reason*, p. 173.

14. Kant, *Prolegomena*, p. 43.

15. Kant, *Critique of Pure Reason*, p. 610.

16. Kant, *Prolegomena*, p. 65.

17. *Ibid.*, p. 59.

18. *Ibid.*, p. 59.

19. H. Feigl, *op. cit.*, p. 511; *supra*, pp. 11–12.

20. Kant, *Critique of Pure Reason*, p. 148; quoted on p. 51 *supra*.

21. Kant, *Prolegomena*, p. 59.

22. Kant, *Critique of Pure Reason*, pp. 534–35.

23. *Ibid.*, p. 303.

24. *Ibid.*, p. 533.

25. *Ibid.*, p. 147.

26. *Ibid.*, p. 623.

27. *Ibid.*, p. 411.

28. *Ibid.*, pp. 536–41.

29. *Ibid.*, p. 546.

30. *Ibid.*, p. 544.

31. Kant, *Prolegomena*, p. 113.

32. Kant, *Critique of Pure Reason*, p. 546.

33. Kemp Smith, *op. cit.*, pp. 559–60.

34. Kant, *Critique of Pure Reason*, p. 546.

35. *Ibid.*, pp. 302–303.

36. *Ibid.*, p. 48.

37. *Ibid.*, p. 97.

38. *Ibid.*, p. 306.

39. *Ibid.*, pp. 487–95.

40. *Ibid.*, p. 306.

41. *Ibid.*, p. 563.

42. Kant, *Prolegomena*, p. 97.

43. Kant, *Critique of Pure Reason*, p. 239.

44. *Ibid.*, p. 241.

45. *Ibid.*, p. 493.

46. *Ibid.*, p. 533.

47. *Ibid.*, p. 307.

48. Kant, *Prolegomena*, p. 97.

49. Kant, *Critique of Pure Reason*, p. 534.

50. *Ibid.*, p. 513.

51. *Ibid.*, p. 534.

52. *Ibid.*, p. 450.

53. *Ibid.*, p. 563.

54. *Ibid.*, p. 533.

55. *Ibid.*, pp. 515–16.

56. *Ibid.*, p. 499.

57. *Ibid.*, p. 466.

58. *Ibid.*, p. 534.

59. *Ibid.*, p. 610.

60. *Ibid.*, p. 581.

61. *Ibid.*, pp. 183–84.

62. Kant, *Prolegomena*, p. 67.

63. *Ibid.*, p. 49.

64. Kant, *Critique of Pure Reason*, p. 162.

65. *Ibid.*, p. 200.

66. C. I. Lewis, *A Survey of Symbolic Logic*, (Berkeley, University of California Press, 1918), p. 341n.

67. Kant, *Critique of Pure Reason*, p. 240.

68. *Ibid.*, p. 579.

69. Kant, *Prolegomena*, p. 59.

70. Kant, *Critique of Pure Reason*, p. 93.

Chapter 4. Kant and Lewis

1. Clarence Irving Lewis, *Mind and the World-Order*, (New York, Dover Publications, Inc., 1956), p. 37.

2. Clarence Irving Lewis, *An Analysis of Knowledge and Valuation*, (La Salle, Illinois, Open Court Publishing Company, 1946), p. 35.

3. *Ibid.*, p. 94.

4. Lewis, *Mind and the World-Order*, p. 37.

5. Lewis, *An Analysis of Knowledge and Valuation*, p. 30.

6. Lewis, *Mind and the World-Order*, p. 114.

7. Lewis, *An Analysis of Knowledge and Valuation*, pp. 182–84.

8. *Ibid.*, p. 17.

9. *Ibid.*, p. 20.

10. Lewis, *Mind and the World-Order*, pp. 139–40.

11. Lewis, *An Analysis of Knowledge and Valuation*, p. 208.

12. *Ibid.*, pp. 20–21.

13. *Ibid.*, p. 236.

14. *Ibid.*, p. 242.

15. Lewis, *Mind and the World-Order*, p. 312. Cf. Kant, *Critique of Pure Reason*, p. 610, quoted *supra*, p. 70.

16. Lewis, *Mind and the World-Order*, p. 320.

17. *Ibid.*, pp. 373–75; cf. Kant,

Prolegomena, p. 65, quoted *supra*, p. 56.

18. Lewis, *Mind and the World-Order*, p. 259.

19. *Ibid.*, p. 396.

20. Kant, *Critique of Pure Reason*, pp. 180–81.

21. *Ibid.*, pp. 181–83; Lewis, *An Analysis of Knowledge and Valuation*, pp. 131–35.

22. *Ibid.*, p. 137.

23. *Ibid.*, p. 46.

24. Lewis, *Mind and the World-Order*, p. 130.

25. Lewis, *An Analysis of Knowledge and Valuation*, p. 361.

26. Lewis, *Mind and the World-Order*, pp. 141–42.

27. *Ibid.*, pp. 305–306.

28. Lewis, *An Analysis of Knowledge and Valuation*, p. 338.

29. *Ibid.*, pp. 344–47.

30. *Ibid.*, pp. 263–64, 336–37.

31. *Ibid.*, p. 362.

32. *Ibid.*, p. 354.

33. *Ibid.*, pp. 349–50.

34. *Ibid.*, p. 353.

35. *Ibid.*, p. 342.

36. *Ibid.*, p. 339.

37. *Ibid.*, p. 353.

38. *Ibid.*, pp. 341–42.

39. *Ibid.*, p. 362.

40. Lewis, *Mind and the World-Order*, pp. 305–306.

41. *Ibid.*, p. 353.

42. Lewis, *An Analysis of Knowledge and Valuation*, p. 345.

43. Lewis, *Mind and the World-Order*, p. 397.

44. *Ibid.*, p. 305.

45. *Ibid.*, p. 345.

46. *Ibid.*, p. 195.

47. *Ibid.*, Preface, p. viii.

48. *Ibid.*, Preface, pp. ix–x.

49. *Ibid.*, p. 145.

50. *Ibid.*, pp. 200–204.

51. Lewis, *An Analysis of Knowledge and Valuation*, p. 38.

52. *Ibid.*, pp. 158–61.

53. *Ibid.*, p. 159.

54. Kant, *Critique of Pure Reason*, p. 215.

55. Lewis, *An Analysis of Knowledge and Valuation*, pp. 161–63.

56. Lewis, *Mind and the World-Order*, p. 349.

57. *Ibid.*, p. 221.

58. *Ibid.*, pp. 320–21.

59. *Ibid.*, p. 214.

60. *Ibid.*, pp. 215–16.

61. *Ibid.*, p. 215.

62. *Ibid.*, pp. 231–32.

Chapter 5. Lewis and the Applicability of the A Priori

1. Lewis, *Mind and the World-Order*, pp. 230–31.

2. *Ibid.*, pp. 265–66.

3. *Ibid.*, p. 266.

4. *Ibid.*, p. 268.

5. *Ibid.*, p. 231.

6. *Ibid.*, p. 197.

7. *Ibid.*, p. 13.

8. *Ibid.*, p. 312.

9. *Ibid.*, pp. 302–305.

10. *Ibid.*, p. 315.

11. *Ibid.*, pp. 300–301.

12. *Ibid.*, p. 307.

13. *Ibid.*, p. 285.

14. *Ibid.*, pp. 287–88.

15. *Ibid.*, p. 290.

16. *Ibid.*, Preface, p. x.

17. *Ibid.*, pp. 312–13; cf. Kant,

Critique of Pure Reason, p. 592, quoted *supra*, p. 38.

18. *Ibid.*, p. 431.
19. *Ibid.*, p. 368.
20. *Ibid.*, pp. 383–85.
21. *Ibid.*, Preface, pp. x–xi.
22. *Ibid.*, p. 323.
23. *Ibid.*, pp. 350–51.
24. *Ibid.*, p. 11.
25. *Ibid.*, p. 263.
26. *Ibid.*, pp. 11–12.
27. Kant, *Critique of Pure Reason*, p. 227.
28. Lewis, *Mind and the World-Order*, p. 20.
29. *Ibid.*, p. 96.
30. *Ibid.*, p. 93.
31. *Ibid.*, p. 110.
32. *Ibid.*, pp. 20–21.
33. *Ibid.*, pp. 91–92.
34. *Ibid.*, p. 21.
35. *Ibid.*, pp. 297–98.
36. *Ibid.*, p. 259.
37. *Ibid.*, pp. 271–72.
38. *Ibid.*, pp. 268–70.
39. *Ibid.*, p. 299.
40. *Ibid.*, pp. 111–12.
41. *Ibid.*, pp. 358–59.
42. *Ibid.*, p. 141.
43. *Ibid.*, p. 307.
44. *Ibid.*, p. 146.
45. *Ibid.*, pp. 262–63.
46. Cf. *supra*, p. 57.
47. Lewis, *Mind and the World-Order*, pp. 398–400.
48. *Ibid.*, p. 265.
49. *Ibid.*, pp. 258–60.
50. *Ibid.*, p. 304.
51. *Ibid.*, p. 398.
52. *Ibid.*, p. 399.
53. *Ibid.*, p. 263.
54. *Ibid.*, p. 12.
55. *Ibid.*, p. 269.
56. *Ibid.*, pp. 210–13.

57. Lewis, *A Survey of Symbolic Logic*, pp. 324–25.
58. C. I. Lewis and C. H. Langford, *Symbolic Logic*, (New York, The Century Company, 1932), p. 247.
59. *Ibid.*, p. 244.
60. Lewis, *Mind and the World-Order*, pp. 209–13.
61. *Ibid.*, p. 210.
62. Lewis, *An Analysis of Knowledge and Valuation*, pp. 24–25.
63. *Ibid.*, pp. 66–67.
64. *Ibid.*, pp. 105–106.
65. *Ibid.*, pp. 112–13.
66. *Ibid.*, p. 106.
67. *Ibid.*, p. 39.
68. *Ibid.*, p. 43.
69. *Ibid.*, pp. 55–56.
70. *Ibid.*, p. 108.
71. *Ibid.*, p. 43.
72. *Ibid.*, p. 56.
73. *Ibid.*, p. 57.
74. *Ibid.*, p. 25.
75. *Ibid.*, p. 97.
76. Lewis, *Mind and the World-Order*, p. 109.
77. Lewis, *An Analysis of Knowledge and Valuation*, p. 53.
78. *Ibid.*, p. 57.
79. Kant, *Critique of Pure Reason*, pp. 177–79.
80. *Ibid.*, p. 182.
81. Lewis, *An Analysis of Knowledge and Valuation*, p. 57.
82. *Ibid.*, p. 71.
83. *Ibid.*, p. 84.
84. *Ibid.*, p. 86.
85. *Ibid.*, p. 78.
86. *Ibid.*, p. 75.
87. *Ibid.*, pp. 86–88.
88. *Ibid.*, pp. 93–94.
89. *Ibid.*, p. 94.
90. *Ibid.*, p. 88.
91. *Ibid.*, pp. 83–84.

Chapter 6. Kant and Reichenbach

1. Kant, *Critique of Pure Reason*, pp. 534–35; see *supra*, pp. 59–60.

2. Lewis, *Mind and the World-Order*, pp. 361–62.

3. *Ibid.*, p. 333.

4. Lewis, *An Analysis of Knowledge and Valuation*, p. 343.

5. *Ibid.*, pp. 303–306.

6. *Ibid.*, p. 290.

7. *Ibid.*, p. 362.

8. Hans Reichenbach, *Experience and Prediction*, (Chicago, University of Chicago Press, 1938), pp. 139–40.

9. *Ibid.*, p. 360.

10. Hans Reichenbach, *The Rise of Scientific Philosophy*, (Berkeley and Los Angeles, University of California Press, 1951), pp. 17–18.

11. *Ibid.*, p. 252.

12. Reichenbach, *Experience and Prediction*, p. 203.

13. *Ibid.*, pp. 205–207.

14. *Ibid.*, p. 221.

15. *Ibid.*, p. 224.

16. *Ibid.*, pp. 220–21.

17. *Ibid.*, p. 220.

18. *Ibid.*, p. 225.

19. Reichenbach, *The Rise of Scientific Philosophy*, p. 48.

20. *Ibid.*, pp. 179–80.

21. Reichenbach, *Experience and Prediction*, p. 139.

22. Reichenbach, *The Rise of Scientific Philosophy*, p. 158.

23. Hans Reichenbach, *Elements of Symbolic Logic*, (New York, The Macmillan Company, 1947), pp. 358–61.

24. *Ibid.*, pp. 355–56.

25. Kant, *Critique of Pure Reason*, p. 177.

26. Reichenbach, *Elements of Symbolic Logic*, p. 395.

27. Kant, *Critique of Pure Reason*, p. 239.

28. Reichenbach, *Elements of Symbolic Logic*, pp. 396–98.

29. *Ibid.*, p. 70.

30. Reichenbach, *The Rise of Scientific Philosophy*, p. 73.

31. *Ibid.*, p. 66.

32. *Ibid.*, p. 72.

33. *Ibid.*, p. 42.

34. *Ibid.*, p. 44.

35. *Ibid.*, p. 48.

36. Reichenbach, *Experience and Prediction*, p. 346.

37. Reichenbach, *The Rise of Scientific Philosophy*, p. 40.

38. *Ibid.*, p. 129.

39. *Ibid.*, pp. 44–46.

40. *Ibid.*, pp. 46–48.

41. Reichenbach, "The Philosophical Significance of the Theory of Relativity," in *Albert Einstein: Philosopher-Scientist*, p. 307.

42. Reichenbach, *The Rise of Scientific Philosophy*, pp. 47–48.

43. *Ibid.*, pp. 139–40.

44. *Ibid.*, pp. 132–33.

45. *Ibid.*, pp. 133–37; cf. Reichenbach, "The Philosophical Significance of the Theory of Relativity," in *Albert Einstein: Philosopher-Scientist*, p. 299.

46. Reichenbach, *The Rise of Scientific Philosophy*, p. 139.

47. Reichenbach, "The Philosophical Significance of the Theory of Relativity," in *Albert Einstein: Philosopher-Scientist*, p. 307.

48. *Ibid.*, pp. 298–99.

49. Reichenbach, *The Rise of Scientific Philosophy*, p. 187.

50. *Ibid.*, pp. 181–86.

51. Reichenbach, *Experience and Prediction*, p. 139.

52. Reichenbach, *The Rise of Scientific Philosophy*, pp. 112–13.

53. *Ibid.*, p. 189.

54. *Ibid.*, p. 186.

55. Reichenbach, *Experience and Prediction*, p. 334.

56. *Ibid.*, pp. 335–36.

57. Kant, *Critique of Pure Reason*, p. 98.

58. Reichenbach, *Elements of Symbolic Logic*, p. 2.

59. Reichenbach, *Experience and Prediction*, p. 335.

60. Reichenbach, *Elements of Symbolic Logic*, pp. 164–67.

61. *Ibid.*, p. 183.

62. Reichenbach, *Experience and Prediction*, pp. 335–36.

63. Reichenbach, *Elements of Symbolic Logic*, pp. 2–3.

64. *Ibid.*, p. 186.

65. *Ibid.*, p. 166.

66. Reichenbach, *Experience and Prediction*, p. 336.

67. Reichenbach, *Elements of Symbolic Logic*, pp. 187–91.

68. Kant, *Critique of Pure Reason*, pp. 554–55.

69. *Ibid.*, p. 391.

70. Reichenbach, *Elements of Symbolic Logic*, p. 191.

71. *Ibid.*, p. 3.

Chapter 7. Reichenbach and the Applicability of the A Priori in Probable Knowledge

1. Reichenbach, *Experience and Prediction*, p. 320.

2. *Ibid.*, p. 301.

3. *Ibid.*, pp. 307–308.

4. *Ibid.*, p. 337.

5. *Ibid.*, pp. 350–51.

6. *Ibid.*, pp. 337–38.

7. *Ibid.*, pp. 320–21.

8. *Ibid.*, p. 338.

9. *Ibid.*, pp. 350–54.

10. *Ibid.*, p. 359.

11. *Ibid.*, pp. 330–31.

12. *Ibid.*, p. 340.

13. *Ibid.*, pp. 348–50.

14. *Ibid.*, pp. 340–41.

15. *Ibid.*, p. 359.

16. *Ibid.*, p. 400.

17. *Ibid.*, p. 342.

18. *Ibid.*, pp. 313–14.

19. *Ibid.*, pp. 352–53.

20. *Ibid.*, pp. 365–70.

21. *Ibid.*, p. 333.

22. *Ibid.*, p. 364.

23. *Ibid.*, pp. 371–72.

24. Reichenbach, *The Rise of Scientific Philosophy*, p. 243.

25. *Ibid.*, pp. 237–38.

26. *Ibid.*, p. 308.

27. Reichenbach, *Experience and Prediction*, p. 192.

28. Reichenbach, *The Rise of Scientific Philosophy*, p. 242.

29. *Ibid.*, p. 247.

30. Kant, *Critique of Pure Reason*, pp. 127–28.

31. Reichenbach, *Experience and Prediction*, p. 342.

32. *Ibid.*, p. 346.

33. *Ibid.*, pp. 359–60.

34. Reichenbach, *Experience and Prediction*, p. 360.

35. *Ibid.*, p. 362.

36. Reichenbach, *Experience and Prediction*, p. 360.

37. *Ibid.*, p. 402.

38. Reichenbach, *Elements of Symbolic Logic*, p. 398.

39. Reichenbach, *Experience and Prediction*, p. 277.

40. *Ibid.*, p. 370.

41. Reichenbach, *The Rise of Scientific Philosophy*, p. 233.

42. Reichenbach, *Experience and Prediction*, p. 333.

43. *Ibid.*, p. 370.

44. *Ibid.*, p. 362.

45. Reichenbach, *The Rise of Scientific Philosophy*, pp. 172–76; 186–90.

46. *Ibid.*, p. 185.

47. *Ibid.*, pp. 172–73.

48. *Ibid.*, pp. 188–89.

49. *Ibid.*, p. 247n. Reichenbach's reference is to Bertrand Russell, *Human Knowledge: Its Scope and Limits*, New York, Simon and Schuster, 1948.

50. Reichenbach, *Experience and Prediction*, p. 401.

Chapter 8. Things: As Known and in Themselves

1. Kant, *Critique of Pure Reason*, p. 287.

2. *Ibid.*, p. 274.

3. Einstein, "Maxwell's Influence on the Evolution of the Idea of Physical Reality," in *Ideas and Opinions*, p. 266.

4. Einstein, "Physics and Reality," in *ibid.*, pp. 291–95.

5. Einstein, "Reply to Criticisms," in *Albert Einstein: Philosopher-Scientist*, p. 680.

6. Einstein, "The Problem of Space, Ether, and the Field of Physics," in *Ideas and Opinions*, p. 277.

7. Einstein, "Maxwell's Influence on the Evolution of the Idea of Physical Reality," in *ibid.*, p. 266.

8. Quoted by H. Margenau, "Einstein's Conception of Reality," in *Albert Einstein: Philosopher-Scientist*, p. 262.

9. Einstein, "Physics and Reality," in *ibid.*, pp. 315–16.

10. Einstein, "On the Method of Theoretical Physics," in *ibid.*, p. 276.

11. Einstein, "Physics and Reality," in *ibid.*, p. 291.

12. Einstein, "Maxwell's Influence on the Evolution of the Idea of Physical Reality," in *ibid.*, p. 266.

13. Einstein, "On the Method of Theoretical Physics," in *ibid.*, p. 272.

14. Einstein, "Physics and Reality," in *ibid.*, p. 303.

15. Einstein, "Maxwell's Influence on the Evolution of the Idea of Physical Reality," in *ibid.*, p. 266.

16. Einstein, "On the Method of Theoretical Physics," in *ibid.*, p. 274.

17. Einstein, "Physics and Reality," in *ibid.*, pp. 294–95.

18. Reichenbach, *Experience and Prediction*, p. 101.

19. *Ibid.*, p. 31.

20. *Ibid.*, p. 101.

21. *Ibid.*, pp. 48–49.

22. *Ibid.*, p. 101.

23. *Ibid.*, pp. 111–12.

24. *Ibid.*, pp. 150–51.

25. *Ibid.*, p. 203.

26. *Ibid.*, pp. 164–65.

27. *Ibid.*, p. 90.

28. *Ibid.*, p. 167.

29. *Ibid.*, pp. 206–207.

30. *Ibid.*, p. 165.

31. *Ibid.*, p. 199.

32. *Ibid.*, p. 220.

33. *Ibid.*, pp. 50–52, 55.

34. *Ibid.*, pp. 105–11.

35. *Ibid.*, pp. 120–24.

36. *Ibid.*, p. 133.

37. *Ibid.*, pp. 158–60.

38. *Ibid.*, p. 133.

39. *Ibid.*, p. 27.

40. *Ibid.*, pp. 123–24.

41. *Ibid.*, pp. 202–203.

42. Lewis, *An Analysis of Knowledge and Valuation*, pp. 182–84.

43. *Ibid.*, p. 242.

44. *Ibid.*, pp. 197–98.

45. *Ibid.*, pp. 180, 184–85.

46. *Ibid.*, p. 230.

47. *Ibid.*, pp. 241–44.

48. *Ibid.*, p. 236.

49. *Ibid.*, pp. 186–87.

50. *Ibid.*, p. 338.

51. Lewis, *Mind and the World-Order*, pp. 192–93.

52. Kant, *Critique of Pure Reason*, p. 159.

53. *Ibid.*, pp. 222, 224.

54. Lewis, *Mind and the World-Order*, p. 190.

55. *Ibid.*, pp. 166–69.

56. *Ibid.*, pp. 174–76.

57. *Ibid.*, pp. 184–85.

58. *Ibid.*, pp. 189–91.

59. *Ibid.*, p. 175.

60. Lewis, *An Analysis of Knowledge and Valuation*, p. 187n.

61. Lewis, *Mind and the World-Order*, p. 417.

62. *Ibid.*, p. 165.

63. *Ibid.*, p. 380.

64. *Ibid.*, pp. 179–81.

65. Lewis, *An Analysis of Knowledge and Valuation*, p. 229.

66. *Ibid.*, p. 230.

67. *Ibid.*, pp. 197–200.

68. Lewis, *Mind and the World-Order*, p. 193.

69. *Ibid.*, pp. 61–65, 64–65n.

70. Lewis, *An Analysis of Knowledge and Valuation*, pp. 213–16.

71. *Ibid.*, p. 212.

72. *Ibid.*, pp. 217–19.

73. *Ibid.*, p. 223.

74. *Ibid.*, pp. 227–30.

75. Reichenbach, *Elements of Symbolic Logic*, pp. 401–402.

76. Lewis, *An Analysis of Knowledge and Valuation*, p. 228n.

77. *Ibid.*, p. 212.

78. *Ibid.*, p. 227.

79. Dewey, *Experience and Nature*, p. 140.

80. Dewey, *Logic*, p. 523.

81. *Ibid.*, p. 126.

82. *Ibid.*, p. 129.

83. Dewey, *Experience and Nature*, p. 154.

84. Lewis, *An Analysis of Knowledge and Valuation*, chapter IX.

85. Dewey, *Logic*, p. 154.

86. Dewey, *Experience and Nature*, pp. 156–58.

87. John Dewey, *The Quest for Certainty: a Study of the Relation of Knowledge and Action*, (New York, Minton, Balch and Company, 1929), p. 104.

88. Dewey, *Logic*, pp. 458–59.

89. Dewey, *The Quest for Certainty*, p. 98.

90. *Ibid.*, p. 103.

91. *Ibid.*, p. 95.

92. Dewey, *Logic*, pp. 531–32.

Chapter 9. Kant's Doctrine of Things

1. *Supra*, pp. 6–8, 29–31.

2. Kant, *Critique of Pure Reason*, p. 244.

3. *Ibid.*, p. 219.

4. Kemp Smith, *Commentary*, p. 83.

5. Kant, *Critique of Pure Reason*, p. 220.

6. *Ibid.*, p. 441.

7. *Ibid.*, pp. 219–20.

8. *Ibid.*, pp. 242–43.

9. Kemp Smith, *Commentary*, pp. 305, 308.

10. Kant, *Critique of Pure Reason*, pp. 244–46.

11. *Ibid.*, p. 346.

12. *Supra*, pp. 189–90.

13. Kant, *Critique of Pure Reason*, pp. 346–47.

14. *Ibid.*, p. 354.

15. *Ibid.*, pp. 346–47.

16. *Ibid.*, p. 72.

17. *Ibid.*, p. 24.

18. Kant, *Prolegomena*, p. 37.

19. Kant, *Critique of Pure Reason*, pp. 355–56.

20. Kant, *Prolegomena*, p. 37.

21. Kant, *Critique of Pure Reason*, p. 27.

22. *Ibid.*, p. 352.

23. *Ibid.*, p. 82.

24. *Ibid.*, p. 439.

25. *Ibid.*, p. 83.

26. *Ibid.*, p. 82.

27. *Ibid.*, p. 287.

28. *Ibid.*, p. 356.

29. Kant, *Prolegomena*, p. 62.

30. *Ibid.*, p. 56.

31. Kant, *Critique of Pure Reason*, p. 65.

32. Kant, *Prolegomena*, p. 38.

33. Kant, *Critique of Pure Reason*, p. 378n.

34. *Ibid.*, pp. 268–69.

35. *Ibid.*, pp. 270–71.

36. *Ibid.*, p. 442.

37. *Ibid.*, p. 271.

38. *Ibid.*, p. 271.

39. *Ibid.*, pp. 265–68.

40. *Ibid.*, p. 271.

41. *Ibid.*, p. 344.

42. Kant, *Prolegomena*, p. 60.

43. Kant, *Critique of Pure Reason*, pp. 266–67.

44. *Ibid.*, pp. 268–71.

45. *Ibid.*, p. 266.

46. *Ibid.*, pp. 272–73.

47. *Ibid.*, p. 297.

48. Cassirer, *Kant's First Critique*, pp. 225, 288; cf. Paton, *Kant's Metaphysic of Experience*, Vol. II, pp. 439, 442–43, 454; Kemp Smith, *Commentary*, pp. 204, 409–12.

49. Reichenbach, *The Rise of Scientific Philosophy*, p. 253.

50. *Ibid.*, p. 66.

51. Lewis, *An Analysis of Knowledge and Valuation*, p. 15.

52. Lewis, *Mind and the World-Order*, pp. 177–79.

53. Dewey, *Logic*, pp. 531–32; *supra*, p. 202.

54. *Ibid.*, p. 518.

55. *Supra*, p. 222.

56. Kant, *Critique of Pure Reason*, pp. 266–67.

57. Kant, *Prolegomena*, p. 36.

58. Kant, *Critique of Pure Reason*, p. 74.

59. *Ibid.*, p. 86.

60. Russell, *Human Knowledge*, pp. 180–81, 449.

61. Kant, *Prolegomena*, p. 36.

62. Kant, *Critique of Pure Reason*, p. 72.

63. *Ibid.*, p. 172.

64. *Ibid.*, pp. 272–73.

65. *Ibid.*, p. 83.

66. Kant, *Prolegomena*, p. 99.

Chapter 10. Kant Today: *A Reappraisal*

1. Paul Kecskemeti, "Some Recent Attempts at 'Meaning,'" *Modern Review*, Vol. III, No. 1 (Summer, 1949), pp. 74–78.

2. Lewis, *Mind and the World-Order*, p. 179.

3. Reichenbach, *Experience and Prediction*, p. 360.

4. Dewey, *Logic*, p. 459.

5. Kant, *Critique of Pure Reason*, p. 93.

BIBLIOGRAPHY

(Only works consulted in the preparation of this book are mentioned.)

Cassirer, Heinrich, *Kant's First Critique* (New York, The Macmillan Company, 1954).

Dewey, John, *Experience and Nature* (New York, W. W. Norton and Company, Inc., 1925, 1929).

——, *Logic: the Theory of Inquiry* (New York, Henry Holt and Company, 1938).

——, *The Quest for Certainty* (New York, Minton, Balch and Company, 1929).

Einstein, Albert, *Ideas and Opinions* (New York, Crown Publishers, Inc., 1954).

Feigl, Herbert, "Some Remarks on the Meaning of Scientific Explanation," in Herbert Feigl and Wilfrid Sellars, eds., *Readings in Philosophical Analysis* (New York, Appleton-Century-Crofts, Inc., 1949).

Hempel, Carl G., *Fundamentals of Concept Formation in Empirical Science* (Chicago, University of Chicago Press, 1952).

Kant, Immanuel, *Prolegomena to Any Future Metaphysic*, trans. by Lewis W. Beck (New York, The Liberal Arts Press, 1951).

——, *Immanuel Kant's Critique of Pure Reason*, trans. by Norman Kemp Smith (London, Macmillan and Co., Ltd., 1953).

——, *Immanuel Kants Kritik der reinen Vernunft*, herausgegeben von Benno Erdmann (Hamburg und Leipzig, Leopold Voss, 1889).

Kecskemeti, Paul, "Some Recent Attempts at 'Meaning,'" *Modern Review*, Vol. III, No. 1 (Summer 1949).

Lewis, Clarence Irving, *An Analysis of Knowledge and Valuation* (LaSalle, Illinois, Open Court Publishing Company, 1946).

——, *Mind and the World-Order* (New York, Dover Publications, Inc., 1956).

Lewis, Clarence Irving, *A Survey of Symbolic Logic* (Berkeley, University of California Press, 1918).

—— and Langford, Cooper Harold, *Symbolic Logic* (New York, The Century Company, 1932).

Margenau, Henry, *The Nature of Physical Reality* (New York, McGraw-Hill Book Company, Inc., 1950).

Paton, H. J., *Kant's Metaphysic of Experience* (New York, The Macmillan Company, 1936), 2 vols.

Pearson, Karl, *The Grammar of Science*, Everyman edition (London, J. M. Dent and Sons, Ltd., 1937).

Reichenbach, Hans, *Atom and Cosmos, the World of Modern Physics*, trans. in collaboration with the author by Edward S. Allen (New York, The Macmillan Company, 1933).

——, *Elements of Symbolic Logic* (New York, The Macmillan Company, 1947).

——, *Experience and Prediction: An Analysis of the Foundations and Structure of Knowledge* (Chicago, University of Chicago Press, 1938).

——, *From Copernicus to Einstein*, trans. by Ralph B. Winn (New York, Philosophical Library, 1942).

——, *The Rise of Scientific Philosophy* (Berkeley and Los Angeles, University of California Press, 1951).

——, *The Theory of Probability, an Inquiry Into the Logical and Mathematical Foundations of the Calculus of Probability*, trans. by Ernest Sutton and Maria Reichenbach (Berkeley, University of California Press, 1949).

Russell, Bertrand, *A Critical Exposition of the Philosophy of Leibniz* (London, George Allen and Unwin, 1937).

——, *Human Knowledge: Its Scope and Limits* (New York, Simon and Schuster, 1948).

Schilpp, Paul Arthur, ed., *Albert Einstein: Philosopher-Scientist* (Evanston, Illinois, The Library of Living Philosophers, 1949).

Einstein, Albert, "Reply to Criticisms"

Margenau, H., "Einstein's Conception of Reality"

Reichenbach, Hans, "The Philosophical Significance of the Theory of Relativity"

Smith, Norman Kemp, *A Commentary to Kant's Critique of Pure Reason* (New York, The Humanities Press, 1950).

Weldon, T. D., *Introduction to Kant's Critique of Pure Reason* (Oxford, Clarendon Press, 1946).

White, Morton G., "The Analytic and the Synthetic: an Untenable Dualism," in L. Linsky, ed., *Semantics and the Philosophy of Language* (Urbana, University of Illinois Press, 1952).